AN AMERICAN UTOPIA

AN AMERICAN UTOPIA

Dual Power and the Universal Army

FREDRIC JAMESON, JODI DEAN, SAROJ GIRI, AGON HAMZA, KOJIN KARATANI, KIM STANLEY ROBINSON, FRANK RUDA, ALBERTO TOSCANO, KATHI WEEKS

EDITED BY SLAVOJ ŽIŽEK

VERSO
London • New York

First published by Verso 2016

1 3 5 7 9 10 8 6 4 2

Verso
UK: 6 Meard Street, London W1F 0EG
US: 20 Jay Street, Suite 1010, Brooklyn, NY 11201
versobooks.com

Verso is the imprint of New Left Books

ISBN-13: 978-1-78478-453-9 (PBK)
ISBN-13: 978-1-78478-452-2 (HBK)
ISBN-13: 978-1-78478-454-6 (US EBK)
ISBN-13: 978-1-78478-451-5 (UK EBK)

British Library Cataloguing in Publication Data
A catalogue record for this book is available from the British Library

Library of Congress Cataloging-in-Publication Data
A catalog record for this book is available from the Library of Congress

Typeset in Fournier by Hewer Text UK Ltd, Edinburgh
Printed in the US by Maple Press

Contents

Foreword: The Need to Censor Our Dreams

Slavoj Žižek

Fredric Jameson's *An American Utopia* radically questions standard leftist notions of an emancipated society, advocating—among other things—universal conscription as the model for the communist reorganization of society, fully acknowledging envy and resentment as the central problem of a communist society, and rejecting dreams of overcoming the division between work and pleasure. Endorsing the axiom that to change society one should begin by changing one's dreams about an emancipated society, Jameson's text is ideally placed to trigger a debate on possible and imaginable alternatives to global capitalism.

This volume brings together Jameson's pathbreaking text, especially revised for this edition, with an original short story by Kim Stanley Robinson that plays upon some of Jameson's motifs, philosophers' and political and cultural analysts' reactions to Jameson, and Jameson's short epilogue. Although the reactions are often critical toward Jameson, they all agree on the need to radically rethink the leftist project.

Many leftists (and especially "leftists") will definitely be appalled at what they encounter in this volume—there will be blood, to quote the title of a well-known film. But what if one has to spill such (ideological) blood to give the left another chance?

1

An American Utopia

Fredric Jameson

1.

We have seen a marked diminution in the production of new utopias over the last decades (along with an overwhelming increase in all manner of conceivable dystopias, most of which look monotonously alike). Can these developments be dated or periodized in some way? I have always been tempted to mark the end of utopian production with Ernest Callenbach's great *Ecotopia* of 1975, a work whose most serious flaw, from today's standpoint, is the absence of electronic or informational technology. Maybe the utopian form, then, cannot integrate such technology, or maybe on the other hand the Internet itself has soaked up many of the available utopian fantasy impulses. Or was it the triumph of Reagan-Thatcher financial deregulation in the late 1970s and early 1980s that spelled the end of utopian thinking, at the same time that it seemed to seal the victory of late capitalism over all imaginable, let alone practicable, alternatives?

In fact, the possibilities for utopian thinking were always bound up with the fortunes of a more general concern, not to say obsession, with power. The meditation on power was itself an ambiguous project. In the 1960s this project was a utopian one: it was a question of thinking and reimagining societies without power, particularly in the form of societies before power: here Lévi-Strauss's revival of Rousseau gave rise to the utopian visions of early Baudrillard, of Marshall Sahlins in his *Stone Age Economics*, of Pierre Clastres, and of that supreme utopian vision, *The Forest People* by Colin Turnbull.

Yet at a certain point the inquiry into societies without power begins to turn into an inquiry into the emergence of power in early human societies; this theoretical problem slowly links up with practical politics, in the form of an anti-institutional and anarchist preponderance on the left whose causes are clearly multiple. They range from the failure of May '68 and the disillusionment with the old Communist Parties to the disillusionment with African decolonization, not to speak of the sorry fate of Third Worldism and of the triumphant wars of national liberation, from Algeria to Vietnam. At some such general point the reflection on power acquires its ideological foundations in the work of Michel Foucault and others, reinforced by "revelations" about the gulag, and becomes a dystopian obsession, a quasi-paranoid fear of any form of political or social organization—whether in the formation of political parties of one kind or another or in speculation about the construction of future societies radically different from this one—as well as a desperate brandishing of the terminologies of freedom and democracy by leftists, who ought to know better and to appreciate the quasi-ownership of this language by Western "democracies" or, in other words, by late capitalism. At any rate, these developments in the field of utopias seemed to go hand in hand with the virtual dissolution of practical politics of all kinds on the left. This is the situation in which I want to propose a project about which I can't be sure whether I am proposing a political program or a utopian vision, neither of which, according to me, ought to be possible any longer.

Why not? Well, the left once had a political program called revolution. No one seems to believe in it any longer, partly because the agency supposed to bring it about has disappeared, partly because the system it was supposed to replace has become too omnipresent to begin to imagine replacing it, and partly because the very language associated with revolution has become as old-fashioned and archaic as that of the Founding Fathers. It is easier, someone once said, to imagine the end of the world than the end of capitalism: and with that the idea of a revolution overthrowing capitalism seems to have vanished. Well, let's be fair: the left did have another political strategy, whatever you think about it, and that was reformism—sometimes, in contradistinction to revolutionary communism, called "socialism." But I'm afraid no one believes in that any longer either.

The reformist or social-democratic parties are in a complete shambles: they have no programs of any distinction, save perhaps to regulate capitalism so it does no really catastrophic or irreparable damage. There is omnipresent corruption both in these parties and in the system at large, which is, in any case, too enormous and too complex to be susceptible to any decisive tinkerings which might improve it, let alone lead to something you could truly call systemic change. Social democracy is in our time irretrievably bankrupt, and communism seems dead. Thus, it would seem, neither of Gramsci's celebrated alternatives—the war of maneuver and the war of position—seem any longer theoretically or practically adequate to the present situation.

Fortunately, there exists a third kind of transition out of capitalism which is less often acknowledged, let alone discussed, and that is what was historically called "dual power." Indeed, dual power will be my political program and will lead to my utopian proposal.[1]

---

1 I am grateful to Alberto Toscano and Sebastian Budgen for indispensible guidance in researching this theme.

The phrase is, of course, associated with Lenin and his description of the coexistence of the provisional government and the network of soviets, or workers' and soldiers' councils, in 1917—a genuine transitional period if there ever was one—but it has also existed in numerous other forms of interest to us today. I would most notably single out the way organizations like the Black Panthers yesterday or Hamas today function to provide daily services—food kitchens, garbage collection, health care, water inspection, and the like—in areas neglected by some official central government. (If you like current Foucauldian jargon, you might describe this as a tension or even an opposition between "sovereignty" and "governmentality.") In such situations, power moves to the networks to which people turn for practical help and leadership on a daily basis: in effect, they become an alternate government, without officially challenging the ostensibly legal structure. The point at which a confrontation and a transfer take place, at which the official government begins to "wither away," a point at which revolutionary violence appears, will of course vary with the overall political and cultural context itself.

It is not necessary to supply a historical catalogue of these anomalous structures of transitional coexistence, which range from the dualities of church and state in some periods to that of local communes in the French Revolution (most notably, the first Commune de Paris that supported Danton's still informal power). It might be more useful to indicate the kinds of events or structures that cannot be considered relevant examples of dual power: enclaves, for example, such as Chiapas or Ecotopia, or the free zones of the maroons, which are spatially separate from the dominant state and have their own geographical autonomy. I would also suggest that the current form of the mass uprising, from the Arab Spring to Occupy, does not really qualify either. The first of these two revolutionary phenomena—the enclave—stands as a kind of state within a state; the second—the uprising—as a spatial event that pioneers information technology as a substitute for political organization. (This is not to discount the survival of this or that local armed uprising or guerrilla struggle—this terrain has mostly been reoccupied by militant Islam, which has filled the void left by the mass destruction of radical or revolutionary, secular movements in the former Third World.)

As for the older political parties, the so-called progressive ones such as the Democrats or the various European social democracies, nothing much is to be hoped for from them—at best a holding operation and at worst the pursuit of capitalist ends by other means, such as NAFTA and all kinds of new international arrangements whose ultimate goal and effect lies in the "improvement" of free trade and its construction of new monopolies and the perpetuation of the so-called free market. In that sense, representative democracy is irreparably corrupt and incapable of fulfilling its promises (or "rising to the level of its concept," as Hegel might say); and the left parties always capitulate whenever they come to power.

This is not to say, however, that they have no function whatsoever. Indeed, in the heady days of a kind of utopian anthropology, the ethnologists of pre-power societies explained that in such tribes there already existed chiefs and leaders, but that in the absence of the bodyguards, retinues and priesthoods they would acquire later on after the state had come into being, their role was quite different and probably now unimaginable to us, except in the dynamics of small groups and sects. For in those early times chiefs had but one function, namely to talk, to talk and talk, upon which their alleged subjects simply guffawed or consulted among themselves. The chief was a powerless figure with a purely ritualistic function, to take the floor, to hold forth, to secure the event of the group meeting; and no more, and certainly not the function of the dictatorial, charismatic orator or the secret and ominous source of orders and sentences.[2]

---

2 On this function of the chief, see Pierre Clastres, *La Société contre l'État*, Paris: Minuit, 1974, especially Chapter 2.

Such might be the role of our parties, but with a useful twist and in a very different situation. I believe that it was Stuart Hall who originated the luminous phrase "discursive struggle" (and this is the moment to pay tribute to his memory and his extraordinary theoretical and pedagogical achievements). Discursive struggle—a phrase that originated in the defeat of the Thatcher years and the interrogations around that victory—discursive struggle posited the process whereby slogans, concepts, stereotypes, and accepted wisdoms did battle among each other for preponderance, which is to say, in the quaint language of that day and age, hegemony. Stuart saw that one of the fundamental strategies at work in that victory lay in the deligitimation of the language of its adversaries, in the tireless discrediting of all the slogans, such as nationalization, that were associated with a postwar labor hegemony. And this is a process which is at least relatively distinct from either ideology or propaganda; it is one which deprives the political enemy of its conceptual weapons and at one stroke ages its programs and turns them boring and old-fashioned, unmodern, overused and over-familiar, a thing of the past. The proof is that free-market rhetoric (and that of the "modern") has become omnipresent—that virtually everyone believes, as Mrs. Thatcher did, that there is no alternative—indeed, that there are many people today, perhaps a majority, who believe that the free market actually exists, besides being eternal.

This is then the situation in which the old social-democratic and liberal parties may still be said to have a function: they can serve as vehicles and platforms for some renewed public legitimation of hitherto repressed and stigmatized transformational policies. It was some such function, for example, that the plays of George Bernard Shaw (along with Bertolt Brecht, one of the few great political playwrights of modern times) fulfilled in the British interwar period, a hidebound reactionary and aristocratic period if there ever was one, for Shaw cunningly inserted into all his drawing-room comedies a secondary character, a socialist chauffeur or footman, who by exercising properly left discourse gradually respectabilized it for the fearful upper classes and made its postwar triumph less terrifying. So today it would be incumbent on our otherwise impotent social-democratic parties to "talk socialism" and to breathe life back into the slogans withered and desiccated by the triumphant poison gas of Mrs. Thatcher's breath. (Bernie Sanders, indeed, seems today to have begun to assume such a function.)

This is of course a matter of collective rather than individual rhetoric, with its own intricacies and technological and collective novelties; nor is this the place to explore them. But surely the most important achievement of any such exercise in discursive struggle is the rehabilitation of nationalization, and behind that, the replacement of the universally detested target of "big government" with the more stirring realities of collective commitment. It is the rehabilitation as well of that even more viscerally repugnant social entity called "bureaucracy," by way of a historical reminder of the glorious roles that social stratum has played in the great literacy campaigns, in the struggles for unionization, in the commitment of teachers to the displacement of superstition-ridden clerical schools in the France of the early Third Republic, or the self-sacrifice of socialist doctors in the first days of the national health services in Britain and in Canada—in short, some welcome renewal of an acknowledgement of the altruistic fervor and sacrifice such as we witness historically in the movements of social workers through the ages.

As for the themes to be floated and relegitimized in this way, surely none is more actual than the nationalization of finance, of banks and insurance companies and investment institutions of all kinds; even though, more recently, what has come to seem more immediately urgent, particularly in the era of climate change now upon us, is the wholesale seizure of all energy sources, the appropriation of the oil wells and the coal mines and the destitution of the immense transnational companies that control them. This is not to neglect the other urgent issues confronting people on a daily basis: the need for draconian taxation of the great corporations, if not their outright appropriation; the gradual redistribution of wealth, not excluding the eventual abolition of inheritance as such; the establishment of a guaranteed annual minimum wage; the dissolution of NATO; popular control of the media and the prohibition of the most noxious right-wing propaganda; universal wi-fi; the abolition of tuition and the reconstruction of free and universal public education, including substantial reinvestment in teachers' salaries; free health care; full employment; and so on and so forth, in no particular order.

Besides these substantive policies, which the political parties might well wish artificially to endorse, thereby educating a public otherwise carefully screened from them by media self-censorship, there is a whole politics of words and terms implicit in the Thatcherite "discursive struggle." This presents another promising, if related, terrain of struggle: the word "austerity," for example, harbors within itself a whole neoconservative economic theory as well as a concentrated verbal slogan and target for political demonstration. In a more positive direction, meanwhile, the word "debt," as it was dramatized by the Occupy movement, suddenly crystallized a whole new theoretical perspective on capitalism as well as a practical-political program of a positive and substantive nature; indeed, "debt" quickly became an "empty signifier" capable of mobilizing a number of distinct political strategies at one and the same time. It should be understood that under the current system of representative government, the political parties can never accomplish any of these things, but they can talk about them, they can make them thinkable and conceivable once again, they can plant the seeds and rekindle the possibility of imagining future praxis—and they can reestablish these themes in their legitimate place in the public sphere.

2.

As for the realization of such monumental changes, that can only be the task of dual power as such; and it is now time to examine our society as it is today in order to weigh the chances for dual power and to identify those already existing institutions which could be its vehicle. Traditionally, of course, it is to labor unions which the left has always turned to as its base and its natural constituency: the very nature of the proletariat has been transformed and enlarged by the transformation of peasants into farmworkers, by underpaid service industries, and by the white-collar workers in a now immense government bureaucracy. On the other hand, as everyone knows, the original industrial character of work has itself been reduced by information technology and the power of the unions greatly diminished; traditionally, in any case, there was always a tension between the unions and the political parties, which had different aims. Nor must we underestimate the success of anti-union propaganda during the dissolution of the New Deal, that is, for the whole of the Cold War, by way of alleged association with the Mafia, with corruption, and with the stigma of identification as a "special interest," as we call lobbying groups in this country. The defeat in Wisconsin, after one of the most encouraging political developments in recent years, is sad proof that this kind of anti-union prejudice persists unabated. Unions no longer offer an effective chance at dual power, if they ever did.

But even a renewed unionization movement faces new and major structural challenges in the postmodern era. For one thing, everyone assures us that in the new era there will be no such thing as stable employment in a single line of work, let alone a single enterprise—assuming there is any employment at all. In fact, we are entering an age of massive structural unemployment, in which the fundamental organizational problem is no longer that of unifying workers assembled in a single locality and sharing concerns about a clearly defined work process but rather organizing the unemployed, who not only do not share a workplace or shop floor but may not even have semi-permanent housing. They do not share routines or priorities, they do not even communicate with each other, and no particular signal can assemble them in meetings; at best they are unified by soup kitchens and flophouses, and not even the same ones from night to night.

The second problem is that the predominant mode of employment in this new era of unemployment is that of what has been called the "gray market": not illegal work in the sense of criminality, drug smuggling and distribution and the like, but rather ad hoc work from job to job and from place to place, on the order of mobile food trucks or informal car repair from neighborhood to neighborhood out of your own pickup. Small business now trends in this direction; if it is not altogether absorbed into those larger monopolistic networks into which dry-cleaning establishments and fast-food restaurants (for example) are forced, then it shrinks in the other direction into individual services, which face a different kind of monopolization, as we shall see in a moment. At any rate, it is clear that the transformation of small business (already immune to unionization) into such individualistic service provision makes for a population for whom union organization can only mean something political, not a fundamentally economic form of self-protection and collectivity. Maybe we should conclude that in this society it is in fact the Mafia which offers the most suggestive example of already existing dual power; however, its effectiveness in a national context seems to have waned as significantly as that of the unions themselves.

Indeed, books like Roberto Saviano's *Gomorrah* suggest that as a business, the Mafia itself (using the term now in a generic sense) has been transformed by globalization and, unlike the unions, has taken on many of the features of a transnational institution. This might suggest a model for world government (we might relate it to paranoid fantasies of that omnipotent UN readying its black helicopters to destroy local American institutions), but it means that in the national context, the local power of crime has been as seriously weakened in its effectiveness as the unions themselves.

Perhaps the emergence of gangs and the drug trade is a symptom and a compensation for this institutional weakness. Thus the globalization of crime leaves a local void into which different kinds of small-scale collectives flow: a void filled by gangs and groupuscules organized along neo-ethnic and identity-political lines, and suggesting a more general pattern of development: a dialectic whereby the well-known "weakening" of the nation-state gives rise to a new reorganization of binary oppositions and a new set of coordinated but polar developments.

Global and local: this idiotic formula, which has known extraordinary and indeed worldwide success in furnishing a brand-new stereotype for new yet still incomprehensible developments, is little more than a caricature of a dialectic of space acted out on all conceivable levels of postmodernity, from the economic and the social all the way to culture and individual existence. On all these dimensions, entities (seemingly of an institutional kind) which are somehow "larger than life" and thus unrepresentable in the form of individual existence move further and further away from a micro-level of human experience, in which everything seems to have been reduced to a present of time without a temporal context. The "global" becomes unimaginable, while the "local" becomes unthinkable and accessible only to bodily sensation and experience. It is a reorganization of oppositions which has left its afterimage on the historically sensitive philosophical template in the form of a seemingly new, yet also very old, struggle between universals and what are no longer particulars but rather singularities. The category of individuality, which was once a kind of Hegelian "synthesis" between universality and particularity, has dissolved altogether, and one finds oneself confronting a complex of terms or semes in which, characteristically, the fourth position remains enigmatic and unfilled, mysterious, the object of conjecture and philosophical speculation:

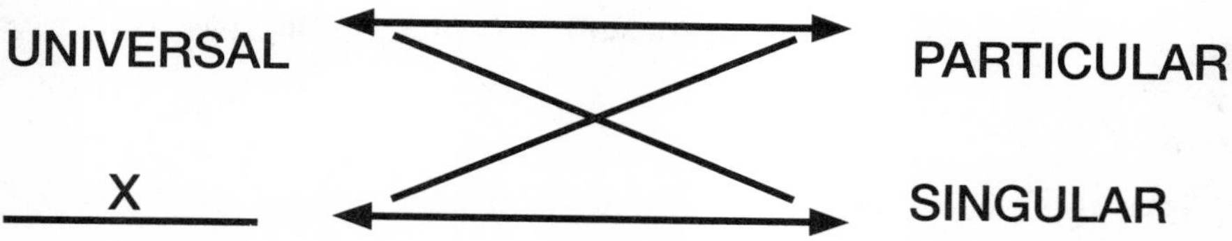

I would propose, but only provisionally, that the empty slot that might stand at one and the same time for the nonparticular and the antisingular be penciled in as sheer standardization, the production of entities of equal value (in the Marxian sense) that have no longer anything distinctive or particular about them, but which also cannot count as unique in the sense of singularities. They are thus grotesque shadows of universalities that no longer function to organize anything but which are equally inaccessible to either reason or sense alike: both tasteless and unthinkable all at once.

The new standardization, which can still be thought of, if one likes, in terms of Marx's analysis of commodities, also reminds us of Cartesian extension, a kind of underlying substance which is neither Kantian *Ding an sich* nor a Spinozan attribute but which, unlike the formless concept of "matter," is historical in its essence and existence. It is the identity of difference, foretold by Hegel's *Logic* and replayed in all its possible combinations by Derrida's tireless mental exercises, whose only flaw was the omission of prophecy—for standardization was something that deserved to be prophesied historically and then reconfirmed, *après coup*, as a prophecy which came true.

We will call it space, and thereby complete the diagnosis of the supersession of time by space in a description of postmodernity which was also meant to be a historical and political diagnosis. It is a development which can now be dramatized politically, for I want to suggest that it is strikingly confirmed by the evolution of politics itself, whose extraordinary verities throughout history seem today, on the global scale, to have been themselves reduced and standardized on a well-nigh global scale. I will put a very simple proposition to you: namely that today, all politics is about real estate. Postmodern politics is essentially a matter of land grabs, on a local as well as a global scale. Whether you think of the question of Palestine, the settlements and the camps, or of the politics of raw materials and extraction; whether you think of ecology (and the rainforests) or the problems of federalism, citizenship, and immigration, or whether it is a question of gentrification in the great cities as well as in the *bidonvilles*, the *favelas* and the townships and of course the movement of the landless—today everything is about land. In Marxist terms, all these struggles result from the commodification of land, the dissolution of the last remnants of feudalism and its peasantries, and their replacement by industrial agriculture or agribusiness and farmworkers.

Where is time in all this? It is to be found in the new flash crowds enabled by cell phones and texting: the new mass demonstrations of Seattle and of Eastern Europe, of Tahrir Square and of Wisconsin and of Occupy. These truly mark the emergence of what my friends Michael Hardt and Toni Negri call "multitude"; they are no longer the politics of duration but the politics of the instant, of the present, what Negri himself has called constituent power, as opposed to the constituted kind. Postmodernity in general is characterized by this new kind of present of time, a reduction to the body. In this new dialectic of omnipresent space and the living or temporal present, history, historicity, the sense of history, is the loser: the past is gone, we can no longer imagine the future. We will return to space shortly in a different context; but it is clear enough that this waning of history, of historicity or historical consciousness, confronts those of us still committed to radical systemic change with some very real political problems, and in particular with the obligation to think revolution in a new way, one here conceptualized as dual power.

3.

We have thus been led to a search for institutions within the already existing state capable of producing or at least making possible and conceivable a situation of dual power. And we have unexpectedly arrived at the possibility of formulating some historically new preconditions required for such an eventuality. Obviously, it has been clear that the need for a revolutionary concept of dual power to fill in the gaps left by the disappearance of the older twin Gramscian concepts of revolution had everything to do not just with the end of the Cold War but above all with that globalization which spelled an end to the way global class struggle had hitherto been waged—both in its political-practical and its ideological forms. So from the outset we might well have formulated our quest in this way: What form can a situation of dual power take in the new world of globalization—of the communicationalization of capital, the globalization of finance capital and of a new kind of extractive neo-imperialism, of a post-national world fitfully controlled by a capitalist hegemon?

But now we may add yet another feature, for we have found that globalization also entailed the preponderance of space as such, and that our framework needed to be enlarged in order to include this fundamental component in its questions. Yet, at the same time, the absence of globalization from our initial framework is explained by our deliberate attempt to reduce this issue to the US context, and it is therefore at once in that context that we need to reformulate the question of space as a new and postmodern problem. I will therefore at this point wish to claim that the unique feature of American space (which I also characterize as a non-national reality) is a historical construction of the American Constitution, and therefore that whoever interrogates political possibility in the United States must necessarily confront the unique problems posed by that counterrevolutionary document, which also claims to be a form of federalism. Indeed, we must anticipate that federalism will remain a fundamental theoretical issue for any utopian projection today. I have argued elsewhere that the collapse of the Soviet Union was not the result of a failure of socialism but rather a failure of federalism, and that the Yugoslavian civil war as well as various federal crises all around the world, from Canada to Spain, from Thailand to Chiapas, are all signs that this is an essentially unsolved dilemma for political theory generally. We will return to it.

At any rate, it is under this triple problematic—globalization, space, federalism—that we return to our incomplete inventory of American institutions capable of assuming a decisive role in a situation of dual power.

What candidates can we identify to play the role of a parallel and non-state power I have been imagining? Almost all of them have suffered the institutional debilitation endemic to late capitalism. Take, for example, the post office. In Europe it is a kind of savings bank as well; here it offers a parallel to the census and could presumably, along with your motor vehicle agency, secure your voting rights. It distributes retirement, pension, and Social Security checks, and is apparently even developing some kind of institutional relationship with its former mortal enemy, the Internet; it mints money, in the form of stamps; it used to be an important source of employment, particularly for those seeking to drop out of the system as inconspicuously as possible; and, generally on foot, it offers a unique, even utopian, experience of nature as well as of urban space and an equally unique relationship to the community, where that still exists. But once again, information technology now stands as an absolute historical break with whatever utopias might have been imagined on the basis of this uniquely relational system, about which Lenin, in *State and Revolution*, took as the Paris Commune's lesson for communism itself: "to organize our whole material economy like the postal system, but in such a way that the technical experts, inspectors, clerks, and indeed all persons employed, should receive no higher wage than the working man."

The professions do not seem any more promising: the legal profession, for example, could scarcely stand in competition with the state insofar as it *is* the state in the first place, something confirmed by the judiciary system's loss of autonomy in our time. Yet the professions—such as lawyers and doctors—possess extremely complex infrastructures capable under certain circumstances of providing an alternate ruling apparatus. Indeed, it might even be argued that the judicial system in this country is already on the point of becoming such an apparatus, with its extensive veto powers on legislation and its virtual population control by way of the penal machinery and its proximity to the various police forces. As in logic, the judgment is the central act around which this system is organized (Kafka's work is something like a caricature or afterimage of a world in which judgment in this sense is the fundamental reality), and it provides an occasion to reflect on how much of life and experience is excluded when judgment, in all its philosophical and practical senses, is the focus through which the latter are exclusively perceived and organized. It is indeed a kind of dystopia distinct from that projected by the conventional image of the military, insofar as power and domination are here replaced by judgment as such, so that the permanent presence of the Other here becomes a far more central (and irresolvable) source of concern and anxiety.

For an aging population, the medical profession might seem to offer more promising material, insofar as its material benefits and necessities come doubled by the sort of moral authority with which Plato wanted to surround his philosopher-kings. But the privatization of the hospitals and the institutionalization of the private practitioner bid fair to strip away that aura, and the doctors have for the most part had to bow to the economic power of insurance companies and pharmaceutical giants, while their guilds—such as the American Medical Association, which functioned in the past as a powerful anti-political lobby on the order of the National Rifle Association—are seemingly no longer very effective.

Yet a society organized around health standards and the production of accessible drugs and foods is certainly conceivable: far more than a utopia of lawyers (Callenbach liked to insist on the beneficial litigiousness of his Ecotopia), it would necessarily presuppose the standard elite of philosopher-kings, given the highly specialized knowledge its decisions would seem to presuppose. On the other hand, such a bio-society (for the currently popular prefix seems nowhere quite so appropriate as in this particular formation) seems ready-made for corruption and inequality, as the current symbiosis with the insurance companies suggests, along with the various science-fictional fantasies about black-market organ transplants and whole syndicates based on their distribution. Money and wealth are at the very heart of such fantasies, to the point where it seems difficult to separate the medical profession out as a distinct structure. Nonetheless, it may not be impossible to imagine crisis situations in which physicians are able to wield social power of considerable significance, in a kind of epidemiological dual structure.

Then there are the churches, many of which do function as a nation within the nation and provide solace and the proverbial "heart of a heartless world" to families alienated by late capitalism. Nor was Robespierre wrong, it seems to me, to call, following Rousseau, for a state religion, a secular religion of reason of some kind, inasmuch as neither had any other concept for what necessarily binds a society together. I suggest that rather than religion it is the fetish as such that provides social cohesion in those instances in which the latter has been possible: the American Constitution, the French conception of the Republic, the Japanese imperial system, certain repressed national languages—these are so many examples of fetishes which have proved more successful than the usual forms of patriotism and dynastic succession, and any possibility for the emergence of a second system of power alongside the first, established and official one, will need to draw on the power of just such a fetish. The fetish—is this to be thought of as a fiction or yet another "as if," the mother's phallus, let alone the phallus itself? Is it a form of belief or religion, let alone the very foundation of all the religions themselves, the bedrock of fanaticism which is somehow to be avoided at all costs, even though it holds everything else together? Or, when we become conscious of it, does it not wither into yet another dried-out, conventional ritual like the flag, thereby becoming useless save for the real believers, who are clearly the most dangerous elements? What, in other words, is the truth of the fetish? Might it not be regarded with that ambiguity of modern art, the reflexive kind, which reminds us that it is itself only an impossible symbol and sends us back to impossibility rather than anything real? Or is a single fetish possible for the multiplicity, and should it not be an empty signifier, capable of taking on any number of local meanings while continuing to be worshipped by all?

Religion, however, is clearly the most dangerous of all candidates for dual power, based as it is on what Kant would have called a subreption, a mistaking of superstructure for base: in fact, the target of the Enlightenment was not religion so much as the priesthood, and it is not the extirpation of religion and any absolute secularization which is required so much as a constant surveillance of the various religious movements. Religion itself, as Cornel West has pointed out, is a fundamental component of American mass culture: it is a place for the organization of small groups and communities and also the pretext for the encouragement of all kinds of manias, fantasies, and wish-fulfillments of an individual as well as collective nature. I will argue in a moment that there is a place for both these things in a different kind of society, but that they should be restricted to the realm of culture as such.

4.

But if business, the professions, religion, even the labor unions (let alone the post office or the Mafia) are inadequate vehicles for dual power, what can then be left in late capitalism as an already organized institution capable of assuming the parallel and ultimately revolutionary role on which alone radical social change depends?

This is the moment to mention a final candidate, the only subsystem left which can function in so truly revolutionary a fashion. It is a thought that must have first come to me many years ago, inspired by an image by one of our greatest political cartoonists. I think it must have been during the first year of the Eisenhower presidency, if not still during the campaign, when the last vestiges of the New Deal still survived in Truman's ill-fated campaign for socialized medicine on the English and the Canadian model. Ike, presumably in full military regalia, perches informally on the edge of the desk in the Oval Office and observes conversationally, "Well, if they want socialized medicine, they have only to join the Army as I did."

This is indeed very precisely the strategy I propose, the recipe for a new form of dual power. Indeed, confirmation comes to us from the far future, in a news report from the future by Terry Bisson: "August 3, 2076. New Veterans Day. Invoking her power as Commander-in-Chief, President Junni inducts 228 million 'draftees' into the National Guard. Their honorable discharge in 24 hours will guarantee medical care for all Americans through the Veterans Administration."[3] I will only add that this bulletin suggests emergency powers already in the power of the president, without any need for congressional debate and approval. It also suggests, along with my cartoon, that the best approach to our proposal is precisely through this matter of health care and not through the army's more obvious military functions. The Veterans Administration hospitals have already been described recently (by Senator Sanders) as a system of socialized medicine with no connections whatsoever to the immense private medical and hospital organizations surrounding it: their woeful conditions and

3 Terry Bisson, "This Month in History," *Locus*, August 2011, p. 19.

deplorable underfunding is then one more illustration, if any more were needed, of the fate of socialist or even public enclaves within an all-embracing late-capitalist system. But it suffices to look at Cuba, even today, to get an idea of a different kind of medical practice in a radically different system (the papers never make much of it when the Cubans send medical teams to assist their non-socialist neighbors during catastrophic emergencies, as they offered to do in Katrina).

At any rate, and returning to the topic at hand, perhaps this particular issue of health care is enough to suggest that the army is a viable candidate for the emergence of dual power I have been imagining here: it is not a utopian scheme but eminently practical. Yet I will have to warn you that we will eventually approach a moment, in evoking radical social change and in describing what it is perfectly proper to call a revolution, when the practical project necessarily passes over into a utopian projection.

Excursus I: On the Withering Away of Political Theory

I have so often deplored the revival of antiquated branches of philosophy—ethics, aesthetics—in a postmodern situation of de-differentiation in which, on the contrary, the various subfields of such a discipline should be asked to fold back on each other and disappear (and perhaps along with them, philosophy itself), that it is a pleasure to be able to include political theory among them as well. It should be obvious that the withering away of the state inevitably brings with it the withering away of that thinking whose object is essentially the state as such (the polis).

Indeed, in order to see this new army—the universal army—in the proper light, it is necessary to understand that it is not a new form of government but rather a new social structure, or better still, a new socioeconomic structure, as we shall see. In the transitional phase—that of dual power—the coexistence of the old state and the new one will indeed seem to be a rivalry of governmental powers; little by little, however, it will be understood that it is the old state which is in reality the "government," and destined as such to "wither away," and the new structure, which is in fact the society at large or, if you prefer, the completion of that "civil society" which Hegel in his own time took to be simply the sphere of private life and of business and commerce. There are suggestive analogies to this process in antiquity: for example, when Augustus founded the Roman Empire as such, he was careful to leave the institutions of the Republic in place. The Senate continued to exist, to meet and deliberate, to give lengthy speeches on the order of those pre-power tribal chieftains of whom we have already spoken, and with the same effects. Meanwhile, antiquity also affords methods of dealing with the fear of dictatorship that inevitably arises in a biological species like our own, in which collectivity is so absolutely sundered from individuation. Indeed, the very word derives from that worthy institution according to which, in a crisis situation, an individual of some unique endowment is accorded exceptional power for a limited period of time, after which he sinks back into equality with the population (or is more often simply banished). The crisis itself is then usefully marked by another ancient institution, the temple of Janus, whose doors are ceremoniously opened at its onset and then closed again to signal the return to normalcy and the conclusion of the imperilment, in an effort to institutionalize what Carl Schmitt famously theorized as the "state of exception." Such states are often thought of in terms of William James's symptomatic American misconception, for in America, wars *are* the moral equivalent of collective action, as witness the great American utopia of World War II. In the twin situation of the economic anarchy of late capitalism and the irreparable ecological damage of nature by contemporary industrial exploitation (whose simultaneity is not accidental), we must invent better temporal models of crisis, long- and short-term, than those afforded by war.

We must also cure ourselves of the habit of thinking politically, for politics is the art of power and of the state. If the latter is effectively to wither away, then we must confidently expect political theory to wither away along with it. As I will continue to snipe at political theory throughout, and to argue for its replacement by a properly utopian kind, I will here explain my fundamental position, namely that the essentials of political theory were already established thousands of years ago by Polybius in his codification of the three types of government (or state) and their degenerate forms. Everything since then (including Machiavelli) has been engineering the invention of forms of statecraft appropriate to these three forms, which are taken as ontology—that is, as given in advance—while Rousseau's cancellation of the scheme, in *The Social Contract*, has rarely been thought through to its utopian conclusion.

Political theory takes as its object problems without solutions; utopian speculation solutions without problems. The first constitutes an ontology which is necessarily obliged to work within the limits of being and of reality as it currently exists. The latter aims at a radical transformation of the present and its system: in that respect, it is the sibling of revolutionary thought and today occupies the place of a revolutionary politics which has not yet fully reemerged from the transformations of globalization and postmodernity, of finance capital on a world scale. Utopian thinking demands a revision of Gramsci's famous slogan, which might now run: cynicism of the intellect, utopianism of the will. A generalized cynicism is indeed one way of characterizing the political transparency of contemporary or postmodern society, in which "they know what they're doing but they do it anyway," in which everyone is a Marxist and understands the dynamics and the depredations of capitalism without feeling it possible to do anything about them.

The problem with representative systems is deeply embedded in the very nature of political thought itself, whose very name conceals a reference to a specific form of political organization based on slavery—the polis. What I would have liked to argue here at greater length is a critique of political philosophy in general: it is already implicit, of course, in the way Marxism seeks to reground social and political interpretation in the economic and in class; but we can come at it from the other side by pointing out the failure of all political theory to constitute its object, which is the collective as such. We have reached a moment philosophically in which people are willing to agree that there is no adequate way of thinking the individual subject, in which various philosophical schools have sought to dispel ideological conceptions of a so-called centered subject and have proposed a variety of untenable alternatives, from multiple subject positions to a radical separation of consciousness as such from various notions of selves or personal identities.

We should be willing to do the same for all the forms in which thinkers have failed in much the same way to conceptualize collective entities. I want to make a philosophical point here; I suppose it is a Kantian one, since it involves the impossibility of thinking certain kinds of things (such as that peculiar thing-in-itself called consciousness, which no human philosopher has ever been able to describe); for it seems to me the same with collective reality. That is, owing to our individuation as biological individuals, the collective is as such also impossible to conceptualize. This is the point Rousseau was trying to make in *The Social Contract* by proposing a kind of unthinkable, unrepresentable "regulative idea" in his "general will"; when Kant praised the emergence of the written constitution, he was not endorsing a type of government or state, but rather singling out the moment when a collectivity comes to "maturity" (or the coming to age at which the individual is liberated from tutelage), by taking the formation of the new society into its own hands, as a deliberate and collective act.

But here I need to pause and to rectify the misunderstandings Kant's formulation is likely to perpetuate, for the dilemma in thinking the collectivity has in modern times generally led to an unacceptable result, namely that from Aristotle to Kant and on, the prejudice that the ultimate aim and endpoint of political theory lies in the drafting of a constitution, conceived as the bringing to an end of revolution rather than its apotheosis. I like Toni Negri's masterful analysis, in which he shows how the arrival of constituted (constitutional) power shuts down that brief moment of freedom of the *constituante*, of the construction of power. But remember that the strength of the universal army scheme is that it cuts across the federal constitution in a wholly novel way, transgressing its boundaries and carefully drawn limits without annulling it, leaving its map intact beneath a wholly different topology.

But to return to my argument about the collective (using the most neutral term for something that by definition cannot be named, let alone conceptualized) and to pursue its thesis about the latter's unrepresentability: one has only to pass in review the various candidates—tribes, clans, groups, communities, *Gemeinschaften*, *Gesellschaften*, mobs, crowds, peoples, nations, democracies, republics, cooperatives, even multitudes (I should add that the concept of social class is not a concept of this kind)—to see that all are in the long run both defective and ideological. I take a Kantian critical perspective on the impossibility for "reason" to think, let alone to name, the multiple and the plural, a dilemma that generally only comes into view when that other unnamable reality—population—makes its scandalous presence unavoidable yet unmentionable. "Un peuple à venir," was Deleuze's wise version of this representational impossibility: implying that any name, by suggesting that such a thing already existed, was an oppression and a normative or repressive ideology. This is why the plural cannot have majorities or minorities either; it is also why political theory cannot be a substantive discipline.

I give a quick example of its insufficiencies before moving on. Recently, the old untenable notion of underdevelopment—unsatisfactory because, as Robert Kurz showed, it implies that development and so-called modernity are still possible—has been succeeded with a new slogan, namely that of the "failed state": a pseudo-concept which really cannot be blamed on the neocons inasmuch as it is today the basis of everyone's foreign policy. This expression is all the more ridiculous in light of the fact that today all states are failed states, very much including this one (the United States). None of them function, none of them can be patched up, even with the usual band-aids of propaganda. Not even dictatorships work anymore, as we have lately seen; and one is, reluctantly or not, drawn back to Samuel Huntington's scandalous conclusion, namely that the more democracy there is, the less governable a state—indeed, that genuine democracy is ungovernable and irreconcilable with capitalism. We must, however, draw the opposite conclusion from his, and as a consequence abandon government altogether.

In fact, no one wants a state any longer, failed or not; all the factions are united in denouncing it. But as the state is the privileged subject matter of political theory, we must abandon political theory as well. I return therefore to the proposition that it is population which is both the conceptual and the social scandal: that philosophically fearful thing called the "Other" which has haunted modern thought in recent years is in reality plural, and it is population as such that constitutes otherness. Not overpopulation, as Malthus thought; not underpopulation, as the early-twentieth-century French thought (along with other countries today); but simply sheer plurality and multiplicity.

Nor is this scandal of the Real to be avoided in the other direction by retreating into nostalgic micro-groups or clans of a fantasy ethnic type, the groupuscules of today's politics, the imaginary players in the so-called "culture wars" of current American politics. These singularities are as ineffectual, in theory as in practice, as the universalities they are supposed to subvert. Yet they are precious symptoms of the inability of late capitalism to provide even the rudiments of collective life; they are the heart of a heartless world, to use Marx's old description of religions and churches. It is not to replace such imagined or, better still, imaginary communities and micro-groups of all kinds that the universal army is called upon, but it seems to me there is a better way of putting them in their place (and allowing them to flourish as they will), and this brings us to the substitution of utopian thinking for politics and political theory.

This is also the moment when we pass from what remains a concrete political program—the conscription of the entire population into some glorified National Guard—to that rather different matter which is the imagining of utopias. And here, to be sure, we enter a no-man's-land (which is also that of dual power), in which assessments of the current situation give way to personal and private visions of all kinds and in which rational revolutionary calculations necessarily give way to fantasy, including those of the crackpots and oddballs who were our great utopian thinkers. This is therefore the moment in which we may all begin to diverge, substituting our private utopian predilections and gadgets for sober analysis.

5.

But we are not yet so far, and for the moment remain with banal historical and political reality. The army we currently have is what is called a volunteer army, that is, a commercial profession like any other. I need not remind us of the history of citizen armies, from the Greeks to Machiavelli, and very much including the French Revolution. These armies, based on the draft, had political missions, most notably in modern times to forge the nation out of a variety of local and provincial populations sometimes not even speaking the national language (itself a political creation of the new national state). To be sure, nowadays the media have already done that for us, but the usefulness of the analogy lies in the fact that, in our federal system, the army is virtually the only institution to transcend the jurisdiction of state laws and boundaries, divisions which were among the most important counterrevolutionary principles embedded in the American Constitution, itself one of the most successful counterrevolutionary schemes ever devised. No genuine systemic change can take place here without an abrogation of the Constitution—a foundational fetish, as I have claimed, and a document the left itself would be as loath to forfeit as the right, owing to the protections of the Bill of Rights. The signal advantage of the army as a system is that it transcends that document without doing away with it; it coexists with it at a different spatial level and becomes thereby a potentially extraordinary instrument in the erection of dual power.

As for the draft, it is preeminently symbolic that Nixon ended the draft in order to put an end to popular, and in particular student, resistance to the war in Vietnam (Johnson had already modified the draft with hosts of class and racial exemptions in order to limit its political impact). More recently, during the Iraq war or what we may call the Rumsfeld period, this professional army has been further privatized—and I insist on the relevance of this word for the way it underscores the relationship with the variety of other economic or free-market privatizations all over the world inaugurated by the Reagan-Thatcher regimes. Rumsfeld further privatized this already specialized and salaried private army by outsourcing many of its functions to private corporations of the Blackwater type, and by introducing complex advanced technology in order to render other portions of the military workforce redundant—that is, by downsizing them via mechanization (a process Marx described in *Capital*). This very significant moment in the history of the modern army had a political purpose above and beyond its adaptation of current late-capitalist business practices: that purpose was to remove this small professionalized group possessing Weber's proverbial monopoly of violence (currently only .05 percent of the population) from any possibility of mass democratic action and, further, to assimilate it to the structure of the police force, which it seems now to have become on a global scale.

So the first step in my utopian proposal is, so to speak, the renationalization of the army along the lines of any number of other socialist candidates for nationalization (some of which I mentioned above), by reintroducing the draft to transform the present armed forces back into that popular mass force capable of coexisting successfully with an increasingly unrepresentative "representative government," and transforming it into a vehicle for mass democracy rather than the representative kind.

Inasmuch as the army continues to be associated with the various *coups d'état* of modern times all over the world, as well as with all the wars it has been called on to wage in recent years, I will at once specify the most important steps in the process. First of all, the body of eligible draftees would be increased by including everyone from sixteen to fifty, or, if you prefer, sixty years of age: that is, virtually the entire adult population. Such an unmanageable body would henceforth be incapable of waging foreign wars, let alone carrying out successful coups. In order to emphasize the universality of the process, let's add that the handicapped would all be found appropriate positions in the system, and that pacifists and conscientious objectors would be placed in control of arms development, arms storage, and the like.

Now I need to remind you of the breadth of the military system, particularly under the pre-Rumsfeld dispensation.[4] We have already begun with medical attention, and in particular the veterans' hospitals, which are currently in desperate straits, at the very moment when hospitals themselves, the private kind, have become

4 See on all this Jennifer Mittelstadt, *The Rise of the Military Welfare State*, Cambridge: Harvard University Press, 2015.

big business in the United States. In our new universal system, of course, the military hospitals would become a free national health service open to everyone (insofar as everyone is now a service person or a veteran) and the entire center of gravity of universal health care, and also, I would add, pharmaceutical production, disease control, and experimentation with and production of new medicines, would now be reorganized and situated within the army itself.

We may also assume a reorientation of education itself under military auspices, not merely for the children of this military population but for various advanced degrees. Nowadays it is difficult to think of any kind of advanced training, save perhaps for business schools, that would not be required within this system (the Army Corps of Engineers is the obvious example). We may think of the socialist (or ex-socialist) countries for models of our situation, in which the various armies included such functions as the manufacture of clothing, the production of films, the eventual production of motor vehicles, and even (as in China) a writers' union, in which intellectuals and writers and artists found their space and income. The army is also notoriously the source of manpower for disaster relief, infrastructural repair and construction and the like; the question of food supply would immediately place this institution (if it can still be called that) in charge of the ordering and supply of food production and therefore in a controlling position for that fundamental dietetic and agronomic activity as well.

6.

The utopian tradition, indeed, offers many different kinds of examples of an attempt to project a future or at least a better social structure from the army as a collective institution, inevitably beginning with Plato's *Republic* (and with the image of Sparta that haunts the ancient world) and fertilizing the monastic system of the Middle Ages (whose open identification with the army is at length disclosed by Loyola). These thought experiments all seem, in various proportions, to deploy emphases on discipline and hierarchy, issues that scarcely vanish from their modern counterparts. But the emergence of the modern armies, with firepower and the transformation of discipline into a new and as it were Cartesian or mathematical kind of exercise (with Maurice of Nassau), introduce a new issue that modifies this traditional semiotic: it is the relationship to the civilian population, or, stated another way, the possibility of a substitution, for the standing army, of citizen militias (Machiavelli), or later on, as its virtual climax, the nation-in-arms of the French Revolution. It is as though the practice of the ancient Greek city-states had reemerged, transformed into a political and social issue by modernity as such (something that could only have been thinkable with the reemergence of the city-state as a form in medieval Italy, along with the charged word "commune," which will have a glorious future ahead of it).

This means that the association of a new utopian state with armies and army organization can henceforth cut both ways: it can serve as a new form of social articulation, as the modern army begins to translate hierarchy into a differentiation of functions, or it can aim at democratizing the army itself and inventing some new relationship between civilian society and this foreign body which has come into extraterritorial existence in its midst. If we take Edward Bellamy and his "industrial army" as the most dramatic exemplification of the first of these tendencies, then it becomes clearer that the articulation in question is historically imposed by the development of industry itself, with its multiplicity of functions and operations. As for the second, it becomes perhaps clearest in Jean Jaurès's proposal for a *nouvelle armée* in the years immediately preceding World War I, when, after the defeat of 1870 and the loss of Alsace-Lorraine, the French were only too conscious of yet another possible conflict with their militarily sophisticated and powerful neighbor. Without trying to assess the cultural limits this mythological conflict places on that internationalist refusal of the war credits so crucial to Zimmerwald and the future communist movement, it is only fair to underscore Jaurès's insistence on the pursuit of an essentially defensive war, a precondition which leads him to the question of the reserves and their use. They must be territorial and integrated into their local societies. Unlike the initial function of national conscription, meant to remove locals from their provincial habitats and instill in them some awareness of the new national framework and the national language, Jaurès's proposal aims at emphasizing the commitment of the reserves to their local terrain and social life, thus foreseeing a resistance of localities on the ground to impede the forward movement of an enemy army of the old style. It is a proposal in which one can recognize the tradition of the militias and the evolving fortunes of guerrilla warfare, from the Spanish resistance to Napoleon all the way to the jihadists of the present day. "The guerrilla must move among the people like a fish in the water," said Mao Ze-dong, in a formula which emphasizes difference fully as much as identity, no longer affirming the assimilation of army and people but rather the emergence of professional revolutionaries. Only in the Cuban *foco* theory (theorized by Régis Debray) will the two entities know a new kind of utopian fusion, but this in a space beyond city and country (bourgeois and peasant) alike—the Sierra Maestra. The generational appearance of a kind of aristocracy of the partisan or revolutionary families and their descendants in postrevolutionary societies is then a development as ominous for future socialists and postrevolutionary states as the emergence of the feudal barons in the Dark Ages.

Trotsky's version of military democracy, more modern than the militia tradition, then returns to Bellamy's model, but in a situation of absolute crisis, in the midst of the war communism of the besieged Soviet state. His aggressive defense of discipline is a welcome antidote to the democratic platitudes of Kautsky and the Social Democrats and of the Mensheviks and their followers, and should today be replaced in the context of a generalized left attack on representative political systems, a critique in my opinion better served by the abandonment of the even more provocative terminology of a "dictatorship of the proletariat," however much its spirit should be affirmed. Terms like "democracy," which are, as it were, the private property of US foreign policy more generally, do not regain their force unless we grasp them in Samuel Huntington's sense, alluded to above, namely that democracy and capitalism are incompatible (big business cannot function in a situation in which budgets and fiscal policies in general are decided by popular vote).

Trotsky is indeed very strong in his reminder that "free" in such contexts has the primary denotation of wage labor: "for the liberal, freedom in the long run means the market."[5] Freedom is not some eternal metaphysical or Platonic concept, it is historically determined, with its fundamental reference anchored in the experience of human temporality, which is to say of labor:

> History has known slave labor. History has known serf labor. History has known the regulated labor of the medieval craft guilds. Throughout the world there now prevails hired labor, which the yellow journalists of all countries oppose, as the highest form of liberty, to Soviet 'slavery.' We, on the other hand, oppose capitalist slavery by socially regulated labor on the basis of an economic plan, obligatory for the whole people and consequently compulsory for each worker in the country.[6]

It is worth observing that this amphiboly of "freedom," a pseudo-concept that slips regularly from labor to the metaphysical, is one of the fundamental roots of anti-utopianism (as well as of the anti-communism into which it is regularly translated). The transcendental content of such metaphysical notions of freedom is itself of course

5 Leon Trotsky, *Terrorism and Communism*, London: Verso, 2007, 132.
6 Ibid.

historical; but it varies less swiftly than the empirical political or social referent which is its other dimension (social hierarchy, business freedoms, gun ownership, etc.) and which is as it were respectabilized and lent the appearance of some eternal philosophical value by the loftier concept with which it is confused. (Foucault, indeed, theorized just such amphibolies as "empirico-transcendental doublet," although he perhaps associated their emergence too narrowly with nineteenth-century historicism.)

But it is time to quote Trotsky's version of "militarism" in more detail:

> One of the Menshevik orators attempted incidentally to represent me as a defender of militarism in general. According to his information, it appears, do you see, that I am defending nothing more or less than German militarism. I proved, you must understand, that the German NCO was a marvel of nature, and all that he does is above criticism. What did I say in reality? Only that militarism, in which all the features of social evolution find their most finished, sharp and clear expression, could be examined from two points of view. First from the political or socialist—and here it depends entirely on the question of what class is in power; and second, from the point of view of organization, as a system of the strict distribution of duties, exact mutual relations, unquestioning responsibility and harsh insistence on execution. The bourgeois army is the apparatus of savage oppression and repression of the workers; the socialist army is a weapon for the liberation and defense of the workers. But the unquestioning subordination of the parts to the whole is a characteristic of every army. A severe internal regime is inseparable from the military organization. In war every piece of slackness, every lack of thoroughness, and even a simple mistake, not infrequently bring in their train the most heavy sacrifices. Hence the striving of the military organization to bring clearness, definiteness, exactness of relations and responsibilities, to the highest degree of development. "Military" qualities in this connection are valued in

> every sphere. It was in this sense that I said that every class prefers to have in its service those of its members who, other things being equal, have passed through the military school. The German peasant, for example, who has passed out of the barracks in the capacity of an NCO was for the German monarchy, and remains for the Ebert Republic, much dearer and more valuable than the same peasant who has not passed through military training. The apparatus of the German railways was splendidly organized, thanks to a considerable degree to the employment of NCOs and officers in administrative posts in the transport department. In this sense we also have something to learn from militarism. Comrade Tsyperovich, one of our foremost trade union leaders, admitted here that the trade union worker who has passed through military training—who has, for example, occupied the responsible post of regimental commissary for a year—does not become worse from the point of view of trade union work as a result. He is returned to the union the same proletarian from head to foot, for he was fighting for the proletariat; but he has returned a veteran—hardened, more independent, more decisive—for he has been in very responsible positions. He had occasions to control several thousands of Red soldiers of different degrees of class-consciousness—most of them peasants. Together with them he has lived through victories and reverses, he has advanced and retreated. There were cases of treachery on the part of the command personnel, of peasant risings, of panic—but he remained at his post, he held together the less class-conscious mass, directed it, inspired it with his example, punished traitors and cowards. This experience is a great and valuable experience. And when a former regimental commissary returns to his trade union, he becomes not a bad organizer.[7]

Two distinct issues are at stake here. The first is the structural parallelism between the army and the seemingly more complex

7 Ibid., 160–1.

mechanisms of productive society: Is the army a miniature version of society, or simply an organic part within that society that might be called upon to fill some of its other functions in an emergency? The situation in which Trotsky is writing his pamphlet corresponds to those emergency moments, but his more general position on the "militarization" of society generally of course demands the first to be argued—it being understood, once again, that militarization here means neither war nor the bearing of weapons, nor even military drills, but rather the discipline involved in ensuring that the functions required for society's existence be secured by something like conscription.

But another theme runs through this passage and is indeed implicit in all the "militarizing" theorists to whom we are appealing here, and that is the pedagogical vocation of the process, which is in effect self-propelling. In order to carry out the new social functions, trainees, recruits, conscripts, former civilians, have to be educated; they have to be taught how to carry out their new duties, and it is an education that may, in situations like that of the nascent Soviet Union, extend as far as literacy itself. Meanwhile, however, once secured, the new tasks propel their users on to higher levels of that education, and on to new skills which will then further complexify the social edifice.

This is what has since come to be identified as "cultural revolution" (a term in fact invented by Lenin) and at first used to designate the literacy campaigns which everywhere transformed peasants into industrial workers and pre-capitalist formations into capitalism (and, in this case, into socialism). It is worth saying another word about cultural revolution, which can abstractly designate the transformation of subjectivities, but which clearly enough bears on education and therefore on culture in general. When the "life of the mind" is no longer the plaything of aristocratic leisure classes and a literal pastime (as in Aristotle), there is initiated an inexorable evolution of knowledge and its ancillary cultures toward the applied. This has meant not only the eclipse of pure or speculative science, but also the rooting out or stifling, in modernity and postmodernity, of the metaphysical impulse and the gradual effacement of artistic production itself, save for commercial and decorative purposes (even the uses of "great art" for financial investment are threatened by the marginalization of the humanities and its transformation into a sandbox affair). It is natural enough, indeed quite inevitable, that in a socialist society this process will be accelerated, inasmuch as the various disciplines and knowledge practices will be ever more transparently interrogated for their social value and assessed in terms of their cost to society. It seems unlikely that the specialized institutes housed within the army by some social formations will be sufficient to shelter what are viewed, whether in the sciences, philosophy or the arts, as sheer gratuitous exercises.

I have elsewhere suggested that we misunderstand an older tradition of "socialist realism" as the mere production of propaganda icons for Stakhanovism; on the contrary, the mission of socialist realism is the relentless critique of bureaucracy, the most dangerous tendency at work in any socialist society and its inevitable structural accompaniment. Let me now add that modernism and its accompanying aesthetics, mostly organized around defenses of the so-called "autonomy of art," paradoxically offer the strongest avenue for the integration of art in a socialist society, for all such apologies insist on the function of art as negation, and it is around the negation of every actually existing society and its practices that the vocation of art needs to be organized and defended. Like the ombudsman in the arena of power, the existence of art is to be justified by the necessity of its negative and critical function, which ranges from outright social content to the very practices of sense perception itself (as in abstract art) and the conduct of daily life. Cultural revolution, as education itself should be renamed in the new dispensation, must necessarily be grasped not only as the acquisition of new skills but also as the experience of an implacable and sometimes even intolerable negativity to be trained against those skills and the positivist and empiricist world they inevitably end up constructing. This would then practically correspond to Delany's "unlicensed sector" in his urban projection of utopia/anti-utopia (see below), and would stand as a perpetual and perpetually exacerbating rebuke of pragmatism, empiricism, the practical, the socially useful, the legal and the normative, the habitual, law and order, and every well-behaved and traditional tenet of social reproduction, very much including, of course, that "discipline" which constitutes the deepest dystopian fear of army life. The complaint—grumbling and grousing—is the most fundamental privilege of modern life, Deleuze once observed; whether it can be thus institutionalized is then a very central challenge to all utopian construction, whose success in that sense is its failure, so that it will urgently need to find a way to make that failure a success.

7.

But the advantage of the military form for the imagination/construction of an American utopia is spatial; and it is time to return to that theme in a more limited and concrete fashion. This will also entail a more direct assessment of the American Constitution in the political organization of a state essentially devised to resist revolutionary transformations (from the right as well as from the left). It has indeed been said that the fundamental feature of the Constitution in this respect has less to do with the well-known governmental separation of powers with the displacement of a different kind of separation in the affirmation of civilian control over the military. It is this, however, that I propose to grasp in spatial terms.

Whatever the historical origins of the original colonies in geographical constraints and the contingencies of settlement, it seems clear that the form of the individual states represents the greatest barrier to social and political transformation, although not necessarily to economic development (inasmuch as the principal function of the Supreme Court lies in assuring the applicability of basic economic practices—such as the actantial unity of the "soulful" corporation—across state borders).

The state form (and now I utilize the word "state" in its local American sense, as something like a unit, a district, a province, and so forth) is now no longer geographical, as one of the fundamental oppositional works of the 1960s—Joel Garreau's *The Seven Nations of North America*, later revised as *The Nine Nations of North America*—argued. It is only when the borders of such unities correspond to essential geographical identities—those that determine unique patterns of survival and thus eventually the distinctive forms of a specifically regional daily life—that the dilemmas and the contradictions of federalism begin to appear. They then take the form of what the Lacanians call the theft of enjoyment on a collective level, or what tradition simply calls envy: most clearly visible when it is a question of the possession of unique mineral rights, or of a rich soil that favors a prosperous agriculture in distinction to one which is unpromising and unforgiving, but in which for that very reason a certain kind of industry has begun incomparably to flourish. This form of collective or even cultural envy can also fasten on seemingly negative features: one can, in other words, envy a peculiarly industrious people whose self-discipline and even sacrifice would seem to be repellent to a population given to taking its ease. (I will defend the political uses of these Lacanian concepts at a later stage.)

Federalism is precisely that conflict and the delicate balancing out of such hostile impulses (just as Fourierism—again, we will come back to this later on—proposes solutions on an individual basis). Federalism is thus very specifically a utopian impulse and a utopian dilemma: Thomas More deftly sidestepped it by dividing his eponymous island into identical counties (which nonetheless correspond allegorically to the radical differences and unevenness of his own historically real London or England). Federalism is, however, to be grasped less as a solution to such dilemmas as rather an embrace of the contradiction, a reveling in its impossibilities and its negativities.

But it is precisely such contradictions which the American Constitution, or rather the development of the state system into which it eventually evolves, is designed to repress, its uniformities serving a purely negative function in their exclusion of any kind of centralizing political project. The jealously guarded autonomy of state law (save, as I underscored, for business practices) ensures the overruling of collective impulses and projects.

This is then the preeminent advantage of the army as a parallel form which is distributed in enclaves throughout the geographical expanse in a way that ignores state boundaries and on a dimension incommensurable with the laws of individual states. It therefore offers the possibilities of a dual power, which has in fact been anticipated in certain historical instances, as when desegregation of the armed forces took place across states still rigidly organized around apartheid and Jim Crow regulations. The network of the universal army (or of military democracy) is one that permits a new kind of decentralization, enabling a variety of collective units from cities to villages to flourish across the former state lines, all of them linked by what is truly utopian about the Internet (whose utopian capacities have too often been celebrated in purely idealistic and anti-institutional ways). Raymond Williams indeed once said that socialism would not be simpler than capitalism, but much more complicated.

The flashpoint in this overlap of two distinct systems lies clearly enough in the existence of the inappropriately named National Guard, a kind of secondary army under the control of the governors of the individual states. It is, for example, conceivable that a nationwide mobilization of the armed forces could find itself in opposition to National Guard units defending the local interests of individual states and their substantive as well as structural resistance to a more extensive and unified revolutionary policy at the level of a nationwide "military democracy" as such. This kind of crisis would then clearly demonstrate the reality of the notion of dual power and its effectiveness as a practical-political strategy. But at this point as well, we begin to pass from issues of political strategy as such to more utopian projections of what might be expected to emerge from such a revolutionary practice. For unlike previous revolutions, in which there has always been a firm—if ideological—distinction between the revolutionary event itself and the new revolutionary order expected to emerge from it (however much this order is recoded as a permanent revolution or an ongoing revolutionary transformation, etc.), the transition proposed here cannot but ensure the persistence of "military" features in any postrevolutionary society. (Trotsky's account comes closest to admitting this continuity and, indeed, to embracing and defending it.) We must therefore at this point shift gears and pass from a political proposal to a utopian one.

8.

It is, however, appropriate at this point to underscore the transformations that the idea of utopia, and indeed its name, have undergone in recent times, where both the connotations of a non-place (U-topia) and a better place (eu-topia) have largely ceased to apply. After the emergence of the very concept of "history" in the French Revolution, where the possibility of an intentional and pragmatic transformation of society became actual for the first time, the utopian will largely came to signify, for practical-political movements, the impractical and unrealizable: this is how Marx used the word, making exceptions for the truly revolutionary social experiments of Robert Owen and the psychological or thought experiments of a Fourier (whom Engels considered little more than a social satirist; as for Owen, Lenin himself came back to him at the end of his life). In fact, we may consider Marx's strictures on utopian socialism (in the *Manifesto*, for example) as acknowledgements of the increasingly political character of utopian movements and the competition they were likely to offer to any genuinely socialist or communist politics.

A further shift in the function of such speculations was then inevitable after the Soviet revolution itself, when various utopianisms (that of Bogdanov, for example) proved likely to have a practical influence on the direction of Bolshevik policy. Meanwhile, all the revolutionary upheavals of modern times have released utopian impulses of all kinds, including the most grotesque forms (such as the interstellar immortalities of a Florensky), and it is essential to include the mark of the subjective daydream and its ineradicable personal singularity in any approach to the utopian system (as distinguished from the political project or proposal as such, which must speak an intelligible collective language). What follows then must necessarily acknowledge its quotient of individual fantasy, as opposed to political tracts which demand practical assessment. However, and it is this which marks the evolution of utopian ideas in our own time, we must also recognize the increasing difficulty of distinguishing the two in a political time in which politics must again begin by igniting individual fantasies, while "utopian" has once again become a designator for certain specific political practices.

This is indeed what happened to the concept in the Cold War period, in which the analogies between the various kinds of political dictatorships gave rise to the ideologeme of "totalitarianism." Particularly since the collapse of the Soviet experiment, it has become fashionable to detect the seeds of the totalitarian within the utopian itself and to transform the hoary folk wisdom of the adage "the perfect is the enemy of the good" into an anti-utopian political position for which the politics of radical change (defined from the outset as unrealizable, for those imperfect and even sinful beings we are) must inevitably lead to violence, as "human nature" is brutally pressed into an unnatural mold and forced to take on utopian and superhuman dimensions. Anti-utopianism is thereby transformed into a vehicle for anti-communism and a generalized anti-radicalism (Nazism no longer being available as a "revolutionary" doctrine, and the religious character of jihadism standing in apparent conflict with secular utopianisms) and the political uses of utopianism thereby hopefully neutralized.

But in the last years, utopia has again changed its meaning and has become the rallying cry for left and progressive forces and a virtual synonym for socialism or communism, now for the moment tainted words or programs. It needs to be said that this is a generational change and that it seems to reflect a wholesale transformation in the social, political, and economic attitudes of those who came to maturity during the 1990s, when the collapse of the traditional left movements made it possible to see just how predatory capitalism was when left to its own devices. This is a generation in a position to see that no real distinctions can be made between capitalism and electoral politics, and that Hayek and Huntington were right when they argued that capitalism was incompatible with genuine mass democracy.

But despite moments like those of Occupy, which have begun to appear fitfully all over the world and in extraordinarily diverse settings, this new utopianism was not a movement like Bellamy's old nineteenth-century political party. Both emerged from the failures of the left: in Bellamy's case the collapse of populism, in the present situation the collapse of liberal, left, and radical movements. Both took place in situations of economic crisis; clearly enough today it is the prospect of permanent unemployment that has reignited a search for some radically different socioeconomic system than the one currently in place. But present-day utopianism remains for the moment a youth movement (using the term in a different sense); other strata of the population have different if provisional allegiances, and in other parts of the world comparable youth movements are often armed and articulated by religious ideologies when not traditional political ones. The fact is that utopianism in the West is not an organized movement of any kind, nor is it unified by any more systematic cultural ideology, even though on the economic level it shares a general consensus on the failure of capitalism (that is, it embraces Marxism as a negative and critical analysis of capitalism, without any longer being attracted to the cultural, social, and political traditions established over a century by the communist movement).

Perhaps, then, the task of utopianism today is rather to propose more elaborated versions of an alternate social system than simply to argue the need for one; the following pages will do just that, with the proviso that, as a thought experiment, they leave open the possibility of very different combinations of the elements which any contemporary politics or social thinking must somehow confront, absorb, or modify.

9.

The utopia of the universal army was based on the presupposition (common enough, I think, to all utopias in the tradition) of the withering away not only of the state but also of politics as such. (See the excursus on the political above.) This leaves two further dimensions of the social order in direct and unmediated confrontation with each other, namely production and culture: what our daily life under capitalism commonly calls work and leisure, or what the Marxian tradition has perpetuated in one of the oldest and most stigmatized stereotypes on the books, namely the distinction between base and superstructure, or in more general terms, between economic production and culture in the broadest sense. There was always, indeed, a slippage and a hesitation in Marxist theory about whether power and politics were part of the superstructure or part of the base; but we have now eliminated that problem by excluding the political altogether, and have thereby not diminished but rather greatly increased the distance between the economic and the cultural (of which our current distinction between work and leisure is little more than an ideological caricature).

I will not pursue the theoretical debate on base and superstructure, which has its own history and complications, except to say that I feel that it is methodologically useful when taken as a starting point for questions and problems, rather than as a solution of any kind. Base and superstructure are in other words a beginning and not a conclusion, a laboratory experiment (whose results are often very different from each other) and not the tenet of some quasi-religious belief or orthodoxy.

Here, however, we are approaching the opposition as a structure, a utopian framework, in which it looks a little more like the famous distinction between the realm of necessity and the realm of freedom, rather than static dimensions of this or that phenomenon or text. There never was a problem about some general identification of the "base" with production; it was always the ways in which culture could constitute its superstructure which remained open to debate, often of the most ferocious kind. But the notion of the base itself raises several problems. The first is working time: how long would everyone have to work (in the sense of ordinary drudgery, the necessary tasks, and the like) in order for everyone's needs to be fulfilled? In the utopian 1960s, in the era of Herbert Marcuse and Rudolf Bahro, these necessary working hours were reckoned to be something like three or four hours a day: I don't know what the calculations would be today, in an age of far greater productivity, but I find it symptomatic and a little sad that the question is never posed anymore and is felt to be of absolutely no practical or theoretical interest.

The other feature is precisely that of productivity and technology, and it seems to me that such developments take care of themselves (under a very different motivational system than what we currently have in capitalism). The real problem is not production and productivity, but rather distribution: and here we return to the reef of federalism, on which so many social experiments, including the Soviet Union itself, have foundered. For however distribution is calculated for individuals—and here I leave to one side one of the greatest of all utopian hobbies, that of inventing new kinds of money, new forms of wages, new techniques of transfer and circulation—we may expect greater quantities of new proposals here. (Mine would be, at least for the transitional stage, a new two-tiered currency system, in which the wealthy—the CEOs, the stockholders, the financiers—are paid in a separate, as it were "foreign tourist," currency whose use is restricted to internal investment, while the rest of us proceed on with our normal everyday cash and our everyday debts and payments.) But, however distribution be calculated for individuals, the larger problem is that of geographical or spatial inequalities, in which richer and more productive regions are asked in effect to support poorer ones, which to be sure people do not want to do. I will come back to this crucial problem in a moment.

As for the other kind of distribution, that of jobs and tasks, necessary or elective, in today's generalized and structural employment crisis we do not need to be told that these are no longer matters of freedom. In Ursula Le Guin's *The Dispossessed*, jobs were assigned by computer according to the talents and capacities of the individuals concerned. Robert Reich has explained that in the future no one should expect to work at the same job for the whole of his or her life, but should look forward to constant displacements and a multiplicity of different kinds of activities and practical responsibilities, if not indeed to permanent unemployment. In our utopian system, full employment is the highest social priority and an absolute presupposition of social organization, and everything must be planned in order to secure it, even when the job in question is not particularly productive. Full employment is far more important than productivity, and I will remind us that in the earliest years of the Chinese revolution, in a period of heady socialist enthusiasm and optimism, even the very elderly and the infirm were given minimal tasks, such as sweeping the sidewalk in the morning, so that the entire society was active in this unimaginably complex set of simultaneities and relationships which make up a functioning social totality. Or, putting it the other way around, in the utopian psychological system we are about to propose, the most damaging pathology is that of unemployment as such.

It is in the distribution of employment, however, that the most crucial utopian problems arise. They have to do with specialization, innovation versus stagnation, efficiency, hierarchy, monopoly, and ultimately with work and leisure themselves. Computerization and information technology are clearly central to all the items in such a discussion; and I have already observed that the question of computers (into which Heidegger's old "question of technology" has today morphed) seems both to have fueled a new kind of utopian enthusiasm and new kinds of utopian fantasies, at the same time that it has virtually shut down the imagination and production of new utopias. It is as though the computer were a kind of black box, capable of solving all problems of organization in a quasi-magical way, so that they do not any longer have to be addressed and concretely imagined or organized into thought experiments. Thus Le Guin's utopias solve their problems—the assignment of work, distribution and the like—by way of computers, which thereby take the place of the traditional philosopher-kings.

If one is not willing to accept this solution, however, there exists another, far more unexpected, disturbing, and paradoxical solution in Barbara Goodwin's conception of the lottery as a central mechanism for the distribution of tasks and goods in complex modern and potentially globalized societies.[8] This is, if you like, a classical solution, a revival of processes in ancient

8 Barbara Goodwin, *Justice by Lottery*, Chicago: University of Chicago Press, 1992.

society which functioned as referenda or other forms of electoral decision-making. In effect, the lottery annuls or sidesteps all the theoretical problems associated with representative "democracy" (see again the digression on the political above) and guarantees a mechanism for equality which replaces the more familiar social or revolutionary proposals for abolishing class and hierarchy. Equally obviously, however, it raises questions of specialization and competence that in an age of new technologies would no longer seem adequately dealt with by Lenin's cook or his postman.

We may assume that certain basic questions of specialization will have been simplified by new forms of education in the army schools, but we may still find it difficult to abandon age-old notions of specific talents or gifts, and wonder how someone without what are customarily called "language skills" or "mathematical gifts" could function efficiently in jobs demanding those activities. This is the point at which to argue against the very notion of efficiency: such an argument is indeed a central component of any properly utopian "cultural revolution," and I open a large parenthesis here on this issue.

10.

There are of course ideological critiques which are an integral part of any cultural revolution, but I suspect they are somewhat different from the more global critiques of what we may call ideological beliefs—free-market fundamentalism, for example, the conviction that capitalism is the only possible system and that fundamental change is impossible, and so forth, ultimately reaching such propositions as the nonexistence of social classes (and that to insist on them is to provoke violence) and so forth.

The specifically socialist ideological critiques I have in mind at this stage have more to do with praxis and daily life, with habit and performance. I would above all want to single out the commitment to efficiency as a fundamental value: an assumption that, presumably based on common sense, fans out into a rationale for austerity as a politico-economic program and a belief in progress as a mode of temporality. Efficiency as a "value" is one of the forms taken by the logic of capitalism, already theorized in a variety of ways, for example in Max Weber's fundamental concept of rationalization, in Adorno and Horkheimer's useful specification of the latter as "instrumentalization," and in much of the protest literature of the sixties. Mathematization, quantification, and the like are also ways we can come at this fundamental reorganization of daily life and practices, which is, we might suggest, the phenomenological dimension of some specifically capitalist "cultural revolution." Paradoxically, these themes—which are all versions of the same general characterization of the procedures needed for capitalism to function in an increasingly "modern" way—also lend themselves to a powerful polemic move, namely a one-sided and self-destructive caricature of Enlightenment itself as a desiccated and alienating promotion of reason over the other human capacities: this critique of the Enlightenment then, particularly in the late nineteenth century and the Industrial Age, developed into a powerful cultural and philosophical movement, with forms reaching from religious revival to vitalisms of all kinds, and one on which the so-called "irrationalisms" of fascism and other anti-modern movements could draw.

The Marxist critique of "instrumentalization," to stick with that particular term for the wealth of critical themes we have only begun to indicate, is not to be confused with this reactionary and anti-modernist attack on the Enlightenment; Marxism is a completion of the Enlightenment rather than a repudiation of it: a proletarian Enlightenment, we might say, which fulfills the promise of the bourgeois (eighteenth-century) Enlightenment that preceded it. This is an affirmation which incidentally involves the reevaluation of Romanticism as such, as the inevitable reaction against the more limited forms taken by eighteenth-century secularisms. Insofar as Romanticism is taken as a wholesale repudiation of Enlightenment, it can obviously be enlisted in the anti-modernisms and reactionary movements of the twentieth century; insofar as we can infer a progressive Romanticism which contains the elements of critique of capitalism (it has not sufficiently been understood, for example, that Edmund Burke's critique of the Jacobins is in fact an attack on capitalism), then such Romanticism becomes a positive resource for revolutionary and utopian movements.

Meanwhile, this profound political ambiguity is prolonged to the present day, when revolution is seen as pulling the emergency brake on capitalism's headlong flight into "progress" (Benjamin) and left programs and projects themselves are grasped in a spirit of conservatism and of preserving the older and more humane communities and ways of living against the inhuman or posthuman development of late-capitalist technology. This is to forget Marx's own enthusiasm for new scientific discoveries and new technologies of all kinds and his conviction that socialism would be a more advanced society than capitalism; it is to encourage an unproductive Luddism and an anarchism with purely negative views of technology, easily accused of a commitment to vandalism and destruction; and it is to distract us from the task of imagining what a genuinely post-capitalist society might look like if it attempted to preserve everything for which today we have a grateful and complicit enthusiasm, even as we disintoxicate ourselves from the older system's powerful addictions.

At any rate, it seems to me that a systematic repudiation of the ideology of efficiency offers a framework for a rethinking of the whole complex of notions which include technology and progress. Indeed, I would go further and suggest that it might well provide a whole new worldview, in which human nature (we may revive the concept in a kind of strategic essentialism) is grasped not as good or evil but rather as essentially inefficient.

What we have historically admired as genius is then simply a form of efficiency in which, for whatever psychic and social reasons, a figure like Napoleon or Edison has been able to project the ramified and complex consequences of an act of which most of us only grasp its one-dimensional appearance in the present. If so, then we may completely reconstruct the equally one-dimensional value of efficiency in new ways which include the future and become properly political rather than ethical or psychological. At any rate, we make a beginning on dismantling the regime of austerity, downsizing, financialization, and the like when we are able to repudiate efficiency in the name of other, even more progressive values. It is a critical reconsideration or refunctioning (Brecht's *Umfunktionierung*) which can then be extended to the other ideological motifs associated with this one, such as instrumentalization (itself in fact simply the reduction of Aristotle's fourfold notion of causality to the priority of a single one, not inappropriately called "efficient causality").

11.

Even if we succeed in removing the value of efficiency from our utopian anxieties, however, the larger issue of creativity remains to be addressed. Efficiency is part of a more elaborate ideological complex which includes issues of progress and change, of invention and inventiveness along with their opposite, stagnation; and which indeed ultimately reaches into the very heart of the unconscious and motivates our well-nigh libidinal commitment to capitalism itself as a system. "Creative destruction" was Schumpeter's excellent word for it, but it is already thoroughly described and indeed eulogized in *The Communist Manifesto*.

To be sure, part of this discussion will today have been transformed (once again) by the existence of the computer, which utterly transforms the nature of labor and its relationship to so-called creativity. Labor, to be sure, had already been fundamentally transformed, first by the application of scientific methods to agriculture (chemical fertilizer) and, concurrently, by the displacement of handicraft by industrial machinery: both "great transformations" in their own right which produced "nature" by relegating it to the past (the fantasy of a return to nature always constituting an imaginary rash the utopian impulse has been eager to scratch). But these twin rectifications of feudal production also strengthened, if they did not themselves produce, the increasingly operative ideology of efficiency, whose role in the next (cybernetic and informational) revolution is less immediately apparent, for it is intersected by that more recent ideology of "immaterial labor," with its insistence on science and "General Intellect" and its peculiar echo of Marx's diagnosis of the "theological" dimension of the commodity itself.

But the social values of efficiency and knowledge are themselves outweighed, in current anti-utopian anxieties, by that of originality and innovation, particularly as they find their fulfillment in the image of the entrepreneur and the glamor of adventure, risk and "modernity" invested in entrepreneurialism and its ethos.

Is the entrepreneur not the very foundation of capitalism as such? I fear not, for the career of the entrepreneur falls into two distinct halves, which we then attempt to recombine in the spurious notion of the businessman. The first part of the entrepreneur's career is that of the inventor, whether of objects, designs, financial "instruments," bright ideas, strategies, or whatever: this is truly the realm of creativity, and one is always tempted to elevate it to the most stirring avatar of the human, even though there is no human nature and therefore no such norm or value. (There is also skill, for example, which is a rather different "virtue"—or virtuosity, as Paolo Virno terms it appropriately.) These vehicles of creativity obviously range from the crackpots and the obsessed to what the term "genius" has often been applied to, which is to say that it is precisely to be regarded as a form of life rather than a value.

Unfortunately, the second part of the life of the successful entrepreneur is that of the businessman, the exploiter of the invention, of which Edison and Ford (and Disney) give us so many American examples, but one might want to extrapolate that into other lines of work as well, such as the academic specializations. This is a wholly different matter, and it no longer means the realm of freedom but reabsorption into the momentum of capital; it leads on into finance and business per se (where there can also be much creativity) and is not to be valorized in and for itself (except perhaps in the sense of its own creativity and invention). This is no doubt the realm of unproductive imperialism, and a new space probably has to be opened up for it: some new "virtue" we might call management in general; if it could ever be separated from money and profit. At any rate, today the bureaucracies are not unified as a force; they are always in the service of something else, whether negative (private business) or positive (social work). They cannot be called upon as an independent force, any more than a garage band could be installed to run a ministry of culture.

Indeed, in a consumer society, the entrepreneur is less likely to be a producer but rather something closer to a designer. The nineteenth-century-type inventors, like Edison and even Ford himself, were indeed the forerunners of such a development, which was not obvious at the time inasmuch as their "designs" actually generated new kinds of objects—electricity and its vehicles, the automobile—which demanded a wholesale expansion of production and the creation of whole new industries, the building of new forms of built space in their factories, and the hiring and training, the transformation, of a workforce that came from the land (a source of labor that no longer exists—except via immigration). Today, such products saturate the market; what is wanted is a redesign of them such that they supply additional needs and wants (or indeed create them in the first place), like the various extras on luxury cars or indeed the smartphone itself, which is little more than a collection of extras in the first place. This is why the great inventor (Edison,

Ford, Disney) is supplanted as a capitalist culture hero by the great designer, whose mythic archetype became the sainted Steve Jobs. Genius in this sense, as we shall see later, is essentially the foretelling of consequences, the capacity to think ahead and trace out a sequence of events in which a given innovation comes up against an obstacle (not this placement of the thumb on the device!) which can then be prophetically displaced in advance.

What is then clear from this development, despite the immense fortunes to be made from moments in which a space for just such new designs (or functional inventions) opens up, is their detachability from capitalism itself. Just as invention of the older type does not require monetary rewards (the careers of the great inventors already mentioned always fell into two halves—the inventive one and then the attempt to exploit the new product as a money-making business, something Ford was better at than Edison, for example), so also the "genius" for design (which can clearly take on its political forms as well) can be imagined as a motivation and a satisfaction in its own right, not particularly affected in its logic by the rewards a different kind of socioeconomic system might offer.

With the critique of the ideology of efficiency and, beyond that, the virtues we have been trained to associate with free enterprise, we have begun to move into a new and larger terrain, only briefly touched on above, and that is that collective transformation of mentalities we have identified as cultural revolution. If the critique of ideology deals with what Brecht called the good old things, cultural revolution itself has to do with the bad new things. But this is a complicated process in which the new cannot simply replace the old but must develop within it somehow, ultimately discarding the old ways like a husk or shell (as Marx put it). This means moving from the plain of doxa, of opinions and stereotypes, of "values," to some deeper level which is no longer that of mere individual psychology but rather the structural one of psychoanalysis (we will discuss psychoanalysis and its role in political and social analysis in another Excursus, below.)

To put it more practically, the proposal must now move from the critique of capitalism and its ideologies to an analysis of the fear of utopia. Utopianism must first and foremost be a diagnosis of the fear of utopia, or of anti-utopianism. The recrudescence and reflowering of dystopias in our present culture suggests deeply rooted anxieties which are a good deal more fundamental than the fear-mongering widely practiced during the Cold War and expressed in various anti-totalitarian tracts such as Orwell's *1984*. We have already mentioned the issue of the state and the anxieties it inevitably arouses: in the long run, what we have to do with here is simply the terror of the collective as such, the existential fear of losing our individuality in some vaster collective being. At this point, however, we have to do with a twofold structure of fears and anxieties layered over this more fundamental one: namely, the specific and substantive apprehensions that attach to the army as a form or to the military as such (and these are empirical as well as formal), and then, at some lower and more general level, the fear of utopia as such. Every psychoanalyst knows (except, apparently, for Freud himself, who simply told his patients outright what was the matter with them, in the process indoctrinating them in his own system) that the best treatment for neurotics lies in indirection: like the sociologists who draw up their questionnaires by making you think they are inquiring about something else, it is best to seem to lead the patients down the wrong path, from which "self-knowledge" rises like a distant glimpse or happy accident (assuming there can be knowledge about something—the so-called self—which doesn't exist in the first place). Utopians must proceed like that: they have to concentrate not on visions of future happiness, but rather on treatments of that stubborn resistance we tend to oppose to it and to all the other proposals for positive change in this now worldwide society. Utopian thinking must first involve the radical therapy for dystopia, its radical treatment and cure; only then can it begin to spin out its own impossible pipe dreams. We hammer away at anti-utopianism not with arguments, but with therapy: every utopia today must be a psychotherapy of anti-utopian fears and draw them out into the light of day, where the sad passions like blinded snakes writhe and twist in the open air. More than that, they must be indulged, for nothing cures a sad passion as fully as its passionate embrace, its wholehearted endorsement.

First, though, a symptomatology must be established and tested: I suggest that the empty signifier to which any number of fears and preoccupations cling, as to a magnet, is the term "freedom," which, following Trotsky (and Kant's terminology), I have suggested to be an amphiboly, in which for an empirical reality (wage labor, as the historical negation of bound labor of whatever kind) is substituted a kind of spiritual essence of indeterminate meaning, itself a stand-in for that even more indeterminate thing which is consciousness itself. It is clear enough that the omission of the material fact of labor from the henceforth supersensible "value" opens the door to any number of fantasy investments, inevitably of the negative or dystopian kind.

But as I indicated above, utopianism is at one with this therapy of the anti-utopian; to use a literary analogy, this kind of cultural revolution is a form which is its own content, like an autoreferential work whose subject is its own composition. This is indeed probably the unique feature about revolutions in general as an event: they essentially grapple with their own possibility or impossibility, unlike the events of daily life or of "normal" history which project their aims beyond and outside themselves in an effort to shape the future or to repeat the past. (Indeed, to insert a gratuitous reference here to another field altogether, it is no doubt in this sense that modernist works are in their autoreferentiality a mimesis of revolution as such, or rather of its afterimage conceived as a kind of ideal event.)

Specifically military fears include issues of violence, of hierarchy and discipline, of regimentation, and ultimately of aggressivity itself, as that is fantasized to be a fundamental feature of human nature or the human "essence" (feminism has thematized this conception of aggressivity as patriarchy or male violence). It is worth reminding the reader that the universal army here proposed is no longer the professional army responsible for any number of bloody and reactionary coups d'état in recent times, whose ruthlessness and authoritarian or dictatorial mentality cannot but inspire horror and whose still vivid memory will certainly astonish anyone at the prospect of entrusting a state or an entire society to its control. Removing such justified and visceral fears would certainly be the first task of any utopian therapy, were it not for the situation of dual power from which the new universal army emerges, which begins life as a parallel force alongside the state and its official army and finds its first tasks, and indeed its vocation, in the fulfillment of neglected social services and in a coexistence with the population of a wholly different type. The "nation at arms" which emerges from this situation is above all a general population in which everyone participates and a principled reaction against just such enclaves which enjoy Weber's "monopoly of violence" and have come to lead an autonomous life independent of society in general. (Current American reactions against isolated police forces present ready-made analogies.)

In recent theory, beginning, I think, with Walter Benjamin's famous essay, there has come to be established a distinction between violence and force. Force is the institutional attribute of entities like the police and the army; it exists invisibly everywhere in daily life in the form of taboos and injunctions and does not have to be manifested physically. Force is the fear and certainty of violence, as Pascal said; more recently, in his discussion of Gramsci, Perry Anderson has compared it to that physical gold which is supposed to back up the claims of paper money to have value in their own right.[9]

Violence will in that case then, virtually by definition, presuppose the "unlawful" in the form of physical outbreaks which define

9 Perry Anderson, "The Antinomies of Antonio Gramsci," *New Left Review*, no. I/100, November–December 1976.

their perpetrators as criminals or revolutionaries, or in any case as antisocial elements. As we are seeing today in the case of so-called terrorism, violence is thus an ideology (whose meaning includes consent to its opposite number, namely "force"). I believe that the use of this word should always be subject to ideological analysis in order to determine the political meaning it is inevitably designed to have, whether that be the preservation of order in well-to-do neighborhoods or the propagation of bodily harm and injury in the service of essentially political tactics or strategy. One does not endorse violence by denouncing its ideological function as a pseudo-concept; rather, this unmasking defamiliarization cannot but clarify the situation to be grasped.

As for the violence of the universal army at issue here, it is probably necessary to add that a social order in which everyone is trained in the use of weapons and nobody is allowed to possess them except in limited and carefully specified situations is probably a safer society than the one we currently live in, and one in which it might be possible to return to that now idyllic condition in which (such as in the Britain of yesterday) even the police are unarmed.

Nonetheless, just as yesterday the business of America was business, so from time immemorial the business of the army has been warfare; and perhaps it is disingenuous to argue, as Jaurès does, for a purely defensive army, despite the fact that all projected utopias, real or imagined—from Winstanley's colony on St. George's Hill to Aldous Huxley's *Island*—have had to fear the hostility of non-utopian neighbors whose interest lay in wiping them out (in *Ecotopia*, that neighbor is the United States itself, held at bay by the Ecotopians' possession of nuclear weapons). In fact, Utopus himself pursued a cunning and highly Machiavellian foreign policy—bribing and corrupting his foreign enemies and hiring mercenaries to neutralize them. The demands of self-defense, from the Greeks to Stalin and passing through the French Revolution, have always been the principal undoing of any number of well-intentioned political arrangements and their deterioration into paranoid, abusive, and self-destructive conditions, complete with elaborate police forces and espionage networks at home and abroad. Indeed, when utopia is diagnosed as the root cause of so-called totalitarianism and terror, it is generally this peril of the effects of self-preservation that is really at issue. The utopias which do not include this foreign hostility as an intrinsic feature of their planning and indeed of their very existence—such utopias, lacking as it were any such utopian foreign policy, have justified themselves in two ways: one, either, as Winstanley quite reasonably thought, the non-utopian population of a non-utopian outside world, seeing the advantages of the new system, will quickly abandon their regimes and their older states; or, two, we will have taken for granted, as Bellamy does, that the rest of the world has at once simultaneously embraced the utopian revolution so that no further "foreign policy" need be provided for. In the real world, the situation of Cuba is enough to demonstrate the vulnerability of any such enclave—in this case, a socialist state at the very heart of Western capitalism.

I have not taken these problems into consideration here, but even their bracketing leaves open the question of military research (atomic weapons and the like). I will only point out how much basic scientific invention and discovery has come from military research and from wartime situations (partly because a civilian population—or its government—is unlikely to spend the tax money warfare demands on purely abstract and theoretical peacetime research). In the universal army, presumably such lines of demarcation will have disappeared. But even bracketing the question of foreign wars, the daily military routine that makes up the life of a peacetime army must now be addressed, and it raises precisely those issues of hierarchy and discipline which have been included in our general review of properly dystopian fears.

One must assume that, as with militias or reserve units, a certain amount of obligatory training would be involved; it might well be combined with a medical regime of prevention and of hygiene, particularly in an affluent population blessed with all the problems of leisure, obesity, and luxury consumption. But for the sake of imagination and the contours of the thought experiment, it need not be feared, as Oscar Wilde famously did, that "socialism" would take too many evenings. In a regime of minimal production, such as the one here envisaged, precious weekends need not be sacrificed to military drills and other forms of physical regimentation or "voluntary labor" (as Trotsky euphemistically put it): such lost hours would be considerably reduced and could be varied according to the specialization allotted to (but also chosen by) the participants.

Regimentation and discipline are serious concerns for any affluent and permissive society like our own, and the threat they seem to pose to our habits and daily life are only exacerbated by the usual ideological confusion around the idea, or at least the slogan, of freedom. Revolutions and revolutionary change generally take place at catastrophic moments (wars, natural disasters) in which the habits of daily life disappear and make place for new ways of living and thinking (and when the older state and its institutions—already demonstrably "inefficient" and incapable of fulfilling its population's most basic needs—have also lost their "legitimacy"). Every reasonable person will understand that as social and economic equality becomes more generalized there will necessarily be a lowering of what are prejudicially termed "living standards" for the privileged (and not only for the rich). The end of World War II in Europe, for example, dramatizes the way in which changes in the work ethic required by reconstruction were accompanied by a certain collective enthusiasm for radical social change and innovation as well (a political hope and optimism which, to be sure, rapidly waned as capitalism was set back in place). Any convincing thought experiment needs to take such factors into consideration; the role played in such objections by our stereotypes of work and leisure need to be discussed in the larger context of a more general cultural revolution.

As for the universal army, however, the association of armies in general with some deep-seated aggressivity in human nature, or perhaps more specifically in some gendered human nature, are of a different type: this is essentialism with a vengeance, and it emerged most dramatically not only in the resistance to the Vietnam War but in the popular explanations for our engagement in it, attributed to the innate male aggressivity of Johnson and his advisors and generals. This is obviously not a particularly materialist explanation, let alone a historical one. On the other hand, the widespread adoption of political strategies of nonviolence is certainly an index of ideological as well as tactical concern; and Callenbach feeds into this general ideological conviction in his sixties' utopia when he describes an annual ceremony of War Games for the collective letting off of steam of the males of this society (whose government is largely staffed by women). In fact, if it is aggressivity as a character trait that is in question here, I would raise some doubt as to whether the machismo of the warrior is much different from that of the great businessman, who used indeed to be called a "robber baron" but whose predatory instincts must necessarily be developed and nurtured at an early age if he or she is to be a success in the competitive world of business today (which is to say, today again, the world of high finance rather than the old proverbial "small business"). In our current situation, far less inclined, it seems to me, to such essentialist views of gender and human nature, it certainly seems clear that the excitement of military action and aggressivity is a more economic and generational matter, attracting unemployed youth to local paramilitary adventure of a paying and valued type, whether in the Mideast or Northern Ireland, Los Angeles gangs or South American guerrillas. William James's famous remark about the moral equivalent of war has of course inspired any number of thinkers to invent equivalents for such lethal remedies for unemployment and its boredom and loss of any sense of personal worth; but revolutions are also notoriously made by young people.

A final motive for anti-utopian resistance, particularly in the area of armies, military service, and the like, must be sought for in a deeper place, which is neither a psychological nor a metaphysical one, I would argue, but very much an instantiation of Sartre's famous conclusion: Hell is other people. It is an originary trauma which explains the function of small groups as protection and which, no doubt, few enough of us are willing to face directly. Those who do have often reached the sobering assessment that the human species is a particularly loathsome biological entity, and this very much owing to its individuality (and freedom) rather than its lack of it. (The idea that humans are naturally good and altruistic is then a secondary corrective to this first metaphysical reaction.) This is why the rich are primarily motivated not by power or pleasure, but by the possibility of radical isolation, of separating themselves off, by way of bodyguards, private property, walls, and the like, from their fellow men (and women).

If this speculative generalization has any merit, it can also explain why the most visceral negative reaction to the very notion of the army, the very prospect of being involved with it in one way or another, has little enough to do with warfare and physical violence: It stems from the fact that the army is virtually the only institution in modern society whose members are obliged to associate with all kinds of people on an involuntary, non-elective basis, beginning with social class as such. This forced association, initially restricted to males, has been a useful mechanism, in the age of nationalism and the modern nation-state, for securing a certain collective unification and leveling (including the imposition of a national language).

So the army is the first glimpse of a classless society, with all the anxieties such a novel social situation has historically (and inevitably) aroused. But class is mediated by a more concrete level of experience, such as gender and the incompatibility of personalities, the distaste we all have for certain other kinds of people and their behavior. That level is initially one of a Bourdieu-type "distinction" and is experienced at first as an educational and class disparity; obvious enough, in the case of gender (for we have specified our universal army as one that no longer functions according to sexual differentiation), the incompatibilities are immeasurably older, not to say primordial, and the discomfort of forced interaction of a purely social type all the more painful (for the male ego, for instance). (I will come back to other, seemingly more superficial psychic incompatibilities later on.) There is probably also some first unformulated notion of violence at work here, which only later gets reorganized in physical form and becomes a source of fear and of the so-called instinct of self-preservation. This experience of social promiscuity, however, is what democracy really means (let's try to avoid that tainted word in the future) and what every utopia must entail: it is species-being, to use Marx's phrase, and to learn its experience and to undergo its pedagogies is perhaps the deepest meaning of the term "cultural revolution," as that designates the transition from one mode of production to another.

On the whole, and except for war movies (and wars still pursued under conscription), Americans do not readily understand that other function of the army so well known to Europeans: a nonmilitary function which is essentially social in nature and is calculated to serve as a vehicle for the fraternization of classes. This is, if you like, a utopia of classlessness, provided you understand that in a purely symbolic sense: for it does not abolish social classes altogether by way of some new social structure, but simply suspends it for the duration of the service (or of the war itself). This forced intermingling of the social classes, or at least of their male members, then turns out to have a somewhat different effect than the one imagined for some genuinely classless or communist utopia, and that is a national or nationalist one.

Before the standardization of the European languages—the elimination of local languages and dialects by legislation, schooling, and the media—the melting pot of military service enforced the hegemony of the official state language and reduced the now provincial languages to secondary status and to the level of local accents. The forced movement of provincials such as the Bretons or the Sicilians to the great national centers then instills, if not patriotism, then at least a sense of the geographic centrality of power and of their own national marginality. To be sure, this outsider status can also under the right circumstances be a source of power, as in the implantation of Mafia-like networks.

In any case, what is produced by this function of military service is the nation itself, and it has little enough to do with warfare as such: the current proposal posits a functional transformation—a Brechtian refunctioning or *Umfunktionierung*—in which this forced class promiscuity becomes the production of genuine classlessness and social leveling. Language is the most delicate feature of this process; one can only point to the polyglot practice of the eastern Mediterranean as a model for a multilingual existence which acknowledges the necessity for some sort of lingua franca without the kind of wholesale dialectal extinction (or linguicide) practiced by the older nation-states in their heydays.

For Americans—their dialects already standardized by the media—the closest experience to this kind of social "melting pot" will have been the school, particularly as epitomized in the undistinguished genre of the high-school movie, in which a variety of social types intermingle and in which the presence of the other sex usefully augments the unisexuality of the Other, more European military model, foregrounding this ultimate utopian frontier as a problem yet to be solved.

In any case, what both these models underscore, and it is an essential feature of any utopian construction or imaginative operation and too often forgotten in the conventional stereotype of utopia as an edulcorated conflict-free zone of social peace and harmony, is the necessarily antagonistic nature of individual life and experience in a classless or communist society. "Classless" in this context means the elimination of collective antagonism and thereby, inevitably, the heightening of individual ones. The absence of any serious attempt, in the standard utopian tradition, to imagine what kind of literature might be produced and consumed in a communist utopia testifies to this unhappy and inveterate lapse in the utopian imagination. In Ivan Efremov's *Andromeda* (1957), for example, only the great natural disasters, such as the loss of a spaceship carrying thousands of people, count as literary material; while in William Morris's *News From Nowhere* (as also in Bellamy's *Looking Backward*) it is the pangs of thwarted love (and the passionate dramas resulting from it) that almost exclusively people the "greatest literary achievements [*sic*]" of those imagined worlds. But can anyone seriously believe that the visceral dislike one individual sometimes feels for another will disappear from a perfect world? Or that rivalry will disappear from the younger generations, no matter what kind of rewards are substituted for sheer cash and profit? Or, indeed, and far more seriously, that generational conflict will not perpetually threaten social reproduction (including the perpetuation of the utopian system itself)? Or, finally—for it has been a central point in many of the analyses here—that envy—the obsession with the theft of "enjoyment" (*jouissance*)—will somehow cease to torment those incomplete biological individuals we are and will not cease to be, even in "paradise"?

The high-school film, then—with all the unpleasantness of its various group bondings, its competitions, its hazing and its exclusions, indeed its unmotivated friendships and enmities, the forms it presents of Kant's "radical evil" or "pathological" inclinations—the high-school drama will come to be acknowledged as a revealing expression of the deepest utopian impulses and the reality principle associated with them. This is the bittersweet parable of a world from which material needs and wants have been somehow removed (and satisfied), and a time from which necessary labor has been suspended. This is a foretaste of the society projected by Lenin in his own utopia, *State and Revolution*, in which "socialist legality" is enforced informally, as a collective habit:

> For when *all* have learned the art of administration, and will indeed independently administer social production, will independently keep accounts, control the idlers, the gentlefolk, the swindlers and similar "guardians of capitalist traditions," the escape from this national accounting and control will inevitably become so increasingly difficult, such a rare exception, and will probably be accompanied by such swift and severe punishment (for the armed workers are practical men and not sentimental intellectuals and they will scarcely allow anyone to trifle with them), that very soon the *necessity* of observing the simple, fundamental rules of human intercourse will become a *habit*.[10]

Indeed, there is something of a shock when one passes from the momentary disorder of the classic "crime of passion" in Morris's Victorian utopia to Le Guin's account of physical violence in *The Dispossessed* (where Shevek is beaten up by another man who simply resents his use of the same—computer-derived—name). I give these instances not to glorify the vigilantes or fistfights but rather simply to dispel our instinctive fear that "utopia" (in whatever form) will be a place without conflict or contradiction—though it is true that Lenin evokes the common sense of "any crowd of civilized people, even in modern society," which as a matter of course "parts two people who are fighting, or interferes to prevent a woman from being assaulted" (340). At any rate, I think it is as a warning against such idyllic expectations aroused by a non-conflictual stereotype of the "classless" utopia that Ernesto Laclau and Chantal Mouffe have insistently expressed their conviction that all societies are founded on antagonism, an insistence which has predictably enough been taken as a repudiation of notions of class and class struggle as such.[11]

10 V.I. Lenin, *Essential Works of Lenin*, New York: Bantam, 1996, 349.

11 Ernest Laclau and Chantal Mouffe, *Hegemony and Socialist Strategy: Towards a Radical Democratic Politics*, London: Verso, 1985.

Perhaps we here need some quasi-Maoist distinction between antagonistic and non-antagonistic antagonisms in order to assure ourselves that a classless society is not to be fantasized as lacking antagonisms of all kinds, which is to say, lacking in the dilemma of the Other as such.

Hobbes thought the fundamental emotion from which society as an institution drew its legitimation was fear; and no doubt, in the context of the English Revolution, through which he lived, the immediate reference, and relevance, of this confession lay in the prospect of outright physical danger, from marauding troops to looters and antisocial elements of all kinds. But the deeper meaning of the insight comes, I think, from precisely this primordial fear of the Other, and above all in its form as other people, in species promiscuity and the bewilderment of the swarm.

Paradoxically, but not undialectically, the other fundamental form taken by this fear of the Other is very precisely the entity Hobbes endorsed to defend himself against that first one, namely the state itself, in its multiple forms as bureaucracy, as court of appeal in last instance, as sheer power and a kind of depersonalized historical subject finding its ultimate *jouissance* in the crushing of individuals, as in the fantasies of a Kafka or, at a lesser level, an Orwell. It is hard to say whether the proliferation of ideologies of power in our time—essentially, as in the care of its leading spokesperson, Michel Foucault, a thematics calculated to displace the economic and to divert politics into more sterile, if possibly more satisfying, directions—is the cause or the effect of such an obsession with the state itself. It will be said that the wars of the twentieth century are explanation enough for this terror of the state, but they did not happen in a void. One may well prefer the attitude of Horkheimer, who famously observed, "He has nothing useful to say about fascism who is unwilling to mention capitalism." At any rate, this fixation has been discussed sufficiently in our earlier Excursus on the political as such. Perhaps, then, this is the moment to insert a second Excursus on the recourse to psychoanalytic doctrines in the context of utopian speculations explicitly designed to deal with the collective rather than the individual.

Excursus II: On Psychology and Psychoanalysis

I have often enough quoted Durkheim's injunction—whenever a social fact is explained psychologically, we may be sure that the explanation is wrong—to find myself obliged to add that this authoritative pronouncement was not meant to endorse the reification of the "social fact" Durkheim advocates, but merely to discredit the claims of psychology as an amalgam of essentially individual observations about motivation, habit, mentality, or behavior (let alone psycho-physical experiment, which seems to be returning in the form of neuropsychology). Collective phenomena cannot be conceptualized as a receptacle containing innumerable individual psychologies any more than they can be attributed to some super-individual "collective consciousness." Meanwhile, Freud's one incursion into this area—*Group Psychology and the Analysis of the Ego*—turned out to be a lamentable reinforcement of Gustave Le Bon's conservative terror of the mob by way of some of the more doubtful psychoanalytic hypotheses such as "identification." The great empirical observers and theoreticians of psychology—La Rochefoucauld, Gracián, Machiavelli—were in fact, as this last name indicates, essentially political thinkers, who tended to apply military and strategic concepts to their social recommendations at the same time that they shrewdly compiled satiric lists of the character types involved in such social maneuvers.

At its best, then, psychology can function as a system of characterology: *qua* science, better than astrology (with which of course it has some connections) but not as respectable as astronomy. Freud said character was destiny, or at any rate, he sharply distinguished between character—the fidgeting or choleric, the treacly or subservient person before us—and neurosis. You can treat the latter, but the former will stay on, except perhaps for the momentous impacts of extreme situations and the secular miracles of conversion. For many of us it will be difficult to mark some absolute break here: Surely character in this (psychological or even literary) sense will have been geologically formed in some early "psychoanalytic" crisis? But psychology at its best will simply be a catalogue of such later and now fairly hardened formations, which may well be organized into cultural systems but which are scarcely the object of what is so often called science. Daily life (and traditional literature) is taken up with the negotiations between such "characters": psychoanalysis with the structure of the individual desire.

The theoreticians of psychoanalysis have always argued at length and in various ways for the radical differentiation of their "science" from that of psychology; it is unnecessary to recapitulate those debates here, nor even to ruminate obsessively on the nature of science. But as most of the references and concepts drawn on here in passing are Lacanian in origin, it will be useful to explain their advantages, if not to endorse or defend Lacanianism as such. We may begin by observing that Marxism has what seems to be its own psychological concepts, whose function is then to mediate between base and superstructure, or, if you prefer, to account for the ways in which the economic—or, in other words, class positionality—articulates its dynamics on the cultural level. The predominant entity which secures this articulation is clearly enough what is called ideology; but increasingly, in late Marxism, another force (already theorized by Marx) has come to play a significant role in Marxian social analysis, and that is commodification, or commodity reification (most notably exemplified in current societies in the form of consumerism, in a situation in which Lenin's rather hasty notion of the bribery of the working class has tended more and more to be replaced by more clinical concepts like that of addiction, which in fact function in much the same "psychological" way).

So a first theoretical problem is therewith at once established: whether the notion of ideology is not itself a psychological one, and if not, what psychoanalysis might usefully have to tell us about it. In the present context, a third consideration becomes inescapable: namely, what role either can be called on to play in cultural revolution. Some history may be appropriate here.

The theoretical polemics of the 1960s (using this term generically rather than chronologically—the latter would prolong our period into the mid- or late 1970s) can be summed up as a twin onslaught on metaphysics and on idealism—two related philosophical pathologies, to be sure, both of them most conveniently characterized as ideologies (we will leave idealism to the side in the present discussion). For ideology itself, like its ancestor, metaphysics, can always be identified by the implicit or explicit promise to answer one of two questions which are ultimately the same. The first is the question about the meaning of nature, while the second is that of the meaning of human nature. Neither of these entities exists, as constructivist philosophy at least as old as Nietzsche (and Sartre) has demonstrated; therefore neither has anything like a meaning, assuming that even that term, so applied, has any meaning. Questions about the meaning of life itself as a biological process belong in the realm of the question about nature; and it may be suspected that origin questions in this area, seemingly scientific since the collapse of theology, still conceal a metaphysical dimension. Meanwhile, all of Nietzsche's diagnoses of the so-called will to power (or, in other words, the social and pragmatic—ideological—uses of seemingly neutral facts and theories) can generally be invoked to discredit the various "psychological" discoveries about human consciousness or behavior (including, to be sure, their alleged ethical implications). All these metaphysical and ideological exhibits, however, once again become productive when one grasps them from a historical perspective, as social and historical symptoms.

The significance of the Althusserian movement was then to have thematized the attack on metaphysics—in a kind of search-and-destroy offensive which tracked its enemy into the most unlikely corners, with often deadly results—in two fundamental forms: humanism and historicism. In hindsight we can identify these targets as follows: Humanism designates a concept of human nature, one which on the one hand expressed bourgeois and Western values, and on the other asserted—against present-day constructivism—that this (bourgeois) human nature was somehow eternal and permanently defined the species as such. Clearly the term can mean many things and was often also, in a related usage, associated with philanthropy and a moralizing politics intent in the long run on avoiding violence. The first of these features was elaborated by Michel Foucault in his complacently perverse view of the way "humane" practices, in medicine and in the penal system, began to replace ritualistic violence and exclusion after the bourgeois revolution. The second feature, the nonviolence associated with Gandhi and Martin Luther King, was taken to be a strategic rebuke to revolutionaries as such, inasmuch as social and Marxist revolutions, with their slogan of class struggle, were taken to be indissociable from violence. (Sartre's rather awkward intervention, "Existentialism is a humanism," was meant to distinguish the politics of the left from a fascism and Nazism then only recently defeated, as well as to promote a conception of freedom utterly distinct from an American Cold War rhetoric of free elections and to underscore the necessity of political commitment. This kind of polemic then clearly muddies the waters and makes any really clear-cut critique of the term "humanism" a space of contradictory cross-currents, particularly inasmuch as a religious and right-wing fundamentalism was also intent on attacking "humanism" as a "godless" atheism.)

As for historicism, I believe that in the beginning it was associated with the Second International belief in an inevitable historical movement toward socialism, or in other words what Benjamin denounced as "progress" and what heretical currents on the left detected as a Stalinist rhetoric of "historical inevitability": one which encouraged passivity and blind trust in the Party and tended to greet independent revolutionary activism with the greatest suspicion, denouncing it in terms of voluntarism and "bad spontaneity," which of course much of it was. The slogan that the time was not ripe or that the situation was objectively not yet a revolutionary one obviously reinforced these positions and called forth a critique of historical telos that, in hindsight, had equal disadvantages. Althusser's own version of the slogan, that "history has neither a subject nor a telos," could then be enlisted in attacks on party organization in general and also (particularly later on, after 1989) called on to reinforce the unconscious Thatcherite conviction that history was not going anywhere and that alternatives were impossible. In hindsight, this attack on historicism had even graver consequences for left and Marxist theory than the denunciation of humanism, which might well be revived in a new and more historically nuanced, "postmodern" way, as I will try to show here. The attack on historicism, however, tended to discredit any forms of historical perspective (those well-known "grand narratives" to be conscientiously avoided), and thereby to blind us to the ways in which anti-historicism could itself be taken as a symptom of the late-capitalist experience of historical temporality and used to support the capitalist ideological doctrine of that "end of history" which had already been promoted as "the end of ideology" and indeed the end of class struggle as such. As a symptom, the critique of historical inevitability (which finally casts doubt not only on the inevitability of socialism but even on its very possibility) cannot be adequately treated by simple counterarguments or reaffirmations of history as such; even the remarkable revival and new efflorescence of Marxian analyses of capitalism and its contradictions remains oddly fixated on an impossible present without any visible historical future, save catastrophe. Rather, genuinely historical thinking can only be revived by a stimulation of speculative images of the future and of perspectives of social change and alternate societies, something which now and for the moment only takes place under the banner of utopianism. The fundamental function of utopianism today, in other words, lies in this seemingly paradoxical revival of a sense of the future with which the ostentatiously "unrealistic" posture of the utopian tradition would seem decidedly at odds. We will return to the political functions of utopia later on.

What it is appropriate to affirm here is that the older slogans of anti-humanism and anti-historicism both need to be renewed (as an ideological task) and corrected by a revision, in terms of which the fundamental targets of critique are identified as psychologism and culture critique. The revision clearly enough reflects that shift from base to superstructure which we have previously emphasized; in other words, it implies some general consensus on the contradictory structure of the infrastructure, of capitalism itself as a mode of production wracked with debilitating and destructive contradictions and ultimately unviable, at the same time that it proposes a shift in the direction of culture and subjectivity, which do seem more accessible to change and a more accessible target for the critiques of intellectuals. But if these critiques do not return to the base itself and articulate new ways in which an anticapitalist praxis can be invented, then they remain sterile, and indeed that sterility is itself the result of the fundamental philosophical flaw Durkheim insisted on at the very birth of sociology as a discipline (without offering any truly alternative mode of analysis of the type such as that available in Marxism and the dialectic), namely that any psychological analysis of collective phenomena is in advance bound to be wrong.

The culture critique indeed is constituted formally by isolating this or that psychological trait ("the culture of narcissism") or this or that psychiatric diagnostic category (Ruth Benedict's classification of cultures as paranoid or schizophrenic) and unifying a set of social observations around it as their fundamental cause "ultimately determining instance." Social change is then predicated on the order of the "cure," a pseudo-utopian illusion if there ever was one and a prospect hotly debated even within the psychoanalytic tradition. Even traditional notions of ideology—particularly those which opposed ideology to truth or science (without even bothering to distinguish these two arenas: the one existential, the other epistemological)—assumed in Enlightenment fashion that some form of class pedagogy would be enough to disabuse supporters or adherents of the system. But the emergence of a generalized cynicism in our own time is enough to discredit this conception of politics as rhetoric or persuasion, even though the very notion of cynicism itself (launched in a rather different context by Peter Sloterdijk in his book on Weimar) risks slipping into just such a psychological trait or entity, into just such a "culture critique," at issue here.

This is then the moment to enunciate several Lacanian concepts which seem useful in any contemporary political analysis. They are: 1) the structural force of gravity of the Other; 2) the theft of enjoyment (*jouissance*); and 3) the permanence of social antagonism on an individual level, or perhaps it would be better to say the disappearance of any concept of normality, the view of society as an ineradicable collection of neurotics. The primacy of desire in Freud remained essentially personal, and included the "otherness" of the family in a merely causal fashion. Lacan was able to insert otherness into the heart of Freud's pathbreaking conception of desire, and to offer a picture of desire from which the presence of the Other—big or small—is never absent, so that in a sense, or rather in all possible senses, individual desire is the desire of the Other, is the Other's desire. This socialization of desire itself now at one stroke renders the attempts to build a bridge between Freud and Marx, between the two great scientific discoveries which characterize modernity, unnecessary. For now the psyche is already essentially social, and the existence of the Other is at the very heart of the libidinal, just as all our social passions are already drenched in the psychic. But we must grasp the originality of this view, whose power is negative rather than positive, for the universal envy which is necessarily at the heart of all social life is not some positive desire, but is rather envy of the *jouissance* or satisfaction of the Other. "Envy," said Thomas Aquinas, "is sorrow for another's good." We find it at work, for example, in that dilemma of federalism to which I referred earlier, for it is not some basely materialist matter when I mourn the mineral wealth and fertility of another's region in comparison to my own barren soil, or when I resent the transfer of my own wealth and prosperity to a less favored neighbor in my commonwealth: rather, both these matters of material inequality are mediated and transmitted, indeed formed at the very outset, by my profound awareness of the theft of *jouissance* by the Other. Indeed, no doubt when we look back at the class-based societies of human prehistory, it is very much just such envy of *jouissance* that is at stake in class conflict and class struggle: my justified rage at the *jouissance* of the masters, and their own, seemingly more subtle resentment of my collective solidarity, my physical strength, my proximity to the earth and to nature, to real work, real life, and the body itself.

The fundamental superiority of Lacanian doctrine over the multitude of other psychoanalyses on offer, including Freud's original one, lies in the way it grasps the Other as being structurally internal to subjectivity itself: the problem with such a formulation remains of course the word "internal," which immediately restores a distinction between the inside and the outside, the self and what is exterior to it, a distinction which was to have been not avoided or eluded, but rather preempted in the first place. Until we reach late Lacan and the drives, all of Lacan is surely to be located here, in this dilemma of the Other, which Lacan inherited from Sartre and which is embodied in everything from the father to language itself, from the social to my own most intimate desires (which are those of the Other, using the genitive in all its ambiguity here), from *das Ding* to my own neurotic attempts to square this impossible circle. This is scarcely the place to map out such an intricate system, but only to observe that here the stereotypical (and ideological) opposition between "the individual" and "society" cannot obtain, since the two are inseparable in an inextricable dialectic of identity and difference. To put it methodologically, where in other systems the operation of transcoding is unavoidable—we must pass from a language of subjective or psychological individuality to a very different terminology governing the social or the collective (a passage involving a mediation I tend to describe in terms of a translation process)—here transcoding is unnecessary and the same code can apply to either reality. Thus where for Freud, in *Group Dynamics and the Analysis of the Ego*, the superego is somehow outside the self, in the form of the dictator and object of fascination he constitutes, here the Lacanian Big Other is within subjectivity, constituting it fully as much as it might be seen to influence it; nor is it some projection of my private desires, as when the Leader somehow symbolically resolves my own oedipal traumas (as for Erickson). Here the "ideal ego" and the "ego ideal" are separated by little more than a grammatical inversion; and the two fundamental political points I here try to make by way of an essentially Lacanian terminology are individual and collective, psychological and sociological, at one and the same time.

Psychologically they might have been named envy and aggressivity, which would, as we have already seen, have at once introduced some notion of human nature back into the societal or utopian picture. Now, however, that contamination is unnecessary, and the "theft of *jouissance*" may serve as a structural or ontological synonym for the psychological property of envy at the same time that it generalizes the phenomenon and grounds it in my unavoidable relationship to the Other and to that "life force" (or death drive) Lacan calls *jouissance*. (Whether this term reinvents a vitalist metaphysics or succeeds in escaping metaphysics altogether is another question that cannot be dealt with here, save to observe that Lacan's is not a philosophy as such but rather, as in Freud and Marx, in a unity of theory and practice.) The essential point to be made here is that *jouissance* cannot be satisfied and that therefore this lack, as a permanent feature of the human condition, is a perpetual invitation to an ontological and cultural envy of the Other that can be expressed in forms that range from Gombrowicz's "immaturity" (the others are grown-ups, I am not) all the way to the bloodiest civil wars.

From this condition—which is neither an emotion nor a political motivation, but rather a structural possibility and an existential fact—to the more generalized conviction about "antagonism" there is but a philosophical step, for antagonism simply denies the possibility of the "cure," whether societal or individual. It denies the possibility of social harmony, whose peaceful regulation was promised, for example, by the various systems of democracy (but also offered by Hobbes's sovereign), thereby opening a path to the construction of a utopian social order that embraces antagonism as such, although perhaps not in so mechanical a way as in Callenbach's War Games. Or better still, as has been suggested above, it excludes the aims and projects of political theory altogether and allows human relationships to develop in other ways.

Freud's therapeutic practice was based on the conviction that within his society and among that largely normal and functioning population, there existed individuals whose psychic mechanisms were blocked or deregulated to the point of making a functioning and productive daily life difficult or impossible. Freudianism then proposed an explanation for such malfunctioning and, in many or most cases, a method for treating it.

In the Lacanian system, taking it as a conceptual system rather than a set of techniques, it is no longer possible to hold this view of a relatively normal society. The internal presence of the Other, which constitutes each of us and ensures our individuality and indeed our consciousness, is not something that can be cured in that sense; it is something with which each of us come to terms in our own existential way (even though our societies and cultures continue to propose and to attempt to enforce traditional "solutions" or conventional ethical guidelines). This means that everyone is neurotic in the psychoanalytic sense and that society, of whatever type, cannot but be a collection of neurotics of various kinds, whose cohabitation can never be regulated in some harmonious or utopian fashion. Lacan's politics—whether you want to call them pessimistic, cynical, or tragic—reflect this conviction; and this is why to whatever form of Lacanian doctrine we adopt must be added the collective practice of a Fourieresque and utopian model which aims to draw its productivity from whatever macro- or microassemblages of human neurotics seem forthcoming. What is, however, unavoidably suggested in the standard culture-critical diagnoses is the secret hope that knowledge will in one way or another bring about a cure of its own and enact epistemological therapies: that awareness of the impossibility of any resolution to this structural relationship to the Other will ultimately lead us to some new place of being, some wisdom of the superman or the posthuman presently unimaginable for us and thereby unavailable. It would be the alternate wisdom of cynicism to be able to live without this secret hope at the heart of all diagnosis: perhaps the utopians have found a way to do that.

12.

The more properly anti-utopian objections to utopia clearly incorporate many of the antimilitary prejudices on a higher or more general level, where they mainly take the form of the various anti-socialisms and anticommunisms. Burke's immortal counterrevolutionary statement was powered by a twofold passion: on the one hand, it becomes clear, when read and examined closely, that his attacks on the Jacobins and their policies were in fact early critiques of capitalism as such (historically, the first powerful critiques of capitalism arose on the right, from a defeated aristocracy, before they were appropriated and developed by a then still nascent left). We may leave these aside. His other stance had to do with time itself and the passing of the old traditional institutions, as well as the hubris of the revolutionary attempt to construct altogether new ones of a purely human fabrication. Contemporary constructivism refutes this in a twofold way, both by insisting on the mirage of traditionalism of a past of transcendental and nonhuman origin ("the invention of tradition," Hobsbawm famously called it) and by glorying in production itself and the human capacity to create its own societies, its own contexts and ecosystems. It is a confidence that might well be tempered by a conviction of human incompetence and ignorance; but we must also make a place in our utopia for the passion for stability and continuity, for Heideggerian dwelling and the security of the land, alongside the delight in acceleration, the new, creative destruction, and perpetual movement. I think that any properly global utopia ought to include immense vacations of displacement, in which the populations of whole cities—New York and Shanghai for example—swap homes and places for a time (this would be the utopian correction for the present-day new industry of commodified tourism), but that city dwellers, prone to novelty, should also leave room for the land itself and deep time, for the metaphysical illusions of some human incorporation into nature itself (even when the latter has ceased to exist).

We need not, I think, spend any further time on the ideological conjunction of utopia with totalitarianism; far more serious is the danger of civil war always inherent in any such attempt to combine the global with the local—the ideologically narrow way in which political theory conceives of federalism. We do not have to enumerate the latter's causalities of federalism in the modern era—Yugoslavia, Spain, Canada, even the Soviet Union itself—to realize how delicate are all such balancing acts, which must avoid the predominance of one province over all the others at the same time that they resist fragmentation and dissolution. The nation was always the sign of the failure of such utopian federalism; there can be no doubt that even the military network we have designed to escape the geographical confines of national or state boundaries in a new way will still be menaced by the rivalry of, say, richer army bases and poorer ones. This is indeed where the Lacanian notion of the theft of *jouissance* comes into play as a historical diagnosis: one can envy industrious populations just as passionately as one can despise lazy and pleasure-seeking ones. Add to this the deeper economic level of geography and raw materials, and indeed the more material resentment of the redistribution of wealth and the investment of tax revenues from the prosperous provinces to pay the expenses of underdeveloped ones, and you have a dilemma of a multidimensional kind for which no ready-made solution exists. More's solution—to make all the subdivisions of his utopia equal in all respects—is a mechanical one, which casts some doubt on the equally mechanical uniformity of its citizens. Federalism is the central political problem of any utopia, using the word "political" in some new sense which is neither internal nor external and which might therefore be just as appropriately replaced by the word "ontological."

13.

This is now the moment to introduce, if not a utopian solution to the dilemma of federalism, then perhaps—in a Lacanian spirit—a utopian nonsolution to it. It is the moment to complete what some might consider the fundamentally pessimistic or even cynical Lacanian view of the impossibility of the social—the permanence of antagonism, the ontologically unavoidable conflict with the (nonexistent) Other—with a different vision of society for which its essential elements and building blocks are not individuals but groups.

This is the extraordinary perspective of Charles Fourier, grandiose and ludicrous all at once, the unlikely thinker of an impossible thought. The madness of his project—for madness is a requisite of any seriously utopian thinker—lies in the mathematical obsessions he shares with Lacan: less, to be sure, with some belief in the scientific objectivity or ideological innocence of the mathematical formula or matheme than in the inexhaustible genius of mathematical permutations and the well-nigh infinite number of sets, groups, and combinations thereby demonstrated. Fourier is no doubt a psychologist, but on the order of La Rochefoucauld rather than the experimental scientists, a Nietzsche without the genealogical interests. No more than those empirical observers do his psychological observations presuppose some concept or essence of human nature, unless it lie in the assumption that human beings and their psychological makeups have no real essence apart from the groups of which they are the parts and organs (and to which, in any utopian system, they ideally ought to belong). Barthes reduced Fourier's psychological makeups to three types or passions, which give something of the flavor of his insights (which Engels compared to those of the great satirists like Molière): these are the butterfly passion (something like an attention deficiency, in which one becomes fixated on one passionate interest after another), the cabbalistic passion, a kind of delight in intrigue and in combining individuals in various conspiracies, and the composite personality, in which the dominant feature is not this or that content, but enthusiasm itself and its powerful and shifting commitments. What is crucial is not this particular account of the human drives, which it would be delightful to combine with Lacanian neuroses and libidinal structures, but rather the fact of the group combinations themselves into which these various passions can productively interact and form their social molecules. Fourier's notion of harmony expresses the conviction that no matter how frustrated and unfulfilled, no matter how neurotic, hysterical, or compulsive, there will always be a collective combination in which the individual bearer of the sad passion in question, of the desperate or antisocial loner, the anorexic or bulimic of desire, the manic convert to ever new and equally unfulfillable hobbies and pastimes, will find relief. Just as Bellamy is the tutelary deity of the universal army and its infrastructure, so Fourier becomes that of a realm of freedom, of culture and its superstructures, and to my mind the only thinker who has thus far discovered the way for a collectivity or a multiplicity to coordinate the ineradicable individualities which make it up. Fourier's "calculus of passions" was a prodigious architectonic which aimed not at repressed potentially antisocial drives and feelings, but rather at harmonizing them in such a way that the negatives became productive. One might argue that his system constitutes the grain of truth at the heart of market ideology, as in Mandeville's *Fable of the Bees*, in which even the most excessive vices and luxuries make the market go round. So here Fourier's delirious yet sober and calculating imagination puts even Spinoza's "sad passions" to use as the cogs and wheels of a lively, ever-changing, self-perpetuating utopia. Today no utopia is viable that promises Thomas More's monasticism or the left puritanism of so many modern revolutionary traditions: rather it must necessarily aim at reducing the inevitable repressions—libidinal as well as security-oriented—that any society interiorizes in order to cohere. The new utopia, indeed, must welcome the most outrageous self-indulgences and personal freedoms of its citizens in all things, very much including puritanism and the hatred of self-indulgence and personal freedoms. It is Fourier who squares this circle, and this is why, alongside a decentralization scattered across its space like the distinctive city-states of Kim Stanley Robinson's Mars trilogy, we must also imagine the emergence of a new kind of institution, destined to supplant traditional government and its agencies and to articulate the superstructural or cultural level of our new society in a post- or trans-Fourieresque spirit.

We may provisionally call this new institution the Psychoanalytic Placement Bureau, and it will, in conjunction with unimaginably complex computer systems, handle and organize all forms of employment as well as all manner of personal and collective therapies. Mediating between the individual and the collective (you may insert innumerable familiar structures and groups in between them), the new institution will combine the functions of a union and a hospital, an employment office and a court, a market research agency, a polling bureau, and a social welfare center. Presumably what is left of the police as an institution will eventually be absorbed into this central agency, which will eventually replace government and political structures equally, the state thereby withering away into some enormous group therapy.

But is this not precisely the political as such? The return of the old centralizing state as the inevitable and necessary mediation between base and superstructure, the arbiter of conflicts of all kinds, the organizer of labor and distributor of its tasks, the very locus of what used to be called bureaucracy and is now, by virtue of the lottery, the black box in which there still dwell, immortal and inescapable, Plato's philosopher-kings?

And is it still possible to reconcile this kind of governing institution, however benign, with the structure of the universal army as a new kind of non-state, a kind of network or exoskeleton of the social needs and functions: something somewhere between a universal democracy, a political party, and a bureaucracy in which everyone is his own bureaucrat, an organizational framework on the order of the kinship system in so-called primitive communism or tribal society? For the kinship system also had the function of assigning tasks in such a fashion that they were not to be seen as the arbitrary result of individual decisions nor grasped as privileges.

In a sense we already live a radical split between base and superstructure, which we call public and private. It is always a delicate matter, in utopianizing, to distinguish between the utopian modification of reality and the symbolic replication of what already exists. Adorno liked to quote the Jewish proverb which describes the world after the coming of Messiah: "The same as this one, only just slightly different." Perhaps, indeed, something like that would hold for a world from which money suddenly disappeared.

Still, it would be worthwhile trying out more strenuous proposals. I envisage a utopia of the double life, in which social reproduction, albeit only involving a few hours a day, is performed in work clothes and in teams, a little like going for army reserve duty. These shifts could be vertical or horizontal, that is, a shift every morning or night, or else a concentrated period of several weeks followed by an equal stretch of what we used to call free time. Each of these temporal rhythms would no doubt generate a habitus, a kind of culture of its own, but what must be insisted on is that, whatever the labor, material or immaterial, it will in one way or another be collective and involve a distinct ontology, that of the collective project, collective life, the team as social being.

In the world of the superstructure, no such specifications hold; the individual is as free to be a recluse as a party person, to practice hobbies or to live out existence as a couch potato, to be a family man or professional mother, to volunteer for hospital work or to climb mountains or to struggle with drug addiction, to gamble on the stock market (some new form of value competition to be invented here) or to write books, to conduct church services, to become a saint, or to live whatever underground life can still be invented. For the superstructure is a matter of invention; and to begin with, one expects its practitioners to distinguish their choices by the most extravagant garments. This is a wholly secular world, in which, as Sartre taught us, everything is performance, everything is social construction. Our existential anxiety lies in the palpable fact that we are always at some slight distance from our choices (and free to change them at any point) and that, in that sense, there is no longer any human nature or any personal identity to weigh us down and offer the security of being one single unalterable personality. To be sure, the variety of individual biologies or bodies will still throw up individual talents or even genius;

and on the other hand, there will always be people who choose to identify so thoroughly with their "work" (their infrastructural morning obligations and tasks) that they know no other existence. There will be those who want the permanency of a home and a nine-to-five job (we may consider this a nostalgic pastiche of capitalism circa 1950) and those who delight in constant change (a pastiche of tourism, homelessness, exploration). This is then the sense in which this new world will look exactly like the old one, with but a few minor modifications (which consist, as we may remember, in the guaranteed wage and in Fourier).

14.

The military utopia was founded, I said, on a separation between base and superstructure as absolute as that enforced in olden times between church and state (and it is worth observing, in passing, how many of those older institutional features have been retained, and yet radically transformed, by their new utopian context and inflection). The realm of necessity and the realm of freedom, it was said: yet not only their relationship to each other (so-called cultural revolution) remains fragile and subject to much tension and renegotiation (particularly across the generational divide), but there are also problems and contradictions within each realm, as I will note in closing.

For the realm of necessity, it is not labor that offers any peculiarly unresolvable or untheorizable problems: necessary production can be calculated, hours reduced, transfers from one kind of work to another programmed on a voluntary basis, sabbaticals for study or retraining institutionalized—a systematic incorporation of information technology and a keen commitment to the development of new kinds of production, the production of new needs and desires, as Marx put it. The guaranteed annual minimum wage, distributed generously enough, removes the desperation that used to course through societies sickened by chronic as well as structural unemployment. As for social and income inequality, I quite like Barbara Goodwin's idea of five-year "life packages" distributed by lottery, and making it possible for citizens to spend a few years in luxurious mansions and a few more improving slums on the point of being reconstructed out of existence.

No, the fundamental problem of the base is money or, if you prefer, capital. Our universal army, or (with apologies to the Iroquois) our military democracy, has changed the very context in which war took on its original meaning. Thus, as has been pointed out, William James's call for a moral equivalent to war, in an older society fulfilled precisely by war itself, is now universally understood to have meant that radical and thoroughgoing social transformation at which our citizen-soldiers work tirelessly every day, secure in the conviction that this new built environment, this new "second nature," this whole newly emerging outside world, is their own production and belongs to them in that primitive sense of ownership Locke ascribed to the world that preceded money.

We may even rewrite a more infamous and sinister dictum of Hegel: namely, that war is the health of nations. Hegel was not himself a German nationalist (he was already thirty-eight when Fichte's notorious *Reden* invented the sentiment); like Goethe, he is more likely to have been a secret admirer of Napoleon. Thus, barring some Callot- or Goya-like bloodthirsty fascination, reasonable interpreters have concluded that he had in mind the kind of momentary surge of collective pride and unity so frequently provoked by the outbreak of a long-impending conflict, such as is familiar in the descriptions of August 1914 all over Europe.

I will, however, propose a different reading, namely that he had in mind the destruction of immense masses of capital as a consequence of warfare: not the annihilation of people but the annihilation of sheer accumulations of money as such. The end of World War II, like a convalescence from a terrible illness, for many countries involved a period of intense revolutionary hope when rebuilding and reconstruction meant radical change and the deployment of new energies, let alone new scientific discoveries and new modes of social action. That did not happen, for the most part and in most places, but that it could even be conceived was, according to me, predicated on poverty and on the destruction of money and capital. The United States today is sick, owing to the toxic accumulation of money and great fortunes which, like an infection, have found outlets only in luxury and the foulest right-wing propaganda. Even the jubilee, and the wholesale abolition of the debt into which the majority of the population has fallen, would count for only a momentary and passing celebration if that ever-increasing stockpile of riches were not destroyed. Utopias are practices of indigence and not collective self-indulgence.

It is said that freedom—the exercise of autonomy that alters subjectivity irrevocably and turns it into agency—cannot be given but only taken. Such is also the benefit of capital as a source of production: it cannot simply be seized from the rich and somehow "applied" to other projects. It must know a moment of laborious and original accumulation, one we want to distinguish from the nightmare of capital's own origin (and its afterimage in Stalin's attempt to build socialism). As for money, it is to be sure the form taken by original sin in most utopian visions, and in much political theory as well; the proposals to eliminate money altogether from a perfect world are as numerous as those which purport to invent harmless substitutes for it, as in Proudhon's labor chits, which Marx so memorably satirized, seizing as in a freeze-frame the moment in which inexorably they turned back into money again. Special relations with this peculiar object have their place in Lacanian/Freudian diagnosis as well as in Fourier's ingenious and nonrepressive remedies for them. Once money is decisively separated from capital in the universal "good sense" of the population, fantasies about its elimination will become less mesmerizing and its relationship to "value" less mysterious.

This does not exclude the establishment of new forms of carnival—resuscitating the potlatch, for example—nor the moral, if not material, need for a recurrent institution of the jubilee, the effacement of all debt. But it minimizes what is innately toxic in this alter ego of the commodity, whose sole utility lies in its ambiguous combination of the "measure" of value and the "means" of circulation.

As for the superstructure, its content can scarcely be predicted, but the unresolvable tensions in its form can certainly be anticipated. This will necessarily be a culture of groups, groups in perpetual emergence, groups in full or gradual dissolution, groups in which individuals join in a collective resistance to groups as such, or in an effort to preserve the cohesion of the institutions which have emerged from them and now seem on the point of outliving themselves. Such groups will no longer take the form of classes, in a society in which the latter no longer exist; are they to be considered "factions" in the sense of those pre-party formations which the ancients (the theoreticians of bourgeois society) so bitterly resisted? The fundamental permissiveness of the new society cannot forbid or exclude them, inasmuch as its Fourieresque spirit prescribes a constant participation of former individuals in groupings and combinations of all kinds, large and small. But groups must be subject to time and mortality, processes whose function generational change can now be expected to take over from the misleading and objectionable organic disintegration of the individual body.

I have often quoted Robert C. Elliott's fundamental observation that a utopia can be judged by the quality and position of the works of art it foretells; most, like More's, are either mute on the subject or distinctly unsatisfying, as in Morris and Bellamy alike. Marx, meanwhile, contented himself with wondering what the Greeks would still have to say to this new world. But I have also proposed that we reconsider the vocation of an older socialist realism as the critique of bureaucracy as such: the Hegelian power of the negative is secured and strengthened here, in the nagging and obsessive sniping at the group itself as it begins to ossify into an institution. The older utopias were perplexed in their contemplation of a future literature still organized around individual subjects, whose suffering and conflicts they now believed to have been solved. Once it is understood that the proper subject of literature is the group—the other arts clearly enough having the collective built into them in one way or another—the renewal of literature in utopia resolves itself and indeed becomes inescapable, in a situation in which the one extreme of the group congeals over into the state and bureaucracy and the other into simmering clashes, small-scale animosities, and civil wars. But the group is formed around the project, and this is why it must not only be called a conspiracy but felt and lived that way; each group project must be a crime underway, the realization of the Universal. Each must be a *new* crime, thereby acknowledging the demands of time itself, which wants fresh blood, which wants to undermine the constitutions and break as many rules as possible.

The political problems, then, are twofold, and they are the same. The first is called federalism (the name of a problem), and it asks how to regulate the antagonisms between the various groups. The second asks the same question about the (necessarily individual) antagonisms within the group, when those are not resolved by the existence of the common project. And what to do about the sad passions?

Hatreds are the easiest and the most insoluble: they ask for reciprocity, and then the twin hatreds are bound together like lovers and must, I suppose, be allowed to consummate their passion. But normally it is envy which is at stake, and which Lacan defines as the theft of enjoyment: I envy the *jouissance* of the Other, which he has in fact stolen from me. To disprove this envy, to assure me that the Other has no more enjoyment than I do, is a barren outcome. What must instead be celebrated is enjoyment itself, that it exists, and that it does not matter who has it inasmuch as no one can really have it in the first place: this is the true overcoming of envy, its elevation into a kind of religion.

It is in that direction also, I suppose, that the "solution" of the most intractable political problem is to be sought, the problem of federalism, the hatred of one group for the other and for its theft of my collective enjoyment (my natural resources, for example, or my big-city mentality, my proximity to nature, my machismo or my metrosexuality). Perhaps this is done by wresting the big cities away from their states and making them universal terrains that belong to everybody and to no one: places of anonymous collective wealth and of orgiastic yet cosmopolitan celebration, where troops of open-mouthed yokels mingle with city slickers, with lots of pickpocketing and outright fistfights. But this space has to be real, somehow, and not staged games à la Callenbach, even if it involves casualties and mortalities. In other words the redistribution of goods and surplus has to be absolute, an iron law like nature itself; trespassing it must be punished, provided the punishment is a pleasure.

Still, the critique of bureaucracy, even heightened into a metaphysical critique of the group itself as a form, is not the only task of a cultural revolution of which we have said that it is necessarily a kind of therapy, a reprogramming of the now disruptive habits of an older society or mode of production into new and productive ones. In an affluent society like our own—economically menaced, in any case, by the redistribution of wealth and the expenses to be paid in a prodigious attempt to establish anything like economic equality—the cultural habit that would seem to demand the most urgent attention is that of consumerism, a kind of universal addiction which can surely not be cured by abstention or criminalization, nor indeed by simple legalization either. But is this association of commodity consumption with the psycho-physical disorder of addiction not simply a regression to those older forms of culture critique already abundantly denounced above? For here we have assimilated a stereotypical public image of the addict (which can be the drug user but also the bulimic or the compulsive gambler, even the compulsive sex addict) with another image, which is that of American social life generally: the buying of food and care, the advertising of any number of name brands, the trappings of a whole affluent society. We combine these two images in such a way that the first reveals or discloses the truth or the skeletal substructure of the latter, peeling an appearance away to disclose a nightmarish underlying reality. This is the use of metaphor as a well-nigh filmic process, a kind of trope in which the tenor is effaced to the benefit of the vehicle. It is not a static trope like metaphor, but it remains a cultural object which is consumed, often with a certain poetic pleasure or satisfaction. (One can become addicted to such pleasures as well, as the plethora of social-diagnostic books in current society testifies.) But this—what I have generally called the "culture critique" in order to underscore its shoddiness and unloveliness as an intellectual operation and artifact—is very far from constituting analysis. The latter must necessarily be formulated as a concept which can structurally and functionally be integrated into the more general structural analysis of capitalism in order to qualify as "knowledge" (or as the opposite of "opinion" [doxa], something which can itself be an object of avid cultural consumption, as is every day apparent in the media). I have no particular revulsion for such consumption and such pleasures, whether those of consumerism or of cocaine—indeed, we must rigorously exclude all moralism from their analysis as well as from that of a given society as a whole—but their construction leads on to no further production any more than a poetic figure generally would, and it is to produce further problematization and theorization that we ought to be concerned here. It would then be desirable to theorize addiction, at least to the point at which it becomes a kind of structural analysis (or "knowledge") on the level with the concept of commodification itself. Indeed, the "spiritual" determinants of the latter ("theological niceties" and the like, in Marx's definition) perhaps give us an opening here, for as Marx describes it, the commodity is no longer a material thing but a kind of amphibious entity, partly corresponding to a need and partly exercising a signifying function which one hesitates to relate to the aesthetic, but which is surely the object of a kind of ideal or aesthetic fascination, all the while retaining the appearance of a bodily need (or something analogous to one).

There might be two ways of approaching the problem. We have already mentioned Marx's diagnosis of the "spiritualization" of the commodity, a process inherent in its very form. But this is not to be understood as a sublimation of some sort; rather, the "theological" dimension is present by way of money itself as a pure form (or empty signifier, if you prefer). Sublimation preserves elements of the concrete desire in a rarefied dimension, so that we still are involved in something determinate when we transfer it to that level. Nothing of the sort is present in the commodity form, from which all physical determination, all relationship to a specific bodily need or function, is absent—an expensive umbrella is as spiritual, as theological, as a priceless can of caviar or a rare book. It is therefore the passage through the money form that empties concrete use value from the object in question and transforms it into a commodity, an object which can be measured abstractly against all the others of its kind. Consumerism as a passion, then, like collecting or hoarding but in its own unique way, has money somewhere in its constitution, and can be expected to wither on the vine in a society in which money no longer plays a central role.

In this first theoretical approach, the body is still present, but in the heavily or lightly effaced form in which use value has been somehow transmogrified into exchange value—the latter still preserving, as it were, the dim memory or the fleeting shadow of an older use, like the lost or buried material foundation of an abstraction. The body will remain crucial in our second alternative, but now in a more Freudian or Lacanian way.

Here, to be sure, we still confront the gravitational pull of the Other (as it is registered in the very structure of exchange, for example), but by way of its absence. The most recent theories of addiction suggest that it is an attempt, in whatever form, to free the subject from the Other and from the mimetic hold of the Other's desire, and to institute a condition in which, with the assistance of this or that external medium, we are able to indulge a desire and its "satisfaction" which is utterly independent of the Other's existence (in a way which, as the Lacanians are able to explain technically, is distinct from the psychotic's "freedom from language" or the pervert's unshakeable certainty about the Other's desire). To consider consumerism as an addiction in this sense would involve a view of "consumer goods" as a kind of objectal medium surrounding us and isolating us from the more agonizing dilemmas posed by every concrete existence of the Other, but also of a world in which isolation from the Other has somehow become an urgent need. For the Lacanians, of course, no solution to the psychic alienation of the Other is possible, but awareness of that impossibility is; it may also be possible to imagine a society in which such awareness is more readily accessible than in our own, along with a Fourieresque relationship to desire which lends the latter's unappeasable insistence a wholly different tone and quality. As for the Marxian alternative outlined at the beginning, mapping our position in the network of production and exchange, of distribution and consumption, would necessarily weaken the psychic investments available to whatever passes as money in that situation, consigning the passionate consumer to some mere local niche in the Fourieresque permutational scheme.

Here, then, we approach the most intractable contradiction in the utopian superstructure: that moment in which the opposition between permanence (institutionalization) and permanent change gradually transforms itself into an opposition between permissiveness and discipline, awakening all the latent forces of cultural envy and in the process awakening in the distance the immense shadow of the Law, or in other words of the antisocial as such, and thereby reenergizing those limits even a utopian society must set for its own self-preservation or reproduction. Or is it possible to imagine a utopia which precisely transcends the societal form as such by doing away with such constitutive limits in the first place (just as Adorno imagined the—to be sure individual—utopia as the place in which individuals gave up their innate drive to self-preservation)? Any insistence on radical permissiveness at the level of culture will necessarily have to deal with the bitterest envies. The guaranteed minimum wage, the freedom to do nothing at all and to drug yourself into oblivion, obviously makes such a utopia into a paradise for slackers: yet this society is wealthy enough to let them go their own way, and a Fourieresque psychoanalysis will help us absorb the envy and bitterness, the sad passions, that will follow them from other workers in this vineyard, such as the religious fundamentalists. What the latter must learn is that such bitterness and envy is itself a *jouissance*, a precious possession, a passion and a satisfaction that is productive in its own right.

The orgiastic vision such freedom inevitably conjures up, however—a world in which drugs and sexual license reign supreme and all the unproductive self-indulgences of a new kind of unemployment sicken the mind—such a vision needs to be understood as the objective fantasy and the ideological opposite number and indissociable component of those dystopias of technological subjection and surveillance, of famine and atomic winters, we have already mentioned earlier. Both complement each other and are the imaginary reflex of a society divided between the freedoms of the rich and privations of the impotent poor, a late-capitalist society whose insurmountable contradictions confine the imagination to a desperate oscillation between impossible solutions and antithetical futures. This opposition is obviously also reflected in the present utopian proposal, which still divides the day into what used to be called work and leisure, namely a regimented morning and an afternoon and evening of aimless free time and potential boredom: what we have identified as base and superstructure. But I hope it is not some essentialist appeal to an eternal human nature to suggest that people are generally not very satisfied with the unproductive, however much it may be identified with pleasure as such, any more than they are resigned to externally dictated activity, let alone workaholism. It is therefore to be expected that in the utopian course of things labor will become cultural and the realm of freedom indissoluble from necessity. This is not to suggest the pseudo-Hegelian reconciliation so many people have attributed to utopia in a pejorative sense: that would be to attribute compromise and uniformity to an insurmountable multiplicity of personal solutions. It would no doubt also conjure up the unthinkable and self-contradictory notion of an end of history, an unacceptable slogan whose circulation merely testifies to our cognitive limitations when it comes to the thinking of utopia itself. In these cases, we must be careful to let the future dispose of our current contradictions as it will, rather than to flail about within them in a thereby self-imposed paralysis of the imagination.

As for crime, or more accurately put, the antisocial: As someone with a horror of the death penalty and of prisons generally, I recommend a return to the old Greek and Tsarist traditions of banishment, but I also propose adoption of Samuel Delany's magnificent institution (in his utopian novel *Triton*) of a so-called "unlicensed sector," where no law exists and anything goes: but it occurs to me that this might in fact be the role of the city itself, as its form survives the great transformation.

Žižek has often quoted Chesterton—a fellow traveler in the perilous effort of coordinating passionate belief with orthodoxy—to the effect that we must see the Law as something even more exciting than crime. Here is the old philosophical crux of the Universal and the Particular, which has such strong political vibrations and reverberations, and of whose Hegelian version Žižek has given us so perverse and pertinent a fresh version: the particular tending always toward the exceptional, it is the exception that ends up constituting the Law, the Universal; the whole generic system thereby tilts and swings upside down, and it is the empirical which ends up being the general, in what he calls the "singular universal."

So now, in the realm of the collective, it is this that must be tested, in the strongest sense of the word. We can then read Chesterton as a way of restoring excitement to the Law: it is to be grasped as a criminal adventure, and this transcends those still too individualistic categories of the act and the event. We must think of gangs and criminal conspiracies, we must think of illegal groups, of small-scale plots, large-scale robberies, raids, takeovers, sorties, elaborate schemes and carefully designed executions, each one on task, everyone in the right place at the right time. This is the point at which the old adage that business (or the state itself) is a conspiracy against the public slowly turns over into its positive form: yes, the Law should also be a conspiracy—all collective action, all collective projects, should have the transgressive excitement of the conspiracy; it is the conspiracy which is the strong form both of crime and of the collective. One, two, many conspiracies: such is the utopian social order, such is the new revolutionary state (or the revolutionary withering away of the state, if you prefer). And this is the truth and wisdom of Žižek's dialectical reversal of Hegel: a friend, André Gide once said, is someone with whom you would be happy to *faire un mauvais coup*. So should be all action, the conspiratorial aim, annulling the individual animosities, the frictions and envies, the incompatibilities of our existence as individuals in society. The stereotypes of army life are above all relevant here, for barracks life, the life of the recruit or draftee, always involves being thrown together with people utterly unlike you, from wholly different and incompatible backgrounds, classes, ethnicities, and even sexes. The instantaneous dislikes and distasteful cultural unfamiliarities, the inescapable elbow-rubbing with people with whom you have nothing in common and would normally avoid—this is true democracy, normally concealed by the various class shelters, the professions, or the family itself (which may well, however, also be felt and lived as just such an intolerable cohabitation of incompatible temperaments and people who get on each other's nerves), and warded off by wealth in its gated communities and walled estates. This is the place of what Laclau called antagonism, which he tended to substitute for class struggle and to bend in a Hobbesian direction: this is the true horror of democracy itself, as the aristocratic distaste of all the reactionary manifestoes testifies. It celebrates its euphoric moments of collective reconciliation in the great mass demonstrations and flash mobs, the "lyric illusion" of the triumphant revolutionary crowds, but then settles down into the daily grind of the petty democratic antagonisms which biological individuals inevitably feel toward one another and from which both empty idealism and Spinoza's "sad passions" derive.

We have only reached the point in which a universal militarization permits the organization of a minimum of necessary production sufficient to satisfy the multiple needs of a given population, from food and housing to education and medical treatment, thereby liberating a free time unexpected and unplanned for in Darwinian evolution and the natural world. This is the moment in which, as Sartre put it, existentialism supersedes Marxism as a philosophic horizon, and we can detect the nature of our own ideological reflexes by way of our reactions to it. However those may be, it is at the very least at least one way in which an alternate future can be imagined as opening once again, a future sealed and effaced by the absolute limits currently imposed by late capitalism as such. So this may not be the place to stop, but also to begin.

2

Mutt and Jeff Push the Button

Kim Stanley Robinson

"Whoever writes the code creates the value."

"That isn't even close to true."

"Yes it is. Value resides in life, and life is coded, like with DNA."

"So bacteria have values?"

"Sure. All life wants things and goes after them. Viruses, bacteria, all the way up to us."

"Which by the way it's your turn to clean the toilet."

"I know. Life means death."

"So, today?"

"Some today. Back to my point. We write code."

"Right, we write."

"Without our code, no firewalls, no finance, no banks, no money, no exchange value, no value."

"All but that last, I see what you mean. But so what?"

"Did you read the news today?"

"Of course not."

"You should. It's bad. Things are falling apart."

"Things are always falling apart. It's like what you said. Life means death. It's messy."

"But more than ever. More than it needs to be."

"This I know. It's why we live in a tent on a roof."

"Yes, but it's getting worse. The food panic is freaking people out."

"Rightfully so. That's the real value, food in your belly. And it isn't fungible. If you have money but you can't buy food, you're fucked, because you can't eat money."

"But that's what I'm saying!"

"No you're not."

"Mutt."

"Jeff."

"Mutt. Hang with me. Follow what I'm saying. We live in a world where people pretend all values are fungible, so money can buy you anything, so money is the point, so we all work for money. Money is thought of as value. People don't see the difference."

"Okay I get that. We're broke and I get that."

"So good, keep following me here."

"What will you pay me for following you?"

"One bitcoin."

"So you'll run your computer all night factoring new numbers for pi, and thus I'm compensated?"

"You'll have a bitcoin you didn't have, put it that way."

"Okay, deal. You promise?"

"Yes."

"Write it down."

"Done. Promissory note for one bitcoin."

"Money in the bank. Okay, your meter is running. Speak on."

"So, we live in a money economy where everything is grossly underpriced, except for rich people's compensation, but that's not the main problem. The main problem is we've agreed to let the market set prices."

"The invisible hand."

"Right. Sellers offer goods and services, buyers buy them, and in the flux of supply and demand the price gets determined. That's the cumulative equilibrium, and its prices change as supply and demand change. It's crowdsourced, it's democratic, it's the market."

"The only way."

"Right. But it's always, always wrong. Its prices are always too low, and so the world is fucked. We're in a mass extinction event, the climate is cooked, there's a food panic, everything you're not reading in the news."

"All because of the market."

"Exactly. It's not just there are market failures. It's the market is a failure."

"How so, what do you mean?"

"I mean the cumulative equilibrium underprices everything. Things and services are sold for less than it costs to make them."

"That sounds like the road to bankruptcy."

"It is, and lots of businesses do go bankrupt. But the ones that don't haven't actually made a profit, they've just gotten away with selling their thing for less than it cost to make it. They do that by hiding or ignoring some of the costs of making it. That's what everyone does, because they're under the huge pressure of market competition. They can't be undersold or they'll go out of business, because every buyer buys the cheapest version of whatever. So the sellers have to shove some of their production costs off their books. They can pay their labor less, of course. They've done that, so labor is one cost they don't pay. That's why we're broke. Then raw materials, they hide the costs of obtaining them, also the costs of turning them into stuff. Then they don't pay for the infrastructure they use to get their stuff to market, and they don't pay for the wastes they dump in the air and water and ground. Finally they put a price on their good or service that's about 10 percent of what it really cost to make, and buyers buy it at that price. The seller shows a profit, shareholder value goes up, the executives take their bonuses and leave to do it again somewhere else, or retire to their mansion island. Meanwhile the biosphere and the workers who made the stuff, also all the generations to come, they take the hidden costs right in the teeth."

"But they got a cheap TV out of it."

"Right, so they can watch something interesting as they sit there broke."

"Except there's nothing interesting on."

"Well, but this is the least of their problems. I mean actually you can usually find something interesting on. Turner Classic Movies, for instance."

"Please. We've seen everything they've got multiple times."

"Everyone has. I'm just saying the boredom of bad TV is not the biggest of our worries. Mass extinction is our biggest worry. Or hunger. Or wrecking kids' lives before they even get a chance. These are bigger worries."

"Granted for the sake of argument."

"So look, it's capitalism. The problem, I mean. It's the market system. We've got good tech, we've got a nice planet, we're fucking all that up by way of stupid laws. That's what capitalism is, a set of stupid laws."

"Say I grant that too, which maybe I do. So what can we do?"

"It's a set of laws! And it's global! It extends all over the Earth, there's no escaping it, we're all in it, and no matter what you try to do, the system rules."

"I'm not seeing the what-we-can-do part."

"Think about it! The laws are on the books by way of being coded into the computers, the Internet, the cloud. Laws are codes and they run the world. They make the value. There are sixteen laws running the whole world."

"To me that seems too few. Too few or too many."

"No. They're articulated, of course, but it comes down to sixteen laws. I've done the analysis."

"As always. But it's still too many. You never hear about sixteen of anything. There are the eight noble truths, the two evil stepsisters. Maybe twelve of something at most, like recovery steps, or apostles, but usually it's single digits."

"Quit that. It's a global economy, so it takes sixteen laws to run it. They're distributed between the World Trade Organization, the International Monetary Fund, the World Bank, and the G20. Financial transactions, currency exchange, trade law, corporate law, tax law. Everywhere the same."

"I'm still thinking sixteen is either too few or too many."

"Sixteen, I'm telling you, and they're isomorphic, and they're encoded. So they can be changed by changing the codes. Look what I'm saying: You change those sixteen, you're like turning a key in a big lock. The key turns, and everything goes from bad to good. The system, instead of hurting people, helps people. It restores landscapes, stops the extinctions, food gets grown, the cleanest techs get deployed. And it's global, so defectors can't get outside it. Bad money gets turned to dust, bad actions likewise. No one could cheat. It would *make* people be good."

"Please Jeff? You're sounding scarier and scarier."

"I'm just saying! Besides what's scarier than right now?"

"Change? I don't know. It just sounds scary."

"What's scary? You can't even read the news, right? Because it's too fucking scary?"

"Well, and I don't have the time."

Jeff laughs till he puts his forehead on the table. Even then he laughs, his head lightly bouncing. Mutt has to laugh to see his friend so amused. They are friends, they amuse each other, they work long hours together writing code that encrypts security for a big flash trader living with his supercomputers on a barge in the Meadowlands. They like their tent on the roof of their building in Manhattan, which lies flooded below them like a super Venice gleaming in the night, majestic, liquid, superb. Their town.

Jeff raises his head. "Look, Ellen has shown me how to break into the WTO computers, and we know how to write code, we are the best coders in the world."

"Or at least in the building."

"No come on, the world! And Ellen's gotten us where we need to go. It turns out the WTO is the best way to start. After that it's a firewall creeper."

"What do you mean?"

"Check it out!" Jeff points at his screen. "We're in there, and I've got the codes ready. Sixteen revisions. Some are little tweaks, some are like complete reversals."

"Now you really are scaring me."

"Well sure, but look, check it out. See what you think."

Mutt moves his lips when he reads. He's not saying the words silently to himself, he's doing a kind of Nero Wolfe stimulation of his brain. It's his favorite neurobics exercise, of which he has many. Now he begins to massage his lips with his fingers as he reads on. This exercise signals worried reflection.

"Tell me what this one means," he says, pointing.

"Speed-trading surcharge, a hundredth of a point per transaction."

"One ten-thousandth of a cent? One millionth of a dollar?"

"It adds up fast. I call it lancing the boil."

"What about this one?"

"Full employment."

"Nice, but, I don't know how to say it, but it looks like you're getting that by drafting everyone into the army."

"That's right, but since everyone's in it, that makes it more like national service. Everyone has to do it."

"For how long?"

"Birth to grave."

"Really? This is your cure?"

"Yeah sure! See what it gets you? Free health care, education, housing, vacations, clothes."

"Well, I always wanted free clothes."

"I know, I put that in there for you. No more trips to the Salvation Army."

"I would miss that."

"You can still do it if you want. So much work gets done by everybody that you'll only have to put in eight hours a week."

"What about political objections? Won't people freak out?"

"Politics becomes like going to the thrift shop. Some people do it for fun, most don't bother."

"No politics?"

"No politics, no business, no psychology, no privilege, no class. Everyone's on the same team, see? It's like when you're in high school."

"How utopian can you get?"

"It's just a different code. We all become bureaucrats."

"You're outdoing yourself."

"You'd become head honcho of the Institute of Mutt."

"I like that. And the speed-trading charge will pay for all this?"

"Not entirely. Look at number fifteen. There's a steeply progressive charge on capital assets. I call that one deoligarchification."

"You're so good with these names."

"That clogged wealth gets distributed equally to everyone, so we all end up with a living wage, which we won't need for the necessities anyway, because they're part of being in the army. So it's a kind of slush fund to fool around with. Because money will always come in handy."

"Bitcoins again?"

"Sometimes. Whatever currency you like. Fucking currencies are fucking fungible. Nothing else is."

"And is number nine here a carbon tax?"

"What's a tax? I don't know what that word means! Number nine is about paying the true cost of things. Same with number two. Number two means we pay the true cost of labor, always."

"Won't that be kind of expensive?"

"What's expensive? It's the cost of living! We pay ourselves the cost of living. Money is just a kind of public utility. Especially once you deoligarchify all the capital assets."

Mutt nods. “Okay, I like that. But, you know, this system doesn’t look like it would be very efficient.”

“Of course not. Efficiency was just a measurement of how fast money moved from the poor to the rich. We prefer the opposite of efficiency, which is to say, justice.”

“There you go with your names again.”

“I think justice is a good name.”

Mutt keeps reading.

Finally he says, “Okay, I see what you’ve got here. I like it. It could be fun. Almost sure to be humorous.”

Jeff nods. He taps the return key. His new set of codes goes out into the world.

They leave their hotello, which is a walk-in tent assembled from a kit, and stand at the railing of their building’s roof balcony, looking down at the drowned city. Lights squiggle off the black water flooring the town. A few skyscrapers around them are very well lit, but most are dark. It’s quiet, weird, beautiful, spooky.

There’s a ping from inside and they go back in the tent.

Jeff reads his computer screen. “Ah shit!” he says. “We’re drafted!”

“Well—congratulations, right?”

Jeff gulps. “Hope so.”

Mutt reads the screen. “Wait, is this drafted, or busted?”

The roof’s service elevator door opens.

3

Dual Power Redux

Jodi Dean

Fredric Jameson's "American utopia" returns to the notion of dual power as a model for revolutionary change. Unlike either Lenin's classic formulation of soviets and provisional government or contemporary anarchist suggestions for institutional counter-power coexisting alongside the state, Jameson's version of dual power uses the state to dismantle the state. In a two-part move, he offers, first, a political program that expands one part of the state, the military, against another part, representative government. Jameson proposes, second, a utopian vision that extends this military arrangement to eliminate the political altogether. From the transitional dual power of active military and ineffective government evolves a new classless society organized in terms of the dual power of base and superstructure, economy and culture, military work and creative leisure (all variations on the same split between a realm of necessity and a realm of freedom). Not only is politics unnecessary in this utopian arrangement, the political has no place.

Jameson's idea of a universal army may seem provocative. However, his fantasy of an end to politics echoes prevailing anti- and post-political sentiments as it eschews the state. The political question of decision—what is to be done and who decides—disappears. It returns in Jameson's utopian proposal in truncated form: a Psychoanalytic Placement Bureau that uses "unimaginably complex computers" to organize employment. This leap of utopian imagination springs from an absence of trust in the people, as if the fact of a divided people implied the impossibility of self-governance rather than establishing its constitutive condition. In place of the sovereignty of the people (understood in Leninist terms as the revolutionary alliance of the oppressed), Jameson gives us the "population" as the subjectless substance to be managed.[1] This vision extends rather than confronts the capitalist view of persons as nothing other than economic units.

At a time when riots and revolutions point to left resurgence across the globe, Jameson's military model of collectivity directs us away from the dual power with actual political potential: crowds and party.[2] In recent decades, an intensifying array of demonstrations, occupations, strikes, and blockades has returned the question of the party form to the center of left politics. Running up against impasses that recur with "predictable if dispiriting regularity," current struggles pose pressing organizational questions.[3] How can our actions scale and endure? How can they link up, reinforce one another, advance an agenda, and achieve political results? In contrast with a utopian proposal distanced from actual movements, "the question of the party-form" takes place "with reference to, and indeed from within the dynamics of, contemporary struggles," as Jason E. Smith rightly points out. Challenged to

---

1 For a discussion of the sovereignty of the people in terms of the revolutionary alliance of the oppressed, see Jodi Dean, *The Communist Horizon*, London: Verso, 2012.

2 On dual power see also Susana Draper, "Within the Horizon of an Actuality: The State and the Commons in the Eternal Return of Communism," *South Atlantic Quarterly*, Fall 2014: 807–20.

3 Jason E. Smith, "Contemporary Struggles and the Question of the Party: A Reply to Gavin Walker," *Theory and Event* 16.4, 2013.

generate and sustain collective energies, political movement thrusts the problematic of the party back onto the terrain of left theory and practice. Peter D. Thomas notes that

> it has been practical experience of the contradictory processes of left regroupment on an international scale—from reconfigurations over the last decade on the Latin American left, to the varying success of coalition parties in Europe such as Die Linke in Germany, Izquierda Unida in Spain, Syriza in Greece and the Front de Gauche in France, to the tentative emergence of new political formations across North Africa and the Arab world—that has firmly placed the question of the party back on the contemporary agenda.[4]

Movement actors increasingly recognize the limitations of a politics conceived in terms of issue- and identity-focused activisms, mass demonstrations that for all intents and purposes are essentially one-offs, and the momentary localism of anarchist street-fighting. With urgency born from intensified economic inequality and the uneven distribution of the effects of planetary warming, they are pressing again the organizational question, reconsidering the political possibilities of the party form.

To the extent that Jameson's utopian proposal contributes to the present task of inciting a desire for organization on the left, its testing of our "ideological reflexes" is useful. But insofar as Jameson repeats the rejection of party and state characteristic of left post-politics, his proposition has already been tried and found wanting. His universal army is an inverted form of the multitude of autonomous, incommunicable struggles celebrated on the left since 1968. For decades, tendencies on the left have disparaged party politics targeting the state and championed social movements targeting society.[5] Where

---

4 Peter D. Thomas, "The Communist Hypothesis and the Question of Organization," *Theory & Event* 16.4, 2013.

5 Differing instances of this same turn can be found in Ernesto Laclau

anarchists and post-Marxists of various stripes try to sidestep the state by urging the pluralization of the economy, Jameson sidesteps the state with the opposite tack: universal conscription into a military responsible for the economy. In each case, the struggle to build and exercise political power, to use the state in the collective interests of poor and working people, is given up. The weakness of Jameson's proposal, then, stems from his imagining of left organization in terms of an economic army of everyone rather than as a political party faithful to egalitarian people's struggle.

Be All That You Can Be

Jameson's political program builds from the idea that the army is the only existing institution capable of exercising a revolutionary function (he qualifies his vision of the army as "pre-Rumsfeldian"). The army is disciplined and democratizing (in the sense of mixing together different groups). It acts across state boundaries, exceeding local jurisdiction. The army provides education, training, and health care. Given this already existing capacity, Jameson argues, the army should be expanded to include everyone between the ages of sixteen and sixty. It can then take over most production and distribution and thereby ensure full employment, Jameson's highest social priority. The ineffective representative government of the present will wither away as the army becomes a new social structure, the exoskeleton of society.

It's hard to tell what makes Jameson's universal army an army. On the one hand, he says that the conscription of everyone into his

---

and Chantal Mouffe, *Hegemony and Socialist Strategy*, London, Verso: 1985; Jean Cohen and Andrew Arato, *Civil Society and Political Theory*, Cambridge, MA: MIT Press, 1992; and Félix Guattari and Antonio Negri, *New Lines of Alliance, New Spaces of Liberty*, New York: Autonomedia, 2010, originally published in French in 1985.

glorified National Guard will make it unmanageable, incapable of carrying out foreign wars or coups. So this is an army that does not fight. On the other hand, Jameson says that conscientious objectors will be employed in arms development and storage. But why would a military incapable of carrying out wars need arms? Given that Jameson reorients disease control, education, disaster relief, infrastructure repair, and food distribution under the army, how is it possible that its units would not be capable of carrying out wars or coups, especially if arms development has continued?

Further complicating the question of how his army is an army, Jameson underplays hierarchy and the chain of command, key elements of military organization. This enables him to avoid dealing with the brutally obscene rituals of hazing endemic to military discipline. It also lets him ignore political power and decision-making and present the military as a decentralized network capable of overcoming federalism's separations. A consequence of Jameson's approach to federalism in general and the structure of the US Constitution in particular, then, is the nature of this overcoming. Is it a fantasy of national unity or of imperial expansion? Jameson proposes that the military absorb the entire population, but population of what? The United States? North America? The Western Hemisphere? The Pacific Rim? The world? This absorption presses all the more intensely the question of the military's purpose: building a nation or conquering the world?

Jameson's utopian military in fact has no political purpose. Its role is economic, concentrated on the base. The military provides full employment, thereby solving what Jameson presents as the most pressing social problem. Full employment, however, is as purposeless a purpose as economic growth and productivity, a repetition of pointless activity for its own sake. Questions of resource allocation, social priorities, and cultural limits remain. These are political questions, sites of antagonism around which collectivity constitutes itself.

The single feature that makes Jameson's universal army a military force is conscription. The army he imagines is a nonvoluntary, nonelective mode of association. People are forced to participate in a common scheme, regardless of their individual differences or preferences. The universal army is a collectivity one does not choose.

The emphasis on collectivity is an advantage to Jameson's approach. He rejects the individualism that has trapped the contemporary left in an iron cage, bringing out the primacy of the collective. Moreover, he anchors his account in Lacanian psychoanalysis, rightly rejecting Freud's attempt to explain group psychology via identification through love for a leader. So why, then, does Jameson follow Freud in treating the army as his model of the collective (Freud's other model is the church)? It could be that Jameson's emphasis on the army is a residuum of his embrace of another element of Freud's discussion in *Group Psychology and the Analysis of the Ego*, envy. Freud explains the demand for equality that structures relations between group members as an effect of an original envy: "Social justice means that we deny ourselves many things so that others may have to do without them as well."[6] Jameson, too, mobilizes envy in the service of his utopian proposition, albeit in a Lacanian-Žižekian guise—"the theft of enjoyment." Jameson treats the theft of enjoyment as synonymous with the idea that *jouissance* cannot be satisfied. That this lack is constitutive, "a permanent feature of the human condition," becomes for Jameson "a perpetual invitation to an ontological and cultural envy of the Other." Where Freud locates group attachment, Jameson finds rupture, the antagonism that prevents social harmony, an antagonism at the heart of collectivity.

Jameson incorporates antagonism into his utopian model in several ways. Drawing from utopian Charles Fourier, he makes the "sad

---

6 Sigmund Freud, *Group Psychology and the Analysis of the Ego*, trans. by James Strachey, London: International Psycho-Analytical Press, 1922, 88.

passions" productive. Antisocial drives will be put to use for the generation of new combinations and assemblages. Rather than repressed, as with Freud, envy and other negative passions will be expressed, even celebrated as enjoyment. This is what the superstructural realm of culture is for: it's the space for self-indulgence and personal freedom. People's time will be divided between their military service, their work obligations (which may be a few hours a week or a few weeks a year), and their free time, the leisure they have to do whatever they like. Big cities can be designated pleasure zones: "places of anonymous collective wealth and of orgiastic yet cosmopolitan celebration, where troops of open-mouthed yokels mingle with city slickers, with lots of pickpocketing and outright fistfights." The Psychoanalytic Placement Bureau, availing itself of "unimaginably complex computer systems," will handle emergent problems, the last remnant of the state now in the form of "some enormous group therapy." In effect, though, it is the split in the social between base and superstructure that takes the place of antagonism. Jameson denies antagonism political expression, replacing it with a society that splits itself between its militarism and its enjoyment, holding the two together via group therapy and computers. No wonder he repeats Adorno's repetition of the Jewish proverb describing the world after the coming of the Messiah: the same as this one, only just slightly different. His "American utopia" re-presents the eroded political of the contemporary United States back to us in utopian form. You want a society of militarism and enjoyment? You got it!

Another Crowd

Jameson prefaces his utopian proposal with a proviso leaving open the possibility of a different combination of elements. One such combination would join Jameson in emphasizing collectivity, but resist its military incorporation and instead begin with the crowd. Here the work of Elias Canetti is helpful.

Arguing that the first task of utopianism is diagnosing the fear of utopia, Jameson posits a terror of the collective: "the existential fear of losing our individuality in some vaster collective being." Canetti begins from a different primal fear: "There is nothing that man fears more than the touch of the unknown."[7] The one place where man is free of this fear is in a crowd. "The crowd he needs is the dense crowd, in which body is pressed to body," Canetti writes, "a crowd, too, whose psychical constitution is also dense, or compact, so that he no longer notices who it is that presses against him."[8] The presence of many relieves us of the anxiety of being touched by the strange or unknown. "Suddenly, it is as though everything were happening in one and the same body." Jameson, in contrast, holds on to biological individuation as an unsurpassable limit.

Canetti's crowd is de-individualizing. It rejects presumptions of individuated embodiment as some kind of natural limit to collectivity. As the crowd coalesces into its heterogeneous being, norms of appropriate proximity dissolve. Conventional hierarchies collapse. In place of the distinctions mobilized to produce the individual form, there is a temporary being of multiple mouths, anuses, stomachs, hands and feet, a being comprised of fold upon fold of touching skin.

Canetti describes the moment of the crowd's emergence as the "discharge." This is the point when "all who belong to the crowd get rid of their differences and feel equal."[9] Up until that point, there may be a lot of people, but they are not yet that concentration of bodies and affects that is a crowd. Density, though, as it increases, has libidinal effects: "In that density, where there is scarcely any space between, and body presses against body, each

---

7 Elias Canetti, *Crowds and Power*, trans. Carol Stewart, New York: Farrar, Straus and Giroux, 1984, 15.

8 Ibid.

9 Ibid., 17.

man is as near the other as he is to himself, and an immense feeling of relief ensues. It is for the sake of this blessed moment, when no-one is greater or better than another, that people become a crowd."[10] Canetti gives us the crowd as a strange attractor of *jouissance*, a figure of collective enjoyment.[11] The libidinal energy of the crowd binds it together for a "blessed moment," a moment Canetti renders as a "feeling of equality" in the shared intensity of the discharge. The feeling won't last. Inequality will return with the dissipation of the crowd. Very few give up the possessions and associations that separate them (and those who do form what Canetti terms "crowd crystals"). But in the orgasmic discharge, "a state of absolute equality" supplants individuating distinctions.[12]

Canetti's crowd equality has nothing to do with the envy driving Freud's imaginary equality of rivals. Nor does it resemble *bourgeois equality* of the sort Marx excoriates in "The Critique of the Gotha Program." This is not the formal equality of a common standard applied to different people, objects or expenditures of labor. Rather, the equality Canetti invokes is one where "a head is a head, an arm is an arm, and the differences between individual heads and arms is irrelevant."[13] De-individuation accompanies intense belonging. Just as Marx parenthetically notes that unequal individuals "would not be different individuals if they were not unequal," so does Canetti associate inequality with differentiation, with the siphoning off of the fluid, mobile substance of collectivity into the form of distinct individuals. The force of equality in the crowd breaks down the always fragile and imaginary enclosure of the individual form, enabling the collective to experience its collectivity. Canetti argues that the crowd's equality infuses all demands

---

10 Ibid., 18.

11 On strange attractors, see Jodi Dean, *Democracy and Other Neoliberal Fantasies*, Durham, NC: Duke University Press, 2009, 67–70.

12 Canetti, *Crowds and Power*, 29.

13 Ibid.

for justice. Equality as belonging —not separation, weighing, and measure—is what gives "energy" (Canetti's term) to the longing for justice.

With the "blessed moment" of belonging in the crowd's discharge, Canetti offers a view of equality fundamentally different from the psychoanalytic association of equality with envy that Jameson adopts. In contrast with the military imagining of a classless society, equality in the crowd is de-differentiation, de-individuation, the momentary release from hierarchy, closure, and separation. "It is for the sake of this equality that people become a crowd and that they tend to overlook anything which might detract from it," Canetti writes. "All demands for justice and all theories of equality ultimately derive their energy from the actual experience of equality familiar to anyone who has been part of a crowd."[14] The press for equality comes not from ressentiment. It's not born of weakness or deprivation. It comes from the strength of many as it amplifies itself, reinforces itself, and pushes itself back upon itself. With shouts, exclamations, and noise—the spontaneous "utterance in common"—the crowd expresses the equality that is its substance.

The crowd's density is its indivisibility or degree of solidarity. Understood physiologically, this density manifests itself in commonality of feeling, for example, the excitement that passes through the crowd, amplifying and feeding into itself. The "skillful enactment of density and equality" engenders the crowd feeling.

In addition to equality and density, Canetti attributes to crowds traits suggestive of what psychoanalysis treats as desire: growth and direction. Canetti's crowd wants to grow, to increase and spread. It will persist as long as it is moving toward a goal. If the crowd is to continue to exist, the goal must remain unattained. Expressed in Lacanian terms: desire is a desire to desire. The urge

14 Ibid.

to increase is a push to be more, to eliminate barriers, to universalize and extend the crowd feeling such that nothing is outside it. The crowd's direction is its goal. When common, the goal "strengthens the feeling of equality." The stronger the common goal is, the weaker the individual goals that threaten the crowd's density. Without its goal, the crowd disintegrates into individuals pursuing their own ends. The goal is outside the crowd, that toward which it is oriented. The goal is not the discharge, although the discharge is the aim.

Crowds are a force of desire exerted by collectivity. When they amass in spaces authorized by neither capital nor the state, they breach the given, installing a gap of possibility. The presence of a crowd is then a positive expression of negation. People act together in ways impossible for individuals, a phenomenon that preoccupied Freud. Pushing against dominant arrangements, the crowd prefigures a collective, egalitarian possibility—but "prefigures" in a completely literal way: "prior to figuration." The crowd by itself, unnamed, doesn't provide or represent an alternative. It cuts out an opening by breaking through the limits bounding permitted experience. People are there, but, through the active desire of the crowd, differently from how they were before, combined into a state of such absolute equality that "differences between individual heads and arms are irrelevant." Together previously separate people impress the possibility of the people as the collective subject of a politics.

Jameson's utopian proposal overlaps with Canetti's crowd theory in several respects. Each approaches the social through the collective: Jameson via the coercive force of conscription, Canetti via the affective pull of the crowd (the relief the crowd provides from the anxiety of being touched by something strange). Likewise, each highlights the constitutive non-satisfaction of desire: Jameson, via envy and Canetti via growth. Finally, each attends to the libidinal dimensions of collectivity. Jameson proposes overcoming envy by elevating it into a kind of religion: "what must instead be celebrated is enjoyment itself, that it exists, and that it does not matter who has it inasmuch as no one can really have it in the first place." Is this not but a description of the discharge, the moment of the crowd's orgasmic intensity when each escapes from the fear and isolation of the individual form in which he had been trapped? Canetti writes: "In the crowd the individual feels that he is transcending the limits of his own person. He has a sense of relief, for the distances are removed which used to throw him back on himself and shut him in. With the lifting of these burdens of distance he feels free; his freedom is the crossing of these boundaries."[15]

Jameson explicitly rejects the crowd as a candidate for dual power. Adopting Hardt's and Negri's terminology, he associates the occupations and riots of the last decade with the constitutive power of the multitude. Mass uprisings such as Occupy and the Arab Spring fail as forms for dual power, he suggests, because they substitute information technology for political organization. Crowds assemble from Seattle to Wisconsin, Eastern Europe to Tahrir Square, as flash mobs enabled by cell phones.[16] Jameson's own utopian proposal for the Psychoanalytic Placement Bureau also substitutes information technology for political organization. This implies that the problem of crowds is not the fact that they are mediated by personal communication devices. These devices are symptoms of something else, namely, the failure of mass uprisings to scale. Mediated crowds concentrate political energy into instances without duration. Unable to grow, theirs is a politics of the instance. For Jameson, this failure to endure is the "true horror of democracy." He writes: "It celebrates its euphoric moments of collective reconciliation in the great mass demonstrations and flash mobs, the 'lyric illusion' of the triumphant revolutionary crowds;

---

15 Ibid., 20.

16 In "Aesthetics of Singularity," Jameson compares flash mobs to the "flash crash" of the stock market in May 2010: *New Left Review* 92, March/April 2015, 101–38.

but then settles down into the daily grind of the petty democratic antagonisms which biological individuals inevitably feel towards one another, and from which both empty idealism and Spinoza's 'sad passions' derive." Jameson sides with the military because it organizes a classless society that can endure.

As already mentioned, the universal army is an economic arrangement. It provides full employment and organizes production. In its utopian form, the universal army presupposes "the withering away, not only of the state but also of politics as such." How the army acquires its orientation and direction is unclear. Does the Psychoanalytic Placement Bureau decide? The Joint Chiefs of Staff? Or is everything already predecided in Jameson's personal fantasy? In any case, the elimination of politics from the universal army depoliticizes the people. They are one unit, but their unity has no political meaning. Any political divisions they might have are replaced by the division between work and leisure, that is, military obligations and free time. Political antagonism is confined to Jameson's initial program of nationalizing the banks, seizing all energy sources, redistributing wealth, establishing a guaranteed minimum annual wage, etc. His initial program is a partisan program—decisive, divisive, appropriate for a communist party. In keeping with this program, the party and the political should be embraced, not replaced by the army.

Jameson acknowledges that his army is something like a party. He introduces dual power with the examples of the Black Panthers and Hamas, networks that provide "practical help and leadership on a daily basis." Even with these examples, though, he treats the party form as if it were irrevocably constrained by the alternative of reform or revolution. No one believes in revolution anymore, he tells us. People have become disillusioned with communist parties. Reform hasn't fared any better. Left parties "always capitulate when they come to power." Jameson's objections to the party aren't convincing, given his military counterproposal. It's not like those leftists disillusioned with communist parties are more enthusiastic about the military.

Although he jettisons the parties of the left, Jameson finds a role for liberal and social democratic parties in his transitional program. Their function is to talk and talk and talk. Although the system of representative government prevents them from actually accomplishing anything, liberal and social democratic parties are vehicles and fora for discursive struggle. They can undermine their opponents' rhetoric, create new vocabularies, and make proposals. Jameson's limited acceptance of parliamentary parties isn't convincing, given his embrace of universal Wi-Fi. Globally networked personal communications provide sites for talk. Detached from policies, actions, and decisions that matter, the circulation of memes and images in the outrage of the day has already superseded the discursive role of parliamentary debate. Where he unnecessarily discards communist parties, Jameson unnecessarily accepts bourgeois ones. At any rate, since bargaining is betrayal and persuasion doesn't work, the remaining option is coercion. Jameson takes the path of the military instead of the party because only the military can get the job done.

But who makes the decisions that matter in Jameson's scheme? Who directs the military? The benefit of Trotsky's version of military democracy (which Jameson invokes) is the supposition of Bolshevik leadership in civil and class war. Politics isn't erased. It takes a leading role, determining the course of military engagement. Jameson, though, imagines a transition in which universal conscription replaces building and exercising political will. In the utopia that follows, the people remain incapable of self-governance, unable to steer their society themselves. They are reduced to elements of machines of work and leisure. Channeled into the military apparatus and through the Psychoanalytic Placement Bureau, the collective power of the people to determine self-consciously the conditions under which they live is utterly foreclosed. Politics has no place. Rather than a communist conception of the people, then, Jameson's universal army takes to an extreme the conception of population that is operative under neoliberal capitalism. There is no active collective of self-governing people making their own history. There are only economic units of production and consumption.

Ensconced in the "quasi-paranoid fear of any form of political or social organization—whether in the formation of political parties of one kind or another or in the speculation about the construction of future societies radically different from this one" that he diagnoses on the left since 1968, Jameson misdiagnoses symptom as cause. The problem is not that we must "cure ourselves of the habit of thinking politically." It is that the left has stopped thinking and acting politically. Preoccupied with identity politics and culture critique (the latter of which Jameson sharply addresses), the left has dissolved itself into liberals interested in including ever more of us into globalized multicultural capitalism and anarchists focused on the micropolitics of small group engagement. Fearful of power after the excesses of the twentieth century, the left has ceded the state to capital acting as a class. Jameson says no one wants a state any longer. This is incorrect. Corporations and the rich lay out billions in their attempts to capture the state, whether via elections or legislation. The US state deploys its murderous force worldwide to insure that its allies control their states. Jameson seeks to circumvent the challenge of building political power by relying on coercion and eliminating the political altogether. But the political cannot be eliminated. What changes is its mode of expression, the forms it takes. In fact, *contra* Jameson, the object of political theory has always been conflict, not the collective as such. The scandal of Marxism, and perhaps even of democracy, is the demand that conflict and connectivity be thought together.

Another Party

Jameson's universal military substitutes the organization of the population for the people as the collective political subject.

Everyone is conscripted into a single organization. This organization is not a vehicle for their subjectivity as a collective. It is a machine for their productivity, anchored in the dissolution of their collective subjectivity insofar as there is no site where they represent themselves to themselves as a collective. In contrast, the party mobilizes a divide within the people. It is a form for a part that struggles on behalf of that part. Not all of the society is included within it. The non-identity between people and party enables each to be more and less than what they are, each to enable, rupture, and exceed the other. Differently put, the party mobilizes the people as a divided subject. The Lacanian concepts important for Jameson's own argument help clarify this idea.

That the subject of politics is collective means that its actions cannot be reduced to those associated with individual agency, actions like choice or decision. Instead, the collective subject impresses itself through ruptures and breaks and the retroactive attribution of these breaks to the subject they expressed.[17] The punctuality of the people as a collective subject could suggest that it is only evental, only disruptive, utterly disconnected from any body, creation, institution, or advance and thus without substance or content. But this would ignore the persistence of the subject in the press of the unrealized. This persistence needs a body, a carrier. Without a carrier, it dissipates into the manifold of potentiality. Nevertheless, with a carrier some potentiality is diminished. Some possibility is eliminated. Some closure is effected. This loss is the subject's condition of possibility, the division constitutive of subjectivity. Political forms—parties, states, guerrilla armies, even leaders—situate themselves within this division. Although they can be and often are fetishized

---

17 See Alain Badiou, *Theory of the Subject*, trans. by Bruno Bosteels, London: Continuum, 2009. For an elaboration of the theory of the party in terms of its fidelity to the egalitarian discharge of the crowd, see my *Crowds and Party*, London: Verso, 2016.

(positioned so as to obscure the loss or to remedy it perfectly, as with Jameson's universal army), the fact of fetishization should not deflect from the prior condition of the gap and its occupation.

The role of the party isn't to reveal to the working class the truth of its desire. Nor is it to represent the interests of the working class on the terrain of politics. Rather, the function of the party is holding open a gap in our setting so as to enable a collective desire for collectivity.[18] "Through such a gap or moment," Daniel Bensaïd writes, "can arise the unaccomplished fact, which contradicts the fatality of the accomplished fact."[19] The crowd's breach of the predictable and given creates the possibility that a political subject might appear. The party steps into that breach and fights to keep it open for the people. To the extent that it is faithful to egalitarian discharge of the crowd event, the party is a communist party (in this vein, Marx heralded the Paris Commune as a glorious achievement of our party).

The psychoanalytic concept of transference depends on and expresses the gap constitutive of subjectivity. In the clinic, the transference registers the effects of an Other beyond analyst and analysand. The analytic relation is not reducible to the interaction between them. Rather, the transference reveals unconscious processes and perspectives contained within the Other. The space of the Other is a crowded, heterogeneous space, a mix of shifting feelings, pressures, and attachments. It has structural features, dynamic features, processes that advance and recede, flow into one another, and shift in importance. Multiple, different figures inhabit and en-form these structures and processes.

---

18 For an account of communist desire in terms of the collective desire for collectivity, see *The Communist Horizon*.

19 Daniel Bensaïd, "Leaps! Leaps! Leaps!" in *Lenin Reloaded*, edited by Sebastian Budgen, Stathis Kouvelakis, and Slavoj Žižek, Durham, NC: Duke University Press, 2007, 158.

Transference contributes to a theory of the party in the precise sense of a "mode of access to what is hidden in the unconscious." The party accesses the discharge that has ended, the crowd that has gone home, the people who are not there but exert a force nonetheless. It is a site of transferential relations. The production of the collective space of the party as a knot of transferential effects is the way people are changed through struggle, the way they maintain a gap in capitalism between its determinations and the political space of their self-determination. Members look at themselves and their interactions from the perspective of the association they create through their association, the party as an Other space. Where Jameson proposes a *machinic* population organized into a universal army, I suggest a militant party faithful to the crowd's egalitarian discharge.

Features of the Other space that Lacan highlights include the ideal ego, the ego ideal, and the superego. As Žižek explains, Lacan gives a very precise inflection to these Freudian terms:

> "Ideal" ego stands for the idealized self-image of the subject (the way I would like to be, the way I would like others to see me); Ego-Ideal is the agency whose gaze I try to impress with my ego image, the big Other who watches over me and impels me to give my best, the ideal I try to follow and actualize; and superego is this same agency in its vengeful, sadistic, punishing aspect.[20]

The ideal ego is how the subject imagines itself. The ego ideal is the point from which the subject looks at itself. And the superego is the judge that torments the subject as it points out its inevitable, unavoidable failure to achieve either of these ideals. These three points are tied together: the ego ideal verifies the image of the subject. Since the ego ideal is supposed to provide this verification, the subject has certain investments in it. The subject needs the ego

---

20 Slavoj Žižek, *How to Read Lacan*, New York: Norton, 2006, 80.

ideal for its stability or sense of autonomy. Because of this need, it is resistant to recognizing that the ego ideal is nothing but a structural effect and resentful of the ego ideal's simultaneous power and inadequacy. Moreover, in trying to live up to the expectations of the ego ideal, the subject may compromise its own desire. It may give up too much, which explains why the superego can exert such an extreme, unrelenting force: it is punishing the subject for this betrayal.[21]

While these features of the space of the Other may appear individual, this appearing is nothing but a Freudian residuum. Not only are the features common, but they attest to the workings of collectivity that Freud encloses in the individual psyche. Such features operate in all collectives, as groups compete with other groups as well as look at themselves from the perspective of other groups. Cities and nations, schools and parties all have self-conceptions formatted via the processes and perspectives of the Other.

The transference that takes place in psychoanalysis reveals two additional features of the Other space: the subject supposed to know and the subject supposed to believe.[22] These elements are configuring suppositions within the subject (again, which is necessarily collective), structural features that the subject posits as supports for its desire. The subject supposed to know is the figure that holds the secret to desire. It knows the truth. God, Socrates, and Freud, as well as institutional roles, such as parent, teacher, and priest, can function as such a locus of knowledge for and of a subject. Consider, for example, the opening of an editorial written by journalist Paul Mason in the aftermath of the 2008 financial crisis:

> One of the upsides of having a global elite is that at least they know what's going on. We, the deluded masses, may have to wait for

21 Ibid., 81.
22 Ibid., 28–9.

> decades to find out who the paedophiles in high places are; and which banks are criminal, or bust. But the elite are supposed to know in real time—and on that basis to make accurate predictions.[23]

Mason presents the global elite as the subject supposed to know. Not only do the elite know the obscene truths of pedophilia and expropriation, but they know them as they happen, "in real time," while the rest of us remain deluded. A persistent question following the economic crisis of 2007 and 2008 was why the elite didn't know. How come no one saw the crisis coming?

Žižek introduces the subject supposed to believe as a more fundamental version of the subject supposed to know.[24] He explains:

> There is no immediate, self-present living subjectivity to whom the belief embodied in "social things" can be attributed, and who is then dispossessed of it. There are some beliefs, the most fundamental ones, which are from the very outset "decentered" beliefs of the Other; the phenomenon of the "subject supposed to believe" is thus universal and structurally necessary.[25]

The subject supposed to believe refers to this unavoidable displacement of belief onto some other. Concrete versions include the maintenance of the fiction of Santa Claus for the sake of children or the positing of some ordinary person who

---

23 Paul Mason, "The Best of Capitalism Is Over for Rich Countries—and for the Poor Ones It Will Be Over by 2060," *Guardian*, July 7, 2014.

24 Slavoj Žižek, *The Sublime Object of Ideology*, London: Verso, 1989, 185. Elsewhere Žižek treats the subject supposed to believe "as the fundamental, constitutive feature of the symbolic order": *The Plague of Fantasies*, London: Verso, 1997, 106.

25 Žižek, *Plague of Fantasies*, 106.

believes in community values. Žižek emphasizes the asymmetry between the subject supposed to know and the subject supposed to believe. Belief is reflective, a belief that another believes. He writes: "'I still believe in Communism' is the equivalent of saying 'I believe there are still people who believe in Communism.'"[26] Because belief is belief in the belief of the other, one can believe through another. Someone else can believe for us. Knowledge is different. That the other knows does not mean that I know. I can only know for myself. No wonder, then, that a frequent refrain in contemporary capitalist ideology is that each should find out for herself. Capitalism relies on our separation from one another, so it does its best to separate and individuate us at every turn.

Although he invokes Lacanian concepts, Jameson reduces the space of the Other to the phenomenon of envy. Absent from his characterization of the universal army is any discussion of the military in its functioning as either ideal ego, ego ideal, or superego. How do its members imagine themselves? From what perspective do they see? How is their enjoyment structured? These are political questions irreducible to the cultural field insofar as the answers to them are inseparable from the collective's self-identity. The army's social role as the collective's working back on itself as a collective, as not simply the entirety of working people but as the people working as universal army, however, does not appear in Jameson's account. Indeed, this effect of collectivity cannot appear because its appearance requires the gap of the political, the torsion of reflexivity. The military does not provide a perspective that the people take toward themselves; nor do the collective people, reduced in Jameson's account to the population, provide a perspective on the military. The two collapse into each other, no symbolic space between them.

To be sure, there is one feature of the Other space for which

26 Ibid., 107.

Jameson makes room: the subject supposed to know. More than assigning occupations and managing group therapy, the Psychoanalytic Placement Bureau, with its unimaginably complex computers, concentrates in a single location the symbolic function of the big Other as that site where actions register. Nevertheless, *how* these actions register, what they register as, is immunized from collective redress or response—that is to say, from politicization. At most, it's a site of mass investment, the continuation of the Internet's service as a zero institution: at least somebody knows what's going on.[27]

Institutions are symbolic arrangements that organize and concentrate the social space. They "fix" an Other, not in the sense of immobilizing it but in the sense of putting in relation the emergent effects of sociality. This "putting in relation" substantializes the social link, giving it its force, enabling it to exert its pressure. A party is an organization and concentration of sociality in behalf of a certain politics. For communists this is a politics of and for the proletarianized, the producers, the oppressed, the people as the rest of us. "Party" knots together within the horizon of communism the effects of ideal ego, ego ideal, superego, "subject supposed to know," and "subject supposed to believe." The particular content of any of these component effects changes over time and place, even as the operations they designate remain as elements of party association.

The ideal ego in communist parties is typically imagined in terms of the good comrade. The good comrade may be a brave militant, skilled organizer, accomplished orator, or loyal functionary. The ego ideal is the point from which comradeship is assessed: How and to what end is bravery, skill, accomplishment and loyalty counted? The party superego incessantly charges us for failing on all fronts—*we never do enough*—even as it taunts us

---

27 For a discussion of the web as a zero institution, see *Democracy and Other Neoliberal Fantasies*.

with the sacrifices we make for the sake of the party—*we have always done too much*. Each of these positions can be varyingly open and closed, coherent or contradictory. Insofar as the party is situated in an antagonistic field, insofar as it is not the state but is a part, other ideals and injunctions enter the mix: this is class struggle within the party, the challenge presented by capitalist consciousness. At the same time, the situatedness of the party means that the space it provides necessarily exerts effects beyond party members, providing images and reference points for those who might join, for allies and fellow travelers, as well as for former members or enemies.

The ideas of "subject supposed to believe" and "subject supposed to know" are particularly useful for thinking about these effects beyond party members. Critics of the communist party chastise the party for claiming to know, for functioning as a location of scientific or revolutionary knowledge. This ostensible expertise has been derided not only as monopolistic but also as false: the knowledge of living with, responding to, and fighting against oppressive power belongs to the people and cannot be confined into a set of iron laws of historical development. Given this critique, which came to be widely shared on the left in the wake of '68, it's surprising that the collapse of the Soviet Union dealt such a mortal blow to communist and socialist organizing in the United States, United Kingdom, and Europe. By 1989, only a tiny few defended the Soviet Union anymore. Most agreed that its bureaucracy was moribund and that it needed to institute market reforms. Why, then, did its collapse have such an effect? The "subject supposed to believe" makes sense of this strange reaction. What was lost when the USSR fell apart was the subject onto whom belief was transposed, the subject through whom others believed. Once this believing subject was gone, it really appeared that communism was ideologically defeated. As a further example, we might consider the prototypical accounts of Communist Party officials with their dachas and privileges. These functioned less as factual exposés than as attacks on the subject supposed to believe: not even the Party believes in Communism. Where the attacks failed, however, is in the fact that they were waged at all. Insofar as they had a target, they affirmed its ongoing function as the subject supposed to believe. The flawed, desiccated Party could still believe for us. Once it utterly collapsed, we lost the Other through whom we could believe.

I've been drawing out what's missing in Jameson's program and utopian proposal: the missing symbolic space of the Other. I've emphasized political dimensions of this loss, particularly with regard to the loss of the gap necessary for reflection, judgment, and critique. Jameson presents his army as an economic organization. It doesn't open the world. Its activities fulfill material needs, particularly the need for employment. Perhaps it is here, then, where we can locate the key difference between military organizing and party organizing. Party organizing breaks with the world given by production. It occupies the political gap between what is given and what could be. The party is a body for collective struggle for something more than provisioning. It presumes struggle and takes a side, fighting to change the world.

Raphael Samuel's memoir of British Communism in the 1930s illustrates my point. Samuel describes British Communists as engaged in an "an endless round of activity that left them very little personal time."[28] Treated as a good in itself, activity not only enveloped members deeply and daily in political work but also installed in them a sense of urgency: what they were doing *had to be done*; it was *vital*, *necessary*, *urgent*. Good Communists involved themselves in a wide variety of day-to-day struggles. The Party held meetings, rallies, and membership drives. It published and distributed a wide array of literature. It organized demonstrations, mobilized strike

28 Raphael Samuel, *The Lost World of British Communism*, London: Verso, 2006, 36. The book is comprised of three essays originally published in *New Left Review* between 1985 and 1987.

support, carried out emergency protests. Committed to direct action and immediate struggle, the Communist Party of Great Britain (CPGB) planned campaigns, developing systems and processes for making its actions more efficient, for following up, and for self-assessment. It worked to concentrate its resources and energies so that it would "seem more powerful than it was." It reviewed tasks, prepared agendas and drew up committees. Members were more than members. They had practical positions and responsibilities far beyond those given to them by their place in capitalism. They had specialized roles such that each was always more than him- or herself. Each was also someone in the Party: organizer, bureau member, instructor, trainer, branch officer, propagandist, literature seller, delegate, agitator. Related to this, Samuel says, "was a positive mania for reports which served both as an elaborate system of tutelage and as a method of accountability."[29] Reporting installed a practice of looking at activity from the perspective of the Party.

Samuel describes Communist organizational passion in detail, treating it as a series of disciplines of the faithful—efficiency in the use of time, solemnity in the conduct of meetings, rhythm and symmetry in street marches, statistical precision in the preparation of reports. What comes through in his account is the affective register of organization. Organization is not just a matter of bureaucracy and control. It's a generator of *enthusiasm*, an apparatus of intensification that ruptures the everyday by breaking with spontaneism. Planning is a matter of collective mindfulness. Samuel writes, "To be organized was to be the master rather than the creature of events. In one register it signified regularity, in another strength, in yet another control."[30] Organization produced a shared sense of strength, of a collective with the capacity to carry out its will.

29 Ibid., 106.

30 Ibid., 103.

The Party meeting connected the local, the immediate, with world-historical events ("think globally, act locally" was communist practice long before it became an activist slogan). Unlike the moves to the personal and political that often disrupt political discussions in an individualist age, comrades drew strength from seeing themselves in a larger setting, from recognizing that, rather than being unique, they were typical, generic. The particular was a bog, a swampy morass in which a group could get stuck and out of which it would have to be pulled. Lessons could then be learned, conclusions drawn, and plans made. Meetings broadened lives by opening them to the political, attaching them to movements and tendencies that took them out of miserable isolation. The world didn't simply happen to communists. They fought to make the world one way rather than another.

Samuel observes that much Party activity was "less instrumental than expressive."[31] Organization had a fantastic dimension, buttressing illusions of control, expressing dreams of power and efficacy as capable of being fulfilled. If weakness was a matter of failures of organization, then strength would accrue as these were corrected. To the extent that organization enabled members of the CPGB to imagine their party as shaping the world, they could believe in what they were doing whether or not their rallies and *Daily Worker* headlines corresponded to any actually significant political influence. But even with this acknowledgement, Samuel rightly refuses to allow the cynical, dismissive, and defeatist attitude of a contemporary left that looks at the world from the perspective of capitalism to fill in the gap of possibility that British Communists were able to maintain. He continues to see from the perspective of the Party. The Party, shortcomings and all, provides an ego ideal or symbolic point from which he views actions as momentous. The Party sustains the perspective it provides such that agitating against imperialism in a colonial society,

31 Ibid., 120.

campaigning against fascism, keeping alive the housing question, and supporting twenty years of Hunger Marches would manifest the heroic work of energetic comrades, communism in the actuality of political movement. Multiple activities are not a differentiated pluralism of possibilities but a singular communist politics, envisioned as and from the perspective of the enduring struggle of the masses.

Samuel's account of Party activity isn't unique to the CPGB. It resonates with the experiences of US Communists. Vivian Gornick writes,

> For thousands of Communists, being a Communist meant years of selling the *Daily Worker*, running off mimeographed leaflets, speaking on street corners, canvassing door-to-door for local and national votes, organizing neighborhood groups for tenants' rights or welfare rights or unemployment benefits, raising money for the Party or for legal defenses or bail bonds or union struggles. Only that and nothing more.[32]

What Gornick calls the "grinding ordinariness" of the life of Party members in the United States, like that in the United Kingdom, involved ceaseless activity. Gornick presents the dream of resolution as external to this activity. But it wasn't the vision that sustained the activity. The activity sustained the vision. Consistent activity on behalf of a politics—particularly planning, meetings, and reports—generated the perspective of the Party that enabled it. Consistency made it possible for the everyday to feel momentous, for neighborhood matters to become more than their immediacy, to become vehicles transmitting the sense of the world. Organization and its symbolization concentrated collective sentiment into a form other than the deprivations of capital and state,

32 Vivian Gornick, *The Romance of American Communism*, New York: Basic Books, 1977, 109–10.

enabling people to see themselves and the world from the perspective of a gap in the given, a gap of hope and possibility.

To solve an economic problem, unemployment, Jameson's utopian proposal eliminates the political sphere. Since representative government cannot effectively address unemployment, or numerous other problems, it withers away, replaced by the population conscripted into a universal army. In his utopian proposal, a *machinic* population is compelled to work. The sphere of culture provides a space for creativity, diversion, relief, drugs, whatever (it doesn't matter). Unimaginably complex computers and a kind of collective group therapy, consolidated into the site of the Psychoanalytic Placement Bureau, provide the single locus of collective symbolic registration, an amalgam of "union and hospital, an employment office and a court, a market research agency, a polling bureau and a social welfare center." The people do not and cannot appear as a collective subject. To the extent that utopian proposals pull out features of the given, arranging them so that we can see our own tendencies differently, Jameson's "American utopia" is effective. It puts before us a society in which the political has been replaced by computers and therapy, and collective action has been displaced by work and leisure. For a left that refuses the political—that rejects the state, abandons the party, betrays the crowd, and mistrusts the people—this is what utopia looks like.

4

The Happy Accident of a Utopia

Saroj Giri

I.

We can start with one basic insight crucial to Fredric Jameson's notion of utopia. He states, "The new cannot simply replace the old but must develop within it somehow, ultimately discarding the old ways like a husk or shell (as Marx put it)." Further, "it is always a delicate matter, in utopianizing, to distinguish between the utopian modification of reality and the symbolic replication of what already exists."

There is a strong sense that not only will the new develop within the old, but the old can also continue—"the symbolic replication of what already exists." The new then comes from the fact that now even the old will rearticulate a new form. Hence, rather than making "global critiques of what we may call ideological beliefs—free-market fundamentalism," Jameson is more interested in unpacking "praxis and daily life, habit and performance" that articulate capitalism. From the "old," from today's capitalist society, particularly neoliberalism, Jameson singles out "commitment to efficiency as a fundamental value." It is easy to show that the ideology of efficiency is connected to free market fundamentalism or austerity. Indeed, we might reject this commitment to efficiency.

But "even if we succeed in removing the value of efficiency from our utopian anxieties, however, the larger issue of creativity remains to be addressed." Efficiency must be grasped without dissolving the element of creativity. Similarly, we must understand the entrepreneur as comprising two sides: the inventor, creative and genius-like, and the businessperson, exploiter of the invention. So creativity and the inventor can continue in the utopian society.

This means that "genius" for design can be detached from capitalist logic: it would no longer appear as the instrumentalist drive for efficiency. This genius "can be imagined as a motivation and a satisfaction in its own right, not particularly affected in its logic by the rewards a different kind of socioeconomic system might offer."

Brechtian refunctioning

Jameson takes this as an instance of how the new (design and genius in a post-capitalist world) cannot simply replace the old but must develop *within* it somehow: the old would now undergo a rearticulation in the utopian society. This would mean "we are able to repudiate efficiency in the name of other, even more progressive values": a move that can best be understood as "a critical reconsideration or refunctioning (Brecht's *Umfunktionierung*)."

Similarly, Jameson subjects consumerism to such a "reconsideration." He finds that consumerism cannot be treated as "a psychophysical disorder," which is what "psychologism and culture critique" does. This approach overlooks the way consumerism discloses the truth "of American social life generally, the buying of food and care, the advertising of any number of name brands, the trappings of a whole affluent society." It ignores the fact consumerism is only an "appearance" concealing "a nightmarish underlying reality."

Here is the key analytical point: "It is therefore the passage through the money form that empties use value from the object in question and transforms it into a commodity, an object that can be measured abstractly against all the others of its kind." The point, then, is to do away with the structural determinations of "consumerism." Once that happens, once the money form or "money no longer plays a central role," consumerism "can be expected to wither on the vine . . . consigning the passionate consumer to some more local niche in the Fourier permutational scheme." Given such a refunctionary "consumerism" can in fact continue in a revolutionary utopia. Hence Jameson is able to make this bold statement: "I have no particular revulsion for such consumption and such pleasures, whether those of consummerism or of cocaine."

Brechtian refunctioning of habit and performance then is a crucial element in ensuring that the utopia is as much a modification of reality as it is a symbolic replication of what exists.

Social antagonism

But once so detached from the reproductive circuits of capitalism, certain praxis and habits can exist, in the revolutionary utopia, as a "free particular," a singularity. That is, they could exist as an individual trait, any kind of quirk or fantasy of an uncharted orientation, happily unhinged from the "base."

For, after all, in this utopia it is only in the field of production, that is, "labor, material or immaterial," where "a collective project, collective life" is insisted upon. But "in the world of the superstructure, no such specifications hold; the individual is as free to be a recluse as a party person, to practice hobbies or to live out existence as a couch potato, to be a family man or professional mother." This utopia is open to "the view of society as an ineradicable collection of neurotics." *This means that a particularity can exist as a singularity and need not (always) articulate itself as a universal.*

No wonder then that in this utopia, collective antagonisms might be eliminated, only to see "the heightening of individual ones." Antagonism and not social harmony must be fully embraced, recognizing the impossibility of the social so that the new utopia would welcome "the most outrageous self-indulgences and personal freedoms of its citizens in all things." It is as though in the midst of such outrageous indulgences and neurotic behavior, with no censoring of capitalism at the behavioral level, utopia would emerge like "a happy accident." Writes Jameson, "Like the sociologists who draw up their questionnaires by making you think they are inquiring about something else, it is best to seem to lead the patients down the wrong path, from which 'self-knowledge' rises like a distant glimpse or happy accident (assuming there can be knowledge about something—the so-called self—that doesn't exist in the first place). *Utopians* must proceed like that." That is why Jameson rejects the idea of utopia as the "cure" or treatment. It is not a utopian solution, but a "utopian non-solution" that is being proposed.

Such overindulgences and overidentifications do not, however, mean a breakdown in production. For the particular traits, habits, and praxis could also be hinged to the base, be integral to the practice of production. But even in that case, the service to production is carried out not through a top-down rule imposition but as a *matter of habit*, as "pedagogical production."

Pedagogical production

In pedagogical production rules become habit, and work is self-propelled. Jameson recalls how for Lenin, in *The State and Revolution*, "socialist legality" is enforced informally, as a collective habit. This is a form of society where "*all* have learned the art of administration, and will indeed independently administer social production, will independently keep accounts, control the idlers, the gentlefolk, the swindlers and similar 'guardians of capitalist traditions.' "[1] This is part of what Jameson wants to call "cultural revolution" rather than education.

1 Lenin, *Essential Works of Lenin*, 349.

The cultural revolution will possess an "intolerable negativity toward the positivist and empiricist world." Against the empirical-practical, Jameson defends the "autonomy of art" and declares that "it is around the negation of every actually existing society and its practices that the vocation of art needs to be organized and defended." This is where we should also consider his approach to the dystopian fear of "discipline" in the army. Here he defends

> a perpetual and perpetually exacerbating rebuke of pragmatism, the practical, the socially useful, the legal and the normative, the habitual, law and order, and every well-behaved and traditional tenet of social reproduction, very much including, of course, that "discipline" which constitutes the deepest dystopian fear of army life.

This means that production produces its own culture, but this culture is not given by production as such, or by the empirical or the practical world. It will not be ruled by practical instrumentalist reasons or by a bureaucracy. Jameson here challenges dominant interpretations of Stakhanovism or socialist realism, stating, "the mission of socialist realism [or of Stakhanovism] is the relentless critique of bureaucracy." The autonomy of art and rebuke of pragmatism mean that the "universal of production" is then always as close as possible to a singular universal.

Here is then the formula, if you like, of Jameson's utopia: *All universals are necessarily singular universals, but not all singulars are (or become) singular universals.* Recall also how, as discussed above, a particularity *can* exist "unhinged," as a singularity, that is, without articulating itself as a universal.

It is a utopia of production, or rather pedagogical production, and also one where existentialism supersedes Marxism: "We have only reached the point in which a universal militarization permits the organization of a minimum of necessary production sufficient to satisfy the multiple needs of a given population, from food and housing to education and medical treatment, thereby liberating a free time unexpected and unplanned for in Darwinian evolution and the natural world. This is the moment in which, as Sartre put it, existentialism supersedes Marxism as a philosophic horizon, and we can detect the nature of our own ideological reflexes by way of our reactions to it."

This dual register of pedagogical production and of existentialist/superstructural freedom defines Jameson's utopia. A utopia that delivers full freedom in individual matters is I think one of the seminal contributions of Jameson's project. He has *found a way to, as it were, "solve" the problem of individual freedom and democracy*, without really valorizing the liberal subject as the repository of capacities that must be enhanced through rights and other endowments—and without giving up on the need for production and discipline. There is, in fact, no real conflict between labor/production/necessity and culture/democracy/freedom, for "in the utopian course of things labor will become embroidered with culture and the realm of freedom preoccupied with necessity."

II

Methodologically, Jameson's approach has three components. The first is of course the Brechtian refunctioning that we discussed above. The second is the structural approach of psychoanalysis, while the third is the topological space of the universal army.

Structural psychoanalysis

Jameson's psychoanalytical approach is crucial when it comes to really understanding why the functional transformation (refunctioning) can indeed detach praxis from the capitalist logic. With this approach, we can see that the habits and praxis do not reinforce themselves in a self-reinforcing circularity—that belief is not already produced in and through the material practices, through the repetition involved in rituals.

Recall how in, say, an Althusserian approach rituals as repetitive practices produce their own beliefs. Writes Judith Butler, "The notion of ritual suggests that it is performed, and it is in the repetition of performance a belief is spawned."[2] Jameson is clearly rejecting such an approach and seems to work with an approach developed by Slavoj Žižek and Mladen Dolar.[3] According to Dolar, Althusser recognizes that "what counts is ultimately not that they [rituals] are material, but that they are ruled by a code, by a repetition," that "they have to be symbolically codified."[4] But, Dolar points out, what "is lacking in Althusser is the conceptualization of the relationship between materiality and the Symbolic." Althusser does not recognize that "sense and subject did not spring up from materiality but from the Symbolic that regulated it," from what Žižek calls the "belief before belief."[5]

"Belief before belief" means the subject assumes there is "a subject supposed to know": the Other. "The Other exists only by the subject's belief in it, the belief that there is a subject to know."[6] So here consumerism or addiction becomes, in Jameson, "an attempt, in whatever form, to free the subject from the Other and from the mimetic hold of the Other's desire." Here "consumer goods" are "a kind of objectal medium surrounding us and isolating us from the more agonizing dilemmas posed by every concrete existence of the Other, but also of a world where isolation from the Other has become somehow an urgent need."

Consumerism, the addiction to certain things and objects, is the result of the individual's unwillingness to accept "the psychic

---

2 Judith Butler, *The Psychic Life of Power*, Stanford: Stanford University Press, 1997, 119.

3 Slavoj Žižek, *The Sublime Object of Ideology*, London: Verso, 1989; Mladen Dolar, "Beyond Interpellation," *Qui Parle*, Vol. 6, No. 2 (Spring/Summer 1993).

4 Dolar, "Beyond Interpellation," 91.

5 Žižek, *The Sublime Object of Ideology*, 40.

6 Dolar, "Beyond Interpellation," 89.

alienation of the Other" and the attempt to evade this problem by succumbing to the mimetic hold of the Other's desire. *But* if the individual is willing to accept this alienation as a "natural" part of the human condition (in an existential mode), then it is possible to not respond to the Other's desire and free the subject from its hold. There is a break possible, a break not from the consumerist acts per se, that is, at the level of capitalist behavior, but from the hold of the Other's desire: a break at the level of necessity.

The Brechtian refunctioning of the old elements producing the new, then, presupposes the structural approach of psychoanalysis. It is this that makes it possible for us to see *how habits, practices, and perfomance now can be reversed, refunctioned without really shunning them as individual acts or "behavior," be it consumerism or the "commitment to efficiency."* For, as we saw, these practices do not move in a circular self-reinforcing loop: the instance of a "belief before belief" is crucial in allowing us to interrupt and reorient them in a new direction—toward a revolutionary utopia.

Now it turns out, this conjunction of refunctioning and psychoanalysis actually presupposes the existence of a new topological space, the universal army—these three elements together must be seen in their simultaneity.

Topological space of the army

Jameson covers a lot of ground in arguing against the practice of the standing army, an army that stands apart from society. He calls for nationalizing the army. He pits the US army tradition with the European traditions of citizen militias and of the nation-in-arms of the French Revolution. He calls for "the renationalization of the army along the lines of any number of other socialist candidates for nationalization and by reintroducing the draft," and for "democratizing the army itself and inventing some new relationship between civilian society and this foreign body that has come into extraterritorial existence in its midst."

The army proposes a *form* that goes beyond federating units, as in the United States. He writes, "The strength of the army is that it cuts across the federal constitution in a wholly novel way, transgressing its boundaries and carefully drawn limits without annulling it, leaving its map intact beneath a wholly different topology." The "signal advantage of the army as a system is that it transcends that document [the Constitution] without doing away with it; it coexists with it at a different spatial level and becomes thereby a potentially extraordinary instrument in the erection of dual power."

"The army is the first glimpse of a classless society." It brings us closer to "true democracy," understood as the "intolerable cohabitation of incompatible temperaments and people who get on each other's nerves," no longer "warded off by wealth in its gated communities and walled estates."

Social promiscuity

The forced class promiscuity or the "forced association" of the universal army *must* itself, if it is not to lead us to just some kind of secular or modern nationalism, undergo a functional transformation. That is why, unlike the national armies that we find today, the universal army posits a different topological space: "the current proposal posits a functional transformation—a Brechtian refunctioning—in which this forced class promiscuity becomes the production of genuine classlessness and social leveling." The universal army that Jameson is proposing *is* that space, the "*spatial* matrix" (without becoming a merely transcendental matrix or an abstract grid) whereby the anonymity, classlessness, and social leveling ("social promiscuity") that the national army (already) offers will itself undergo a functional transformation (refunctioning).

Hence Jameson's proposal for the nationalization of the army and the reintroduction of the draft is to initiate a functional transformation of the army itself. What the topological space of the army does is to dismember the transcendental matrix of capitalism from the social body—where now the social body itself approached as, at base, habits and performance, identifications and investments, undergoes a Brechtian refunctioning and structural rearticulation. For if this refunctioning and rearticulation of praxis and performance were really to break with or exit capitalism, it must now be "plugged into" the topological space of the universal army. Dismembering the capitalist matrix means that the necessity of consumerism (as the attempt to free oneself from "the mimetic hold of the Other's desire"), or the "necessity" in antagonism imposed by the theft of *jouissance* (Lacan), itself gets undermined, given the new condition of "genuine classlessness and social leveling." Hence consumerism as "behavior" or individual antagonism can continue in the revolutionary utopia, without the Necessity—this Necessity being what capitalism really comes down to.

Dialectical contradiction

Here we see (a) the functional transformation, (b) the rearticulation of praxis suggested by structural psychoanalysis, and (c) the topological space of the universal army—all converge to produce a particular form of society. This society is marked by the kind of relationship between the particular and the universal in which the singularities are crucial, as we noted above.

But if such a vortex of society, not as "enclaves of freedom" or supposedly alternative "non-capitalist practices," but as a universalist form, were to emerge, then, given the continuing existence of capitalist society, we would have *a situation of dual power*. Jameson invokes Lenin on dual power, but we must now point out one crucial difference with Lenin.

For Jameson, dual power exists without conflict with the official state power, so that the society of the universal army appears as a parallel force: "the situation of dual power from which the new universal army emerges, which begins life as a parallel force alongside the state and its official army and finds its first tasks, and indeed its vocation, in the fulfillment of neglected social services and in a coexistence with the population of a wholly different type." Further, in such situations of dual power and "transitioning out of capitalism," "power moves to the networks to which people turn for practical help and leadership on a daily basis: in effect, they become an alternate government, without officially challenging the ostensibly legal structure."

However, dual power, as Lenin conceives it, does not emerge parallel to the capitalist state order but actively dislodges it from within. Jameson points to the universal army beginning life as a parallel force, but he does not tell us at what point it will end that status and start "officially challenging the ostensibly legal structure." The point is that the emergence of a new society, in Lenin, has everything to do with the internal contradictions of capitalism. So Lenin would want to mobilize the power of the working class emanating from the internal dialectical contradiction between capital and labor.

Jameson substitutes the structural approach of psychoanalysis for the approach of internal contradiction and dialectics, even as he upholds the Lacanian notion of social antagonism. So while he keeps the universalist emphasis intact and rightly rejects the approach of "enclaves of freedom," like that of Chiapas and even the Arab Spring and Occupy movement for not being able to prescribe a way to transition out of capitalism, it seems that he himself proposes a universalism, in fact, an entire form of society, that exists parallel to capitalism. A utopian universalist world exists in parallel to another universalist world of capitalism.

This parallel utopian universalist world is internally lucid, with praxis, habit, and performance now functionally transformed in a way that neurotic behavior or our overidentifications would happily inhabit the revolutionary utopia. And yet one wants to know if there is any way to mobilize the power within capitalism, held up in dialectical contradictions, toward such a revolutionary utopia—that is, if say the power of the working class could be the crucial link as a power that is internal to dialectical contradictions of capitalism as well as one which points to the "outside," so that now the "parallel" in dual power would only be a temporary stage and not a constitutive or ontological ground of the struggle.

"Impossible present"

To my mind, Jameson is responding to our present predicament, our position "living in the end times," when, as they say, it is easier to imagine the end of human society rather than the more modest task of ending capitalism. Here Jameson finds that "even the remarkable revival and new efflorescence of Marxian analyses of capitalism and its contradictions remains oddly fixated on an impossible present without any visible historical future save catastrophe." This "impossible present" is marked by, as Maurizio Lazzarato puts it, the Indebted Man borrowing from the future, living on borrowed time, annulling the future.[7] Popular culture today is rife with visions of how only an apocalyptic doomsday, taking us (back) to the zero-level of existence, can "restart" History.[8]

In such a scenario, Jameson carries out this formidable task of furrowing deep into our present condition to see if we can rearticulate the present forces and subjects in a new fashion and new form. One can only work with what is there, with the banal and

---

7 Lazzarato dwells on how "living in a society without time, without possibility, without foreseeable rupture, is debt," in Maurizio Lazzarato, *The Making of the Indebted Man*, Los Angeles: SemioTexte, 2007, 47.

8 As a contrast, however, Andrei Platonov's novels, such as *The Foundation Pit*, can be said to assume dystopia or apocalypse as a condition for utopia. It is as though truly only the near-destruction of human life can allow us to escape the trap whereby any utopia we imagine is always bounded by the present, and is carrying what Jameson calls the blood guilt of the present. See Jameson's discussion on this in *The Seeds of Time*, Irvine: Columbia University Press, 1994, 73–128.

the ordinary, and, who knows, to our pleasant surprise, the tide might turn—for good! Without any abstract, transcendental move, keeping us totally close to spatial determinations and our daily life and praxis, Jameson is able to suggest ways to break with the problem of the "end of temporality" without really positing temporality. He cracks open time, temporality, and the subjective figure of the universal army from within the "regime of spatiality" that we famously inhabit today. With Jameson, now, we may discover that imagining a utopia need not necessarily be apocalyptic and destructive, as it might initially seem!

This is in line with Jameson's earlier work where he argued, "History can be apprehended only through its effects, and never directly as some reified force."[9] He argues for an openness to the force of all events and social phenomena. History cannot be understood "as some new representation or 'vision,' some new content, but the formal effects of what Althusser, following Spinoza, calls 'absent cause.' "[10]

But the fact of the matter is that we are dealing not just with "effects" but also with reified force, for example, in the shape of the existence of the power of the bourgeoisie and the state. That is why then perhaps the exit from capitalism must be mediated by another (possibly revolutionary) "reified" force internal to capitalism, tied down to the capitalist contradiction: we know the working class as such a force and such a power, a power which Jameson underestimates. After all, if the existing army itself has to undergo nationalization and functional transformation, it has to break its deep bonds with the bourgeoisie and the capitalist state, and perhaps that can happen only if a power dialectically internal to capitalism can weaken the reified powers of the ruling classes. The pleasures of a "happy accident" or an accidental discovery can perhaps go hand-in-hand with those of strategic success.

---

9 Fredric Jameson, *The Political Unconsious*, London: Routledge, 2006, 88.

10 Ibid.

5

From the Other Scene to the Other State: Jameson's Dialectic of Dual Power

Agon Hamza

> The freedom of mind or spirit is not merely an absence of dependence on an Other won outside of the Other, but won in it; it attains actuality not by fleeing from the Other but by overcoming it.
>
> —G.W.F. Hegel[1]

The Structural Impossibility of the Left

It is nothing new to assert that the left, both as a theory and practice, is in a crisis. Even the most radical anticapitalist left operates within the capitalist horizon. Therefore, the paradox of the left is that ultimately it seems to inescapably be at the service of capital, in the sense that what Marxists traditionally believed to be bourgeois ideals (formal liberty, redistribution of wealth, etc.) are now

1 G.W.F. Hegel, *Encyclopedia of the Philosophical Sciences: Philosophy of Mind*, Oxford: Oxford University Press, 1971, 15.

the ultimate aims of the leftist projects themselves. In other words, the left is not capable today of even minimally disturbing the profound and complicated structure of capitalism. It seems that the most difficult aspect of the contemporary left, on both its theoretical and political levels, is located in the notion that defines it: that is, in the notion of the left itself. What does it really mean to be a leftist today?

Let us distinguish between the theoretical and practical domains inspired and carried out by the left and analyze them separately. The horizon within which the organizations and practices of the left operate today are those of the struggles against neoliberalism, austerity, and racism and in favor of democratization, ecology, gay rights, multiculturalism, and so on. Theoretically, the return to socialism marks its most radical point. Without denying or downplaying the importance of these struggles, however, we should claim their insufficiency insofar as no theoretical orientation can be derived therefrom. Succinctly put, the left is either engaged in false struggles, or in struggles whose field is already overdetermined by the ruling ideology.

In the last instance, we can argue that the terms and the terrain of the political and ideological struggles of the left are decided by its enemies. The case of Syriza is exemplary: while it is a radical left party, it set itself the aim of "saving capitalism from itself." Although its political and government programs are of a moderate Keynesianism, the effects of its governance are the opposite of its aims. This is why the position of communists today is rather a paradoxical one: while all the above-mentioned fields of struggles are of crucial importance, their result or outcome is the restoration of capitalism. The recent upheavals and riots in Brazil testify to this: the problem is not so much the corruption of the Workers' Party as the exhaustion of a political sequence (begun back in the sixties) in which leftism itself was structured as a defense against the dictatorship. This political sequence, with its reformist social-democratic program, has now come to an end, and it is to this exhaustion of the left that the ambivalent new riots testify.[2]

The first emancipatory step, the condition *sine qua non* for any politics of emancipation today, is therefore to abandon the notion and the concept of the left. No matter how paradoxical it might appear, we must maintain that the left is an obstacle to the universal emancipation, perhaps to a comparable degree to capitalism itself. It is both a demoralized and demoralizing ideology and political force. While it remains associated with the image of its past struggles and victories, the left carries none of the organizational and political potency it had before. For leftism which is not communist (and the left, radical or not, seldom is communist), emancipation has very clear borders: they are always national. The emblematic examples are not only the Latin American socialist governments, but also the European left parties, such as Syriza, Podemos, and so forth. Alongside abandoning this term as an identifying mark, we need to cease seeking to identify ourselves through those political practices associated with it, such as the critique of neoliberalism and participation in human rights struggles—no matter how important these struggles remain, we should stop considering them both the principal contradiction of capital and the principal unification principle of emancipatory politics. We seem to have forgotten Marx's basic lesson: capitalism as a social and economic formation is based on a constant self-revolutionization: that is, it only establishes limits to itself in order to valorize the crossing of these national and cultural borders. The principal problem of capitalism is not in neoliberalism or in austerity politics, nor in new forms of authoritarian or apartheid regimes, nor in sexism, homophobia, racism, and so on, but in the capitalist form itself: that is, in the *value form*. Instead of referring to neoliberalism as the cause for our plights and misery, we should (at the risk of sounding archaic) bring back the critique and the

2 Paulo Arantes, *O novo tempo do mundo*, São Paulo: Boitempo, 2015.

overcoming of *capital* as the ultimate goal of our thinking and actions.

In the current conjuncture, in which capitalism is successfully neutralizing all possible resistances and alternatives to it, Slavoj Žižek's reversal of going back from Marx to Hegel gains its relevance. In the terms of conjuncture, we're closer to the Hegelian rather than the Marxian universe. While Marx was writing on a revolutionary situation (1848), identifying and theorizing the contradictions that might lead to the revolution, Hegel was mostly concerned with the effects of the revolution in the postrevolutionary situation. We are in a similar conjuncture: the period of the socialist revolutions is over and capitalism has become a global system. The socialist era is over, and we need to radically rethink the idea of communism.

Marx's famous response to Proudhon's *The Philosophy of Poverty* was to return the message in its inverted form: *The Poverty of Philosophy*. Today, when the value of thinking has become itself measured by the standards of the incessant activity and production that organize all forms of labor, it might be time to supplement Marx's position. The crisis of the left is no longer the crisis of idealism, of a "poor" philosophy disconnected from the material basis that conditions it—ours is a poverty *of* philosophy, a blatant absence of any form of thinking subtracted from the imperative of compulsive activity. A "return to philosophy" has, then, a double role today: one, it is a means to reinvent the critical powers needed in order to transform the world; and two, it is the first movement of constructing something that has no place in our world.

Furthermore, the decision to affirm the critical and transformative power of philosophical thinking also allows us to shed light on our contemporary predicament from a renewed perspective, as the crisis of the left, more than the crises of capitalism, becomes our main concern. Considered from the standpoint of our "poverty of philosophy," it suddenly becomes possible to recognize the imposture at the heart of some of our diagnoses of our enemies and struggles: for example, the supposition, shared by most of the left today, that we live in postideological times, in which all that is left for us to do is to act, or—in its most current version—the idea that "neoliberalism" names our true enemies, a conclusion that all too comfortably allows us to bypass producing new critical resources and therefore confronting our current lack of any robust conceptual framework, given that our adversary is conveniently cut off from its complex political-economic grounding. Paradoxically, today, the impasse of philosophy alone marks the left's most important tasks: to develop a more profound and comprehensive account of the left's failures in the twentieth century and to think the problem of political organization anew.

The problem is, to paraphrase Žižek, how are we to revolutionize an economic and political system which itself is revolutionary? Or, in the terms of Kurz and Postone: wherefrom are we to think this political process if the contradiction between the left and capitalism is overdetermined by capital itself?

The necessity of the utopian dream

The most utopic idea today is, therefore, the dream of overcoming capitalism itself. However, equally utopic is the idea that capitalism will go on indefinitely, as the only viable form of social organization. A serious diagnosis of the present, from a communist standpoint, is thus confronted with the apocalyptic scenario of an omnipotent *and* impotent world system—a capitalist world that is perfectly adequate to the simultaneously absurd and incipient expectations of the contemporary left.

It is in view of this diagnosis that we can measure the ultimate importance of Fredric Jameson's *The American Utopia*. At the same time, this diagnosis is itself part of the nature and the character of his utopian vision, since it relies on the confrontation with the impossibility of our situation. Which is to say, it intervenes in our impotence to even dream of a postcapitalist organization of societies. The material force of the capitalist ideologies is so powerful that it is structuring our imaginations.

Are we simply confronted with the poverty of imagination (and, perhaps in the same mode, the poverty of philosophy and of politics), or we are confronted with political cynicism? Žižek's reversal of Marx's formula, "They don't know it, but they are doing it," is prevalent: "The illusion is not on the side of knowledge, it is already on the side of reality itself, of what the people are doing."[3] We all know what is wrong with global capitalism, nothing shocks us any longer, but nonetheless we act as if . . .

In this sense, the traditional art of the critique of ideology is not productive any longer: there is nothing to expose, unmask, or demystify, because everything is already exposed and open. It is this "cynical reason" that Jameson is also trying to confront. Since ideology sustains late global capitalism, we need to reinvent not only the notion of ideology but also the procedure for its critique. In this enterprise, the limits of "traditional" Marxism are clearly visible. The standard opposition of ideology to science, characteristic of Althusser's work, is in the last instance an ideological position, in the sense that, rather than produce a constructive political vision, we merely "borrow" the constructive capacities of science, remaining ourselves without any proper political orientation. In order to reconstruct a political imagination, we need not only the critique of ideology, but the political inventiveness that fixates itself in the tableaux of utopic constructions.

In this regard, we have (at least) two visions or understandings of utopia. The first is the negative conception, in which a utopia is first of all an ideal: that is, where imagination, at the service of reproducing present conditions, supplements dire reality with an impossible promise of a future that renders the present bearable. It is a negative vision not merely in the sense of being ideologically overdetermined: there are many Marxists, especially those ready

3 Slavoj Žižek, *The Sublime Object of Ideology*, London: Verso, 1989, 32.

to reintroduce Christianity and "ethical socialism" into Marxism, who see this impossible future as a positive and useful guiding star, in a sort of substitute for moral law.

The second view of utopia, however, found for example in Karl Mannheim's analysis of Thomas Müntzer's political organization, considers utopia to be the production and channeling of the people's unreal expectations of current social life.[4] Here it is not the content of utopia that counts, but its form: the utopic form guarantees the "bottom-up" circulation of all those unsatisfied and unsatisfiable expectations of the working class. In other words, like in the case of Kafka's *Josephine the Singer, or the Mouse Folk*, a utopia is a performative component that channels the force of organization, it is a tool for critique: through its narrative articulation of our forms of suffering, in the form of a future where they are institutionally addressed, it also contributes to the consistency of our critical force in the present.

To each of these conceptions of utopia there corresponds a concept of politics: the first, "regulative" conception considers utopic thinking to be a rhetorical device in the political struggle toward a given aim; the second, "formal" conception considers politics as the domain of forms of life, of organization that is not merely a means to an end but an end in itself. One should also understand Jameson's project in this way: a positive conceptualization of a utopian vision that is *also* a political intervention in what he calls cynical reason as a form of ideology. It is in these terms that we should judge Jameson's proposal: not by its practicability or possibility, but by the effects it has on contemporary political thinking as such. In other words, his utopia should be read as a political strategy and utopian program that aims at drawing radical lines of demarcation within today's political impotence and ideological confusion, through *constructive* rather than purely critical procedures.

---

4 See Karl Mannheim, *Ideology and Utopia: An Introduction to the Sociology of Knowledge*, New York: Mariner Books, 1955.

Jameson's utopian vision, however, is peculiar for the simple fact that from his endeavours to define what utopia is, he set himself to creating his *own* utopia.[5] Jameson himself is not certain whether he is proposing a utopian vision for society or a political program, but that should not be our concern at this point. In the present world, the existing economic and social relations are so shattered (poverty, unemployment, violence, exclusion, and so on) that any talk about political change is either doomed to fail or be discredited as utopian (i.e., totalitarian). In a period of profound crisis of the left, the fact that Jameson has moved from the negative critique of capitalism to providing a "positive program" (or idea) is of tremendous importance. Jameson once said that it is easier to imagine the end of the world than the end of capitalism.[6] Today we should amend this dictum and argue that it seems to be easier to truly end the world than to end capitalism. In this sense, the utopia, understood in Jameson's terms as an operation that aims at exposing the limits of our imagination and reality, is the political slogan and program of our predicament. The relation between utopia and politics is not only unresolved but, at a certain level of analysis, presents the crux of our situation.

It is in this sense that we should understand Jameson's utopia as his version of the communist program.

Bureaucratic Versus Political Form of Life

The most important contribution of Jameson's project is to show that his fundamental dialectic of utopia and ideology is

5 See, for example, Fredric Jameson, *Archaeologies of the Future: The Desire Called Utopia and Other Science Fictions*, London: Verso, 2005.

6 Fredric Jameson, "The Future City," *New Left Review* 21, May–June 2003.

also connected to the dialectics of single and dual power and to the overcoming of this duality. One aspect of this duality is that between communists and anarchists—that is, between the politics of determination versus the politics of indetermination. Anarchists, holding to the politics of indetermination, rightfully criticize communists for being incapable of preserving the space for the useless dimension of subjectivity in their determinate vision of the future, while the lack of such a determinate view prevents anarchism from producing a constructive emancipatory project for the masses. On the other hand, communists, thinking politics from the standpoint of determination, correctly argue that the anarchists are capable neither of thinking the principal contradiction of capitalism in its systemic form nor of conceiving a form of organization capable of countering it, while the lack of such indeterminate space prevents communists from properly engaging with the contemporary masses, who no longer identify themselves as workers. One should also note that there are anarchist elements in the work of Marx himself, such as his famous call to "imagine, for a change, an association of free men, working with the means of production held in common."[7] Every anarchist can identify with this. However, what concerns us is the relation of the producers with "their labor and the products of their labor . . . in production as well as in distribution."[8] In Marx's understanding, this division depends on the form of social organization of production and the respective social order.

At one level, Žižek, Badiou,Ranciére, Karatani, etc., are all preoccupied with overcoming the duality of communism and anarchism. Or, more precisely, in a situation in which occupying the state is not a guarantee of transforming it, these contemporary Marxist thinkers are concerned with recuperating dual-power

7 Karl Marx, *Capital*, Vol. 1, London: Penguin, 1976, 171.

8 Ibid., 172.

strategies as a means to disrupt the one power composed by the alliance between capital and the state. Let me briefly point out the main positions of some of the Marxist philosophers on this issue. Alain Badiou argues that "Marxism, the workers' movement, mass democracy, Leninism, the proletarian party, the socialist state—all these remarkable inventions of the twentieth century—are no longer of practical use."[9] He maintains that the third sequence of the communist hypothesis, the situation in which we find ourselves now, is not a question of a proletarian party, nor of a mass movement as bearer of this hypothesis. We find, according to Badiou, a new relationship between the ideology and a political movement. The generic processes are neither "resisting" the state nor trying to take it, but by taking a distance toward the state. It is a dual power that claims to be more universal and more powerful than the state itself—a sort of immanent duality that, though dual, remains more immanent to the situation than the transcendental unity of the capitalist state.

Kojin Karatani proposes to simultaneously create a dual-power movement, through alternative common currencies and markets, and take over the state/capital. In Karatani's view, the triad of capital–nation–state is inseparable; as such, the three ought to be revolutionized together. His solution, as we will see later, is the transformation of the modes of exchange. Žižek, on the other hand, proposes that the party should be conceived as another power (which is not the state, hence dual power) but also that it should become the state (one power). For him, the dichotomy of either the struggle for state power *or* withdrawal from and/or resistance against state power is a false alternative. According to Žižek, this alternative presupposes the premise that the state in its actual form is perpetual. Žižek's wager is that we need a Leninist gesture: the ultimate aim of the revolution is not only simply to take state power, but also to use revolutionary violence

9 Alain Badiou, *The Meaning of Sarkozy*, London: Verso, 2008, 113.

in radically transforming it. As he puts it, we should make the state work in a "non-statal way."[10]

Finally, Jameson suggests a very concrete proposition through which the state/capital apparatus would gradually become the "smaller" of the two powers, when compared with the military complex, which would grow progressively more central. Jameson's idea is a militarized version of Žižek's tetrad of people–movement–party–leader. Jameson departs from Lenin's short text "The Dual Power," written in April 1917, during the coexistence of the Provisional Government and the Soviets of Workers' and Soldiers' Deputies. Lenin designates three main features of the Soviet councils: 1) power comes from below, that is, from the people in their areas ("direct seizure"); 2) in the soviets, the police and army are replaced by arming the workers and peasants *directly*; and 3) the bureaucracy is organized similarly to the armed forces—not by elected officials, but by direct rule of the people. In a sense, Lenin also provides a militarized version of the soviets.[11]

Jameson's idea is simple—but, as Brecht noted, it is only the simple things that are so difficult to do: to inscribe the whole of the American people in the American army complex. The basic premise of his utopia is strictly Marxist: withering away of the state and, with the state, of politics as such. For Jameson, the state is the field of politics. As he puts it, "It should be obvious that the withering away of the state inevitably brings with it the withering away of that thinking whose object is essentially the state as such (the polis)." By doing so, the two levels of social order that have been traditionally thought of as the base and superstructure, that is, the realms of production and of culture, will take on a wholly new dimension through increasing the distance between them. This poses a very important problem that weighs heavily on the Marxist

10 Slavoj Žižek, "How to Begin from the Beginning?" in *The Idea of Communism*, edited by C. Douzinas and S. Žižek, London: Verso, 2010.

11 V.I. Lenin, "The Dual Power," 1917, marxists.org.

tradition. As with Marx's and Lenin's analyses of the transition from capitalism to socialism, Jameson is preoccupied with what he elsewhere calls the "persistence of childbirth." If we recall the famous passages on the "Historical Tendency of Capitalist Accumulation" from Marx's *Capital,* where he talks about monopoly capitalism and expropriating the expropriators:

> The monopoly of capital becomes a fetter upon the mode of production, which has sprung up and flourished along with, and under it. Centralization of the means of production and socialization of labor at last reach a point where they become incompatible with their capitalist integument. This integument is burst asunder. The knell of capitalist private property sounds. The expropriators are expropriated.[12]

Further, Lenin argued that imperialism is capitalism in decay, or in transition:

> When a big enterprise assumes gigantic proportions, and, on the basis of an exact computation of mass data, organizes according to plan the supply of primary raw materials to the extent of two-thirds, or three-fourths, of all that is necessary for tens of millions of people; when the raw materials are transported in a systematic and organized manner to the most suitable places of production, sometimes situated hundreds or thousands of miles from each other; when a single center directs all the consecutive stages of processing the material right up to the manufacture of numerous varieties of finished articles; when these products are distributed according to a single plan among tens and hundreds of millions of consumers (the marketing of oil in America and Germany by the American oil trust)—then it becomes evident that we have socialization of production, and not mere "interlocking," that private economic and

12 Marx, *Capital*, Vol. 1, 929.

> private property relations constitute a shell which no longer fits its contents, a shell which must inevitably decay if its removal is artificially delayed, a shell which may remain in a state of decay for a fairly long period (if, at the worst, the cure of the opportunist abscess is protracted), but which will inevitably be removed.[13]

Following Marx and Lenin, Jameson's utopia aims at transforming the structures or the base of society so that they will become irreconcilable with the existing superstructure. Therefore Jameson is proposing a transgression.

One way to propose such a transgression of the relation between base and superstructure is to find a non-statal functioning of the base. In the preface to first volume of *Capital*, Marx writes that he does not "by any means depict the capitalist and the landowner in rosy colors. But individuals are dealt with here only in so far as they are the personifications of economic categories, the bearers of particular class interests." From his standpoint of analysis, the individual cannot be made "responsible for relations whose creature he remains . . . however much he may subjectively raise himself above them."[14] Capitalism thus appears as an anonymous social organization, without a central body for regulation. As much as capitalism is an anonymous machine, equally the capitalists and the economic follow and are subjected to relations imposed upon them. In the last part of the volume three of *Capital*, Marx presents the formula of trinity: "Capital–profit (profit of enterprise plus interest), land–ground-rent, labor–wages, this is the trinity formula which comprises all the secrets of the social production process," the material conditions of production.[15] There is an impersonal rule in the functioning of capitalism—or the "religion of everyday life," as

13 V.I. Lenin, "Imperialism: The Highest Stage of Capitalism," in *Essential Works of Lenin*, New York: Dover, 1987, 269.

14 Marx, *Capital*, Vol. 1, 92.

15 Karl Marx, *Capital*, Vol. 3, London: Penguin, 1991, 953.

Marx calls it. All the structures (political, economic, social, ideological) are grounded at an impersonal level; that is, they are impersonal structures. Instead, we have that which Marx names as "personification of things and the reification of the relations of production."[16] The lesson here is that the social forms cannot be distinguished from the material content, as expressed in the *trinity formula*. In this regard, when we make individuals the for the effects of the economy or politics on our own lives, we are already at level *zero* of ideology, which is another name for anti-Semitism and other fascist procedures of reification of social relations in a given social group.

Marx writes that the "society does not consist of individuals, but expresses the sum of interrelations, the relations within which these individuals stand."[17] Here we proceed with an Althusserian lesson: class struggle precedes the classes that struggle, and it is in the class struggle that the classes are constituted. They do not exist at the ontic level as part of objective social reality. Various forms of domination, exploitation, and oppression characterize contemporary capitalism, but each one always falls short in encompassing them all. This is why Marx was preoccupied with the economic structures of the capitalist form of social organization. However, even a complete understanding of the capitalist base does not mean that capitalism as a mode of production and distribution is completely understood.

We do not simply need to understand or recognize classes. In Europe, it is the far-right political parties who constantly refer to the working class. What is at stake in today's critique of capitalism is the rehabilitation of class analysis *and* the redefinition of class society as such. Today, instead of referring to entrepreneurs, citizens, employed, civil or other servants, and so on, we need to radicalize the notion and the concept of the proletariat. We shall come back to this later on.

---

16 Ibid., 969.

17 Karl Marx, *Grundrisse: Foundations of the Critique of Political Economy*, London: Penguin, 1993, 265.

The transgression of the relations between base and superstructure is, among other things, what Jameson is concerned with. In this enterprise, however, we should not count all too much on the "power of the people." The people, as a democratic body, are not a political agent by definition. Dual power, in which the existing base is transformed to the extent that it does not correspond to the superstructure, should not be understood as a state of emergency in which people will be permanently mobilized. In this regard, the direct participation of the people in horizontal, self-organized movements should not be mandatory. People have the right to apathy, but not to laziness, in collective life. Bureaucratic life, from making decisions for the collective to implementing them, should be organized by the politicians, who are always-already militants, in a central body called the party.

The whole question of bureaucracy as a form of life hinges on representation versus inclusion. The Communist Party form of organization, in a Jamesonian militarized form, should not represent the people, but rather include everyone in it. This inclusion overcomes the problem of the duality of powers (state versus party) because there is no party-state, but rather a party *instead* of a state. Furthermore, not only the duality of representation versus inclusion but also of representation versus participation is solved.

But what is the real danger of Jameson's proposal of the withering away of both politics *and* the state? As noted, for Jameson, the state is the site of politics. He therefore suggests that the society should be based not on a political but on a bureaucratic form of organization. In my understanding this is the most problematic part of his program, precisely because it is a very tenable proposal. Why? First, on a cynical note, the socialist Yugoslavia, with its concept of self-management, *was* a bureaucratized form of social organization, with clear elements of a market economy: private property was not completely abolished, the workers were not managers but managers were managing the economy, and so on. So the problem of bureaucracy was not the bureaucratic form, but rather that it didn't substitute the value form. This is the true problem: that the distance between the party and the state, while implementing the bureaucratic form of life, also keeps it at a distance from the value form, which is allowed to silently exist "in between" state and party. In other words, party is thought of as the substitute for the nation, for local forms of internationalism.

According to many analysis and critics, the socialist regimes of the twentieth century failed due to, among other reasons, their unification of the state with the party, or because of their despotic character and economic and social misery. But was that really the case? In Stalin's USSR, all property and institutions belonged to the state. However, there was one exception: the Communist Party, which functioned at a distance from the state. Its status was that of *obshchestvennaia*—a public organization. Nevertheless, the party had its cells in each state institution. Apropos this, Žižek's thesis is that the failure of twentieth-century communism was due to its distance from, not its proximity to, power. When he writes about the relation between the state and politics, he writes that

> the failure of the Communist State-Party politics is above all and primarily the failure of anti-statist politics, of the endeavor to break out of the constraints of the State, to replace statal forms of organization with "direct" non-representative forms of self-organization ("councils").[18]

This is a crucial lesson: whatever form of communist organization we are to think, we have to take into account that we need a unified body of state *and* the party. We shall come back to this in a moment.

In his discussion of the reasons for the failure of the socialist experiments, Alain Badiou provides a very provocative but insightful and profound thesis:

---

18 Žižek, "How to Begin from the Beginning?" 219.

> The failure should not be attributed either to the despotic character of socialist states or to their economic shortcomings. It is the withering away of politics which made these constructions untenable for their own leaders. All in all, people played practically no part.[19]

Judging from this, we can argue that the withering away of the state, as the ultimate goal of communism, should not be understood as the end of politics. The risk of both the state and politics withering away is that bureaucratized life will replace politics.

Marx defined communism as "the *real* movement which abolishes the present state of things." He always toyed with the idea that socialism would be far more advanced and revolutionary than capitalism. Remaining faithful to Marx's definition, we can argue that the present can be abolished only by collective political engagement. Indeed, politics is not the "practical" dimension; before everything, politics is a register of thought. The relation between thinking (i.e., philosophy) and politics is very complex, but let the following proposition suffice: the transformation of thought inevitably produces effects in politics. The effects of theoretical (philosophical) work have even a greater effect in the world than practical work. It transforms the very foundations on which the world actually exists and within which politics takes place. Revolutionize the former and the latter will necessarily transform itself. In other words, pure thinking and politics are inseparable. When bureaucracy carries out the functions of politics, social life becomes unbearable: too mechanical and boring. Instead, I propose, in complete agreement with Jameson on the withering away of the state, that we should replace the bureaucratic form of life with the political form of life.

---

19 Alain Badiou, *On the Obscure Disaster—On the End of State-Truth*, Maastricht: Jan van Eyck Academie and Arkzin, 2009, 5–6.

Communism as a Universal Party Organization

The main danger in dual-power societies is that the structures of dual power might not only pose no threat to state power, but could be tolerated or even (silently) supported by the state. The other risk is that while these structures operate in parallel with state structures, that is to say, as *excluded* structures, they will be included in the capitalist circulation. The greatest danger, however, is their normalization: a situation in which they present no risk to the ruling ideology. The common danger to these two ways of dual power functioning as inherent transgressions of the law is the normalization of dual power. That was the case with the Zapatistas, the "parallel structures" during the 1990s in Kosovo, anarchists' liberated zones, "temporary autonomous zones," and so on. Let us name these two risks the *normalizing risks*. For dual power to be successful, it should NOT by all means become acceptable to the state. Otherwise, as someone once said, the zones or territories in which the other power operates risk becoming nice tourist destinations for melancholic leftists.

The other side of this is that, as Jameson notes, there are already structures of dual power at work in our world today, from drug dealers to perhaps even the Islamic State—which has the double function of the army *and* the state, therefore constituting an army-state. On this note, let us point to perhaps one of the most difficult aspects of organization: the lack of emblem and organization. We are witnessing continuous upheavals, revolts, and massive demonstrations all around the globe. However, we are also witnessing their failure in the "morning after"—that is, the inability to formalize these eruptions into consistent political organizations. Writing on the protests in Brazil, Gabriel Tupinambá argues that

> the parallel power exerted by the drug dealers in the slums operates a similar feat [to fascist appropriation of popular dissatisfaction], proposing a figure of potency to the young men who have already

> seen that hard work does not produce any recognition of one's value and place in Brazilian society.[20]

According to him, it is either fascist groups or drug cartels that offer a place, arms, and organization for invisible youth from the favelas. The articulation of a brand and belonging is produced by mafia or fascists, which, in the absence of a leftist brand, allows people from the lower classes to recognize themselves as actors without depending on the institutional recognition of the state:

> Such is, then, the failure—and the challenge—at stake today when trying to combine both direction and confidence in the masses: the difficulty of inventing a political emblem which would cut across the demands for identification which distinguish different sectors of the working class while, at the same time, having confidence that such an emblem is capable of evoking passionate discipline and organization in the masses without turning popular power into a totalitarian tendency.[21]

The urgent task of communist thinking is to break the vicious circle of desperate (and failed) attempts to articulate clear positions and rethink the forms of mass political organization.

According to Karatani, capitalism is not merely the existence of production, but the world economy based on four modes of exchange: A) reciprocity of the gift; B) plunder and protection; C) commodity exchange; and D) the mode which transcends the other three. In our capitalist societies, however, mode of exchange C is *dominant*. The whole point is to overcome the mode of commodity exchange (C): that is, to invent a new mode of exchange that resolves the contradictions of mode C. For Karatani, this means a

---

20 Gabriel Tupinambá, "What Is a Party a Part Of?" *Crisis and Critique* 1(1), 2014, 226, crisiscritique.org.

21 Ibid.

return to mode A: "the mode of exchange D, as the restoration of A in a higher dimension, is in fact only possible with the negation of A."[22] Karatani is well aware that there is no such thing as eradicating commodity exchange. One can eradicate capitalism and capital-based ways of life, but not the form of exchange itself. His solution goes as follows: there is no particular way to solve the problems of capital, nation, and state without privileging one of the three. According to Karatani, what he calls the "UN system" can be the "federation of nations as a world system."[23] Instead of the world republic proposed by Kant or the United Nations proposed by Karatani, let us call our utopia a non-statal World Party. Is a universal party organization of societies thinkable and conceivable?

Departing from Žižek's position that the Soviet Union was a dual form of party *and* state, we will propose a universal party *instead* of a state. Jameson suggests that the militarized power should be "a kind of network or exoskeleton of the social needs and functions: something somewhere between a universal democracy, a political party, and a bureaucracy in which everyone is his own bureaucrat." Let us proceed with replacing the army with the party. Instead of everyone being his or her own bureaucrat, we shall propose militants of the party to replace the bureaucrats. In order for the universal party to function in running society, it has to have potent militants. In doing so, we keep the political invention alive. The universal party should reappropriate the notions of discipline, hierarchy, order, collectivity, and so on. Mao used to say that without an ideological discipline, there can be no order in the party. Let us propose the following thesis: the party is the condition *for* politics. It provides the *suprastatal form* of politics, which in order to exist

22 Kojin Karatani, *The Structure of World History: From Modes of Production to Modes of Exchange*, Durham, NC: Duke University Press, 2014, xi–xii. We should note that for Karatani, the "return to mode A" is done in a Kantian form.

23 Ibid.

has to be organized. The question remains: how do we turn the state against itself, to operate and function in a non-statal form? The absolute precondition is creating strong and efficient party structures, a strong body that will transform the entire social and political life. The abolition of capitalism has to go hand in hand with the *transformation* of the state, which we call a non-statal state or a party. To our previous thesis of politics *as* thought, we should add another element: politics is thought, acting, *and* organization.

But what are its foundations? The most difficult part is the economic class struggle. The status of the worker has changed: it is double in relation to its position in the processes of production and of consumption. Karatani maintains that "consumers are simply members of the proletariat who have stepped into the site of circulation," which, in his understanding, makes the consumerist movement part of the proletarian movement.[24] Therefore, the 1968 slogan "back to the factories" is no longer operative. Perhaps the shift is from the struggle in the factories to struggles in the field of consumption. The traditional relation between power structures and exploitation, or production and society, has to be rethought. The emergence of new forms of production necessitates new forms of exploitation, and with them new forms of domination.

In this regard, we need to reactualize the notion of the proletariat: the proletariat is not only she or he from whom surplus-value is extracted, but who is alienated from the substance of our subjectivity. In this sense, the *Communist Manifesto*'s call "proletarians of the world, unite" is actual: we need a large-scale unification of workers, consumers, the excluded, immigrants, the unemployed, the unemployable and illegally employed, dispossessed farmers, youth with no prospects, and so on.

Jameson writes that "the new utopia, indeed, must welcome the most outrageous self-indulgences and personal freedoms of its citizens in all things, very much including puritanism and the

24 Ibid., 290.

hatred of self-indulgence and personal freedoms." A new ethics should be invented. Jameson proposes that the life of the army barracks is such that

> the life of the recruit or draftee . . . always involves being thrown together with people utterly unlike you, from wholly different and incompatible backgrounds, classes, ethnicities, and even sexes. The instantaneous dislikes and distasteful cultural unfamiliarities, the inescapable elbow-rubbing with people with whom you have nothing in common and would normally avoid—this is true democracy, normally concealed by the various class shelters, the professions, or the family itself.

This is the ethics of Agota Kristof—of the double levels of alienation and solidarity. Already in our societies we are thrown into collectivities with unknown people; we need a radical form of alienation, a ruthless alienation founded on profound solidarity.

Jameson's use of psychoanalysis and Lacan also sheds light into a very complicated matter. His insights are useful in articulating how, in communism, we will have *fewer excuses* for our unhappiness. As such, we are more susceptible to envy and other pathologies, opening up a completely new field of theory concerning *communist pathologies*.

The universal party form of social organizations can also be structured in military terms: each nation forms a division. But, as in the army, it is the central command or the Central Committee that runs the divisions, not vice versa, as is the case with NATO or UN. This division of nations into army brigades should not be seen as a form of federalism; the party form of social organization is unitary.

This form of social organization seems impossible to realize. Maybe it is. But we should always remember that partial emancipation (national, regional, and so on) is equally impossible. Without a global organized movement, revolution is simply unimaginable. If we fail in creating a strong international movement, the probable outcome is yet another world war—and the current conjuncture is certainly leading us toward that situation.

6

A Japanese Utopia

Kojin Karatani

I read Fredric Jameson's "An American Utopia" just as I was beginning to commit myself to various protest movements against Prime Minister Shinzō Abe's bill to enable Japan to dispatch its Self-Defense Forces overseas in collaboration with the United States. These movements, especially street demonstrations, gradually gathered popular momentum, reaching a scale the likes of which has not been seen since the 1960s. The people, including young students, are particularly outraged by Abe's trampling on Japan's post–World War II pacifist constitution, in particular Article 9, which reads:

> Aspiring sincerely to an international peace based on justice and order, the Japanese people forever renounce war as a sovereign right of the nation and the threat or use of force as means of settling international disputes. In order to accomplish the aim of the preceding paragraph, land, sea, and air forces, as well as other war potential, will never be maintained. The right of belligerency of the state will not be recognized.

This provision prohibits Japan from having any military power. It unconditionally denies the right of waging war. Any state may claim the right to defend itself, but Japan abandons it. Apparently, this provision reflects the antiwar Kellogg-Briand Pact of 1928, which can be traced back to Kant's "perpetual peace." I will come back to this point later in more detail.

The mass media expected this bill to pass based on Prime Minister Abe's high approval rating. However, Abe's proposal was met with an unanticipated setback, as he aroused deep resentment outside of the Japanese Diet. This unlikely—but growing—protest seemed to confirm my long-held theory about Article 9. Here I will outline this theory, making references to Jameson's paper.

I had a curious thought while reading "An American Utopia," which goes like this. If my understanding is accurate, Jameson argues that there are no more effective tactics for revolution in America than general conscription, and that is an American utopia. I was deeply moved by Jameson's desperate measure, not to mention the rare candidness of his essay. At the same time, I believe that his theory opens up another possibility. Following Jameson, I would like to call it "A Japanese Utopia." In fact, these two utopias are inextricably connected.

The first thing to say in relation to Article 9 is that it has not been put into practice. Nevertheless, Japan has maintained it intact to the present day. To be more specific, we have the Self-Defense Forces of Japan, which ranks high on international lists of weaponry and military budgets. On top of this, the United States Forces Japan maintains 132 military bases throughout Japan, which are financially supported by Japan. How is such a thing possible under this constitution? It is impossible, of course. In order to cover over this incongruousness, the Japanese government has repeatedly stretched the "interpretation" of Article 9. For example, according to the government, since the Self-Defense Forces renounce the "use of force as a means of settling international disputes," it cannot possibly be an army, nor a military power. Let me draw your attention to the fact that it is called our "forces" and not our "military." Similarly, its members are called "personnel" or "members," not "soldiers."

But no "interpretation" can possibly justify the existence of the Self-Defense Forces in Japan, so long as the Constitution remains in force. Thinking logically, there seem to be two options: abolish the Self-Defense Forces or abolish Article 9. This is normal logic. But Japan has avoided logic. Instead, it has held onto the Constitution it never put into practice while increasingly strengthening the Self-Defense Forces. In order to justify this, Japan continually—and arbitrarily—stretches interpretations of the Constitution to suit its needs.

However, Article 9 cannot be read to justify sending the Self-Defense Forces into overseas battlefields. Even if such a farfetched interpretation is conceded, it would still require a radical departure from that interpretation in order to actually send the Self-Defense Forces personnel to the battlefield at the risk of their lives.

It is quite clear that if Japan really wants to take part in war, it has to amend Article 9 instead of simply changing the interpretation. If this is what the people want as well, no one can stop it. In fact, the ruling strata have long wished to amend the Constitution, but the ruling conservative party has never dared to do so. The reason for its hesitation is quite simple. It has never made a constitutional amendment the main issue in an election campaign. In fact, the Liberal Democratic Party (LDP) has announced plans for a new Constitution several times, but never brought the issue up during elections. A number of politicians have openly supported the idea, but they hold their tongues during election campaigns. Even Prime Minister Abe has done the same. Why is this? The reason is quite simple. They know that making a constitutional amendment the main issue in an election would lead to a sure catastrophe.

Hoping to create the impression that war is imminent, Prime Minister Abe has been inflaming tensions with neighboring nations, thereby manipulating public opinion. This has worked well, and most of the mass media seemed to succumb to it. If this is the case, however, why then is Abe still holding back from openly suggesting the amendment of Article 9, his long-cherished dream? He seems unlikely ever to do so, because—and again—he knows that he and his party would suffer at the polls.

He does not, however, understand why this is so. I assume that he must be optimistically thinking that continually manipulating public opinion to his benefit will eventually earn him the support he needs to launch the amendment process. By the same token, I doubt if the pro–Article 9 camp knows why the people have shown such steadfast support for this Article. I think they fear that if current trends continue, eventually people will start supporting the constitutional amendment.

The pro–Article 9 camp believe something like this: Article 9 is not carried out literally, but we must be content that it still survives and has some deterrent effect. But I want to insist that we carry out Article 9 or else we abandon it. I will come back to this point later. For now I will just point out that my claim seems to resonate with Jameson's ideas.

In the United States the general conscription system was abolished at the end of the Vietnam War. It is said that it is no longer necessary. This is because today's wars require only professional soldiers and robots such as drones, and the drafted public cannot acquire such skills. However, that is not the actual reason why the conscription system was abolished. The truth is that the government was not able to maintain it. Enforcing the system would arouse huge protest movements like the ones in the 1960s.

General conscription is not just a military matter. This is because it came into being along with civil revolution; that is, it came into being with the birth of the nation-state. It is therefore inseparable from such "just causes" as liberty and equality. In the times of absolute monarchy, the mercenary system was employed. In this sense, American wars today hark back to that period. Now that we are in the age of the "absolute monarchy of capital" (neoliberalism), the United States cannot pretend that there is a cause just enough to reintroduce the general conscription system. Besides, general conscription makes today's high-tech wars impossible. In this sense, Jameson's demand implies renouncing war, not to mention denouncing the absolute monarchy of capital.

Let us now consider the Constitution of Japan, which renounces the right to wage war. This was not drawn up nor drafted by the Japanese of their own accord. It was imposed on Japan by the occupation army led by General Douglas MacArthur. The Constitution was meant to eradicate Japanese so-called emperor fascism. In Article 1, the role of emperor, who used to be the sovereign, is prescribed as "the symbol of the unity of the people with whom resides sovereign power." In Article 9, as I have mentioned before, the use of force is entirely renounced.

However, at the same time, it is undeniable that the occupation army had some "idealism," held by many leftist New Dealers. They nurtured and supported Japanese labor movements and agrarian reform. On top of that, they prompted Japan to renounce the right to wage war, in the form of Article 9. A utopia that seemed unrealizable in the United States was actually smuggled into the Japanese Constitution. Although the New Dealers were to be purged soon after this, their will remained in Article 9.

Thus Article 9, which presupposed the United Nations' founding in 1945 and was based upon the Kellogg-Briand Pact of 1928 as well as Kantian thought, was introduced into Japan. Of course there were sympathizers of Kantian peace theory among the Japanese who were involved in the process of enacting the Constitution. Yet it was only through the constraint of the occupation army that this idea was actualized.

It is this fact of the United States's imposition of Article 9 to which the conservative revisionist ideologues repeatedly refer.

But they turn a blind eye to the following fact: When the Korean War broke out, the United States, wanting Japan to join the military effort, demanded that Japan revise its Constitution. That means that the United States at that point no longer had any intention of forcing Article 9 on Japan. Shigeru Yoshida, the prime minister at the time, responded to this demand with a refusal. In this sense, the Constitution was chosen voluntarily by the Japanese.

Prime Minister Yoshida was a pro-American conservative, but in order to reject America's demand he went so far as to request that the Socialist Party organize an anti-rearmament movement. Why was it that he tried to protect Article 9? It is said that he gave priority to the economic recovery of Japan. But my opinion is different: it was because he judged that proposing revision would lead to the collapse of his party, not to mention his administration. It was not a risk worth taking. Meanwhile, Yoshida did accept the formation of the National Police Reserve (the predecessor of the Self-Defense Forces), which he claimed did not infringe on Article 9. This marked the start of the practice of changing the interpretation of the Constitution in place of changing the Constitution itself.

In fact, Japanese soldiers were used in secret in the Korean War. Needless to say, Japan was the US military base during the war. This was the case with the Vietnam War as well. Such was the reality despite Article 9. Nonetheless, Japanese leaders did not abolish Article 9. They only changed the interpretation.

That became the standard method of the LDP thereafter. They never bring up the issue of a constitutional amendment at election time. However, they have also been certain that the time for amendment will come at some point, once Japan rises as an economic giant. Today they still believe that they should be able to change it, on the grounds that the Constitution was not established of Japan's own accord. But things did not turn out as they anticipated. Article 9 has been long supported by the Japanese people.

Why is this? The LDP believes that the Japanese have been brainwashed by left-wing intellectuals and politicians. But this is a sheer misunderstanding. The left wing, for that matter, used to be rather critical of Article 9. They considered forming a people's self-defense force in order to expel the United States Forces Japan. It was only much later that the left wing turned pro–Article 9.

Nevertheless, the conservatives blame the left-wing campaign for the Japanese people's longstanding and steadfast support of Article 9. They cannot make sense of it otherwise. With regard to this, what are the thoughts of the pro-Constitution camp? They seem just as unable to understand the reason for the people's support of the Constitution. They think the Japanese supported Article 9 because they experienced the cruelty of war and repented over the damage Japan caused to its neighboring nations. They also believe that Article 9 was maintained thanks to their own efforts to enlighten people.

But I do not think they have the right picture. The Japanese did not form the Constitution through conscious reflection, as they claim. The fact is that it was imposed by the occupation army. But it is also a fact that the people came to support it. Nevertheless, this did not happen through the intellectuals' enlightenment efforts. If that was the only reason, its popular support could not have lasted so long. And if the people's rejection of war is based upon their own experience of war, their support of the Constitution should have withered as that memory faded with time and with the changing of generations. But that has not been the case with Article 9. It still enjoys strong support in spite of the weakening of the left-wing intellectuals. Pro–Article 9 activists think that they are protecting the Article. We may say, however, that they do not protect Article 9 but are protected by it.

How, then, can we explain this situation, in which the Japanese people were compelled to accept Article 9 by the occupation army but have supported it voluntarily and cherished it, despite continual criticism and manipulation of public opinion?

Here I must refer to Freud, specifically following World War I. Freud supported Austria's participation in World War I. As the war lingered, however, he became negative toward it, but still wrote the following comment:

> It [war] strips us of the later accretions of civilization, and lays bare the primal man in each of us. It completes us once more to be heroes who cannot believe in their own death; it stamps strangers as enemies, whose death is to be brought about or desired; it tells us to disregard the death of those we love. But war cannot be abolished; so long as the conditions of existence among nations are so different and their mutual repulsion so violent, there are bound to be wars.[1]

In his view, the human cruelty seen in war is only an exposure of our ordinarily repressed "life of feeling," unleashed by the state. So he concludes that we may hope for this to disappear after the war. This way of thinking is characteristic of Freud's early writings. At this stage, he was still basing his thought upon the dualism between the pleasure principle and the reality principle. The pleasure principle seeks to actualize the unconscious desire or drive. But since that could put the ego in danger, it needs to be curbed. That is the role of the reality principle, which originates in one's father or in society. Under normal circumstances, the pleasure principle is held in check by the reality principle, but is unleashed under special circumstances, such as in dreams, rituals, and wars.

After the war, however, Freud had to revise his view when he met patients suffering from war neurosis. For them, the war was far from gradually fading away from their memories. The nightmare of the war awoke them every night. Freud noticed something here that could not be explained within the framework of dualism. He wrote: "Enough is left unexplained to justify the hypothesis of a compulsion to repeat—something that seems more primitive,

1 Sigmund Freud, "Beyond the Pleasure Principle," in *The Standard Edition of the Complete Psychological Works of Sigmund Freud*, Vol. 14, trans. J. Strachey, London: Hogarth Press, 1986, 299.

more elementary, more instinctual than the pleasure principle which it over-rides."[2]

Here Freud introduced a new concept, "the death drive," which causes repetition compulsion. With regard to this, he stressed the positive aspects of the death drive; the role it plays is actually more positive than negative. The repetition compulsion in war neurosis is not just a symptom caused by the aftershock of the war, but an attempt to overcome that shock by repeating it.

This led to the notion of the "superego," which Freud posited in *The Ego and the Id* in 1923. He had discussed similar notions earlier in his career, for example the idea of the "censor" in dreams that he mentions in *Interpretation of Dreams* (1900). The censor is explained as the social norms internalized through one's parents. That is a form of the reality principle. But the superego he presents in his *The Ego and the Id* is different from this. Whereas the censor comes from outside, the superego comes from inside—or, in other words, from the death drive. To put it differently, while the censor is heteronymous, the superego is autonomous or self-regulating. By introducing the death drive, Freud locates the basis for human autonomy, which at times exceeds internalized social norms or the reality principle. What is more, he holds that the superego exists in the collective as well. This theoretical turn is more evident in his cultural theory than in his psychoanalysis in the narrow sense, because culture concerns the superego of the collective.

I said that it was not during but after the war when Freud encountered patients of war neurosis (repetition compulsion) and came to think about questions such as the death drive, the aggression drive, and the superego. In this light, I think that we can regard Article 9 as the superego in the unconscious of the Japanese people. Article 9 is not a matter of consciousness. Freud noted that

---

2 Sigmund Freud, *The Standard Edition of the Complete Psychological Works of Sigmund Freud*, Vol. 18, trans. J. Strachey, London: Hogarth Press, 1986, 23.

although the patients of obsessive neurosis are tormented by a guilty conscience, they themselves are not aware of this. He called it an "unconscious sense of guilt."[3]

Such is the case with the Japanese people's relation to Article 9. It is a kind of obsessive neurosis, demonstrating an unconscious sense of guilt. Support for Article 9 does not originate in consciousness. Therefore, Article 9 does not originate in people's sense of guilt. Nor is it maintained through deepening reflection on their past. If such was the case, it would have been abolished long ago. Article 9 involves a strong ethical moment, but it is not conscious or voluntary. For that matter, Freud remarked on masochism as follows:

> The situation is usually presented as though ethical requirements were the primary thing and the renunciation of instinct followed from them. This leaves the origin of the ethical sense unexplained. Actually, it seems to be the other way about. The first instinctual renunciation is enforced by external powers, and it is only this that creates the ethical sense, which expresses itself in conscience and demands a further renunciation of instinct.[4]

Freud's view brilliantly explains the fact that Article 9 was "enforced by the external powers," that is, by the occupation army, but took root deeply in the collective unconsciousness of the Japanese people. To put it differently, in the beginning was the "renunciation" of aggression enforced by the external powers, which, however, "created the ethical sense" or conscience that "demands further renunciation" of war. Let me say this once

3 Sigmund Freud, *The Standard Edition of the Complete Psychological Works of Sigmund Freud*, Vol. 19, trans. J. Strachey, London: Hogarth Press, 1986, 166.

4 Sigmund Freud, "The Economic Problem of Masochism," in *The Standard Edition of the Complete Psychological Works of Sigmund Freud*, Vol. 19, trans. J. Strachey, London: Hogarth Press, 1986, 170.

again. Article 9 was not made by the people's voluntary agreement, but enforced by the external powers. Yet it took root deeply all the more for it.

Currently, and perhaps from this time on, the conservative administration wants to urge the Japanese to participate in war under various pretexts. They might temporarily succeed in this, but it would sooner or later provoke tremendous resentment, which would then press them into carrying out the Constitution more literally. The Japanese would then be bound to Article 9 for good. This is why I am optimistic as well as pessimistic regarding the future of Japan.

I attach importance to Article 9 because it is grounded in the Kantian idea, about which I want to make two points. First, regarding the common critique that it is idealistic: When Kant proposed a federation of nations, Hegel criticized it as idealistic. He argued that in order for the federation to function effectively, there would need to be a superpower with the ability to punish other states for violation of rules. Therefore, peace is unlikely without a hegemonic power. This argument is employed even now to criticize the United Nations.

In fact, the Kantian idea was totally ignored throughout the nineteenth century, but was revived toward the end of the century as the imperialist wars took place and bore fruit as the League of Nations following World War I, as well as the Kellogg-Briand Pact. This later led to the formation of the United Nations in 1945. It is self-evident that the Kantian idea was behind all of these events. As a matter of fact, Article 9 presupposed the existence of the United Nations, as is stated in the preamble of the Constitution.

In this regard, the Kantian idea did not remain a mere idealism. It was actualized to a considerable degree. Why? Earlier I mentioned that Hegel criticized the Kantian idea of peace as idealist and unrealistic. Such critiques have been repeated to the present day. However, Kant was far from a naïve idealist. Concerning human nature, Kant shared the same negative view as Hobbes;

Kant thought humans have an intrinsically "unsocial sociability" (*ungesellige Geselligkeit*) and that this cannot be removed. This "unsocial sociability" can be seen as synonymous with what Freud called the "aggression drive." Consequently, Kant never thought the federation of free nations would be realized through human reason or morality. To the contrary, it would be this "unsocial sociability," or war, that would eventually realize it. Such a view can be called "the cunning of nature," in contrast to what Hegel called "the cunning of reason."

Secondly, I want to argue that Kantian perpetual peace means not a mere question of peace, but revolution. Kant published "Perpetual Peace: A Philosophical Sketch" in 1795, just before the outbreak of a world war that later came to be called the Napoleonic Wars. He put forward the idea of a world federation of nations in this essay not simply because a war was looming. He had written a thesis to the same effect in 1784, but for a different purpose. At that time he was in support of the Rousseauian civil revolution, although Kant was skeptical about this in one respect: Rousseau, Kant argued, thought of revolution only within a single state. However, if a civil revolution took place in one nation, it would be immediately interfered with and crushed by the neighboring old regimes (absolute monarchical states). To prevent this, Kant thought, a federation of free states would be necessary.

In fact, a civil revolution did take place in France in 1789. Neighboring states like Austria meddled with the revolution in order to overthrow it. France then started a defensive war, from which Napoleon emerged as a military leader. It was around this time that Kant published his essay on perpetual peace. It drew attention only in terms of the question of war, and it was forgotten that this was originally related to the question of civil revolution.

Things took a similar course in the years that followed, but civil revolution and the federation of nations always remained decoupled. For instance, two world-historical incidents took place after World War I: the Russian Revolution and the formation of the

League of Nations. It is believed that the former was based upon Marx's thought and the latter upon Kant's thought, but the two are inseparable from a Kantian as well as a Marxian viewpoint. Marx thought of abolishing the state, but realized that it would be impossible within a single state, because the state exists vis-à-vis other states. Thus, he concludes, "communism is only possible as the act of the dominant peoples all at once and simultaneously."[5] Similarly, when Kant emphasized perpetual peace as distinct from temporary peace, the implication was the necessity of a civil revolution in each state as a prerequisite. In this sense, it may be said that Kant too thought of the simultaneous civil revolution of all nations.

In this way Kantian and Marxian thought are interconnected. Nevertheless, they were considered irrelevant to each other, and this led to the failure of these world-historical events. The Russian Revolution took place within a single state and was immediately met with interference and invasions by the surrounding powers. This warped the nature of the socialist revolution. That is to say, faced with crisis, the revolutionaries, who intended to sublate the state, had no choice but to first strengthen the state in order to resist this intervention. Meanwhile, the League of Nations failed to function. It was in practical terms nothing more than an alliance of the imperialist states, and on top of that the superpower, the United States, refused to take part. As a result, the League of Nations in its actually existing form remained far from a realization of the Kantian idea.

The powerlessness of the League of Nations was revealed in its inability to prevent World War II. The United Nations, which was established to take the League's place after that war, was far more efficient in comparison, but still not powerful enough to curb the hegemonic powers. It has grown even more powerless in recent years.

---

5 Karl Marx and Frederick Engels, "The German Ideology," in *Karl Marx and Frederick Engels Collected Works*, Vol. 5, Moscow: Progress Publishers, 1976, 49.

In retrospect, it turns out that the socialist revolutions of the twentieth century were doomed because the two moments, civil revolution in each nation and a federation of nations, were decoupled. Now we have a good picture of what our possible revolutionary movements should look like. They must be based upon countermovements against capital-state in each nation and upon the solidarity and association among them. But the latter is no mean feat, as it is likely to be divided and crushed by capital-states, just as the Second International was dissolved by the First World War. The Third International was solid, but in that case one nation dominated the others.

Now only one possibility seems to remain: coupling Kant and Marx, so to speak. On the one hand we carry out countermovements against capital-state in each nation, while on the other hand prompting the UN to change into an organ where these movements can be united. Were these things realized, what seemed impossible would become possible, whether that would be Article 9 or the general conscription system. I think that is a simultaneous world revolution.

7

Jameson and Method: On Comic Utopianism

Frank Ruda

It has become common prejudice to claim that utopia . . . is not possible. It follows that the spell under which most people live is not the spell of the materialism that is said to be so awful. The real spell . . . is that of a vulgar idealism that has long since forgotten its own assumptions.

—Theodor W. Adorno[1]

We first of all have to engage in a cultural revolution.

—Alain Badiou[2]

That's impossible! From history to politics

What kind of text is one effectively reading when one reads Fredric Jameson's "An American Utopia"? What kind of method, what

1 Theodor W. Adorno, *History and Freedom: Lectures 1964–1965*, Cambridge: Polity, 2006, 68.

2 Alain Badiou, "True and False Contradictions of the Crisis," *Liberation*, trans. David Broder, May 29, 2015, http://www.versobooks.com/blogs/2014-alain-badiou-true-and-false-contradictions-of-the-crisis.

kind of methodology is here employed? Jameson's title seems to suggest that such questions are not really worthy of being raised at all. Isn't one here clearly confronted with a utopia? So, why bother? One should nonetheless not hasten to give too swift an answer, since Jameson himself, close to the very beginning of his text, states that he "can't be sure whether I am proposing a political program or a utopian vision" and then adds that "neither of which, according to me, ought to be possible any longer."[3] The text itself therefore presents a proposal of which it is unclear if it is a utopia or a political program, yet what is clear is that it does something that is not or at least ought not to be possible any longer. One might then infer that the difficulty of how to classify the very status of Jameson's proposal, the difficulty of classifying it as a program or a utopia, is internally linked to, if not derived from, the very impossibility that characterizes his proposal. To clarify the very status of the text itself, if distinctly determinable or not, an exercise in formal analysis is needed. It will investigate the specific locus from which Jameson's proposal is enunciated. This is not an external starting point, but—dealing with an author so preoccupied with the analysis of form—this will rather directly lead into the heart of the matter.[4] Before entering directly into the argument of the text, I will thus demonstrate that it is instructive to first specify the text's peculiarly impossible status—and in this precise sense I will begin by examining Jameson's methodological starting point. One can do so by differentiating between six different aspects that are at the same time conceptually interwoven.

The *first* reason why Jameson's text has an *impossible* status is *historical*, since the proposal it presents is not impossible as such, but rather impossible in the specific time in which it is articulated:

3 Fredric Jameson, "An American Utopia."

4 Here one just has to recall his classic: Fredric Jameson, *Marxism and Form: Twentieth-Century Dialectical Theories of Literature*, Princeton, NJ: Princeton University Press, 1974.

that is, it is only impossible relative to its own historical situation. This is why the impossibility of Jameson's proposal is first and foremost not ontological but rather historical, insofar as it is produced within a particular situation and thus mediated by the historical circumstances in which it appears.

Therefrom, one can infer that Jameson's proposal *secondly* appears to be *epistemologically impossible*. For if impossibility is not a neutral modality but one that is produced in a historically specific setting and its modal functioning therefore has to be historicized (as in point 1), then such an (historically specific) impossibility is generated by means of presenting some things, some thoughts, as being unthinkable. In short, this is to say that there is always a historically specific rendering of what "here and now" can possibly be imagined and thought.

Here it is *thirdly* important to note that the historically specific determination of what is *epistemologically* considered to be *impossible* ultimately *has ontological effects*. This is because that which is determined as impossibility within and by the historical situation does necessarily not appear as simply being an impossibility relative to the present state of things.[5] Rather, it cannot but appear—at least from within (the perspective of) the situation—as being impossible as such, impossible in itself.[6] The historical production of impossibility thereby necessarily ontologizes (and naturalizes) its own modal product. It therefore seems as if what appears

5 A (maybe) more or less complex example for this dynamic: The historically specific claim that communism historically failed and that it is therefore impossible to realize any such form of organization, although it declares itself to be a historical claim (one learned this lesson from history), nonetheless draws nonhistorical consequences from this, namely that communism was flawed and conceptually (or substantially) doomed to fail from the very beginning and is therefore an impossibility as such.

6 I will subsequently return to the question if there is or can(not) be another perspective than the perspective of the situation and will ultimately argue that there is one, but it is a peculiarly impossible one.

impossible now will have been impossible since forever.[7] This is why Jameson's proposal does not only appear historically specific (1) or epistemologically impossible (2); rather, it is also linked with its ontological effects (3). In short, and paradoxically put, Jameson's place of enunciation therefore itself appears ontologically impossible, something like a historical, epistemological, ontological, modal "no-man's land."[8] But how is it possible—since it is impossible—to tackle such a peculiar concatenation? To answer this, one has to introduce another aspect.

It is *fourthly* crucial to note that the concoction of the first three determining aspects of impossibility has *practical as well as political consequences*. The (determining) move from historical specificity to epistemology to ontology thus leads back to the very historical situation where it originated. That is to say: if something is rendered within a certain historical situation as being impossible to conceive of, this ultimately turns this very "something" into an ontological impossibility, and this also determines patterns of possible and impossible actions.[9] Jameson's text is literally—in the double sense of the term—doing something impossible. But how

---

7 It therefore follows the logic nicely captured by Jean-Pierre Dupuy, who once noted: "An object possesses a property x"—for example to be possible or thinkable—"until time t; after t, it is not only that the object no longer has the property x; it is that it is not true that it possessed x at any time. The truth-value of the proposition 'the object O has the property x at the moment t' therefore depends on the moment in which the proposition is enunciated." The same holds for the proposition "the object O is thinkable / unthinkable." Jean-Pierre Dupuy, "Quand je mourrai, rien de notre amour n'aura jamais existé," unpublished typescript, cited in: Slavoj Žižek, *Absolute Recoil: Towards a New Foundation of Dialectical Materialism*, London: Verso, 2014, 187).

8 To my mind, this is why Jameson can justifiably call this no-man's-land "also that of dual power."

9 The sense in which I here characterize the different aspects of impossibility is very close to what Alain Badiou calls "the state (of a situation)." For this, see Alain Badiou, *Being and Event*, London: Continuum, 2005, 81–112.

do these patterns appear? This is where the fifth aspect of impossibility enters the scene.

The *fifth* aspect has to do with what Jameson in a different context once referred to as the "widespread paralysis of the collective or social imaginary."[10] Why is there a link between *impossibility* and the paralysis of the collective *imaginary*? One way to answer this would be to refer to Althusser's famous definition of ideology as imaginary relation to the real conditions of existence—which would then mean that it is precisely the imaginary relation within which the first four aspects would be inscribed, as something that Jameson once called "the axiomatics of ideology."[11] Another, more precise way of answering this question is to take up a diagnosis from the beginning of "An American Utopia": that if one today seeks to think radical political change, one immediately seems to face conceptual impasses. There seems to be no alternative to the influential and history-making distinction between the "political program" of the left, revolution (or communism), and its alternative "political strategy," reformism (or socialism). Yet, in the present historical setting, this distinction is saturated. Neither of its sides presents any imaginable and/or mobilizing political option any longer.[12] The idea of revolution became essentially unbelievable (who is going to make it? with what to replace the

10 Fredric Jameson, "Totality as Conspiracy," in *The Geopolitical Aesthetic: Cinema and Space in the World System*, Bloomington: Indiana University Press, 1995, 9.

11 Fredric Jameson, *The Political Unconscious: Narrative as a Socially Symbolic Act*, New York: Routledge, 1983, 171. It is here important to remark that Jameson leaves out the dimension of the symbolic—that is, for him, representation—a dimension to which I will return below.

12 One could, and I think should, supplement this diagnosis of saturation on the side of the "left" with a saturation on the other side, of the right, which opts for returning to a—generically fascist—variety of substantialisms (of race, religions, etc.) to counter the present situation and its self-proclaimed nonideological pragmatist-"realism" of what one can and cannot do.

current system? etc.); reformism from the very beginning proved to be corrupted by the very system it allegedly sought to reform.[13]

If this is true and "Gramsci's celebrated alternatives—the war of maneuver and the war of position—no longer seem theoretically adequate to the present situation," one today seems to be stuck with old fashion. Not only with an old-fashioned language of revolution that no one believes any longer (and with old-fashioned corruption on the other side), but also with an old-fashioned distinction between two unfeasible political (non) options. One may here see in what precise sense a historically specific setting generates the very epistemological impossibility that is ontologized and thereby determines practical and political behavior by making certain things unimaginable: if one is stuck with a distinction in which both sides of the distinction do not work, the only way out is to denounce both options ("No, thanks, both are worse"). Although this rejection indicates an option that was not present before, such a maneuver also comes with the danger of ending just as an abstract rejection (although one, even then, is better off than before). But it should be clear that being stuck with a conceptual instrument that hinders imagining radical change is precisely what paralyzes the collective imaginary.

The paralysis is thus a symptom of a situation in which there seems to be no way out, no exit option with regard to the current state of things. This is how late capitalism, in Jameson's term, swallows and absorbs time—the future can be no real future if one cannot imagine any difference to the present state of affairs any longer. "This is the sense in which the very advances in our own system, late capitalism, interpose themselves between ourselves

13 This account of the limitations of the revolution/reformism distinction is consistent with the claim that the impossibilities one is here dealing with are (1) a historically specific, (2) make certain things unthinkable and therefore also (3) appear to be ontologically impossible. This generates (4) practical effects that are effectuated by determining (5) the imaginary.

and the future"—a future that thereby becomes a repetition of the past and thereby time as such is lost.[14] This assumption "of an end of history . . . merely testifies to our cognitive limitations when it comes to the thinking of utopia itself." This is to say that one's imaginary powers are paralyzed when one is in a situation in which what is a historically specific impossibility is conceived of being ontologically impossible and there is practically nowhere to go to. If there is no time left, all politics becomes a politics of space: "all politics is about real estate," about grabbing, keeping, and administering territory. (Globalization is currently the most influential name of such real-estate politics.) Any countertendency ultimately turns out to be "politics of the instant" that does not last and conceptually abandons conceptions of permanent organization and sustainability—its paradigm is the slightly anarchic flash mob (and theoretically it is best captured by what Antonio Negri defined as "constituent power").[15] So one stays and is stuck, as one cannot imagine where to go or even that there is an elsewhere any longer. The fifth reason shows that Jameson's proposal is *impossible* in an *imaginary* sense. But how is it then at all possible to formulate an impossible proposal?

Cynicism as Anti-Utopianism

This is where the *sixth* aspect of the impossibility comes in, which is related to why *it is unclear* if Jameson's proposal is a utopia or a political program. Where does this *impossibility to discriminate* come from? If Jameson's proposal were a clear political program for realizing political transformation, it would necessarily be a

14 Fredric Jameson, *The Seeds of Time*, New York: Columbia University Press, 1994, 75f.

15 Antonio Negri, *Insurgencies: Constituent Power and the Modern State*, Minneapolis: University of Minnesota Press, 1999.

political program for revolution—and since this is not possible, it is not possible. This is a kind of *Petitio Principi*: a political program for radical change articulated in a time where such a program is unimaginable, because ontologically impossible, must therefore itself be impossible. Therefore, Jameson's proposal can only be utopian in the strictest sense of the term. Since the very functioning of utopia is to imagine what one cannot possibly imagine by means of its form, a form "which insists that its radical difference is the answer to the ideological conviction that no alternative is possible, that there is no alternative to the system."[16] But if this is the case, why is it then unclear, even to Jameson himself, if he proposes a utopia or a political program? Because the very rendering of present-day impossibilities makes even utopias seem impossible. Utopias were never "mere fictions," but always presented something as possible that broadened the historically specific constructions of ontological possibility and impossibility. Yet these very constructions today seem to prevent utopia-production ontologically.

Why? One can answer this by referring, *inter alia*, to today's "generalized cynicism . . . in which everyone is a Marxist and understands the dynamics and the depredations of capitalism without feeling it possible to do anything about it."[17] Utopias become unimaginable when one cannot imagine that there is anything left to imagine. In short, when knowledge—this is why one is here dealing with cynicism—obstructs the very functioning of the

16 Fredric Jameson, *Archaeologies of the Future: The Desire Called Utopia and Other Science Fictions*, London: Verso, 2005, 232.

17 Jameson, "An American Utopia." A similar claim—that everyone has become Marxist today—can already be found in the opening pages of Lenin's *State and Revolution*. I analyze this in greater detail in Frank Ruda, "Was ist ein Marxist? Lenins Wiederherstellung der Wahrheit des Namens," in *Namen. Benennung, Verehrung, Wirkung (1850–1930)*, ed. Tatjana Petzer, Sylvia Sasse, Franziska Thun-Hohenstein, and Sandro Zanetti, Berlin: Kadmos, 2009, 225–42.

imaginary.[18] For precisely the form in which knowledge is presented or, in short, the form of knowledge itself, can be the reason why this knowledge does not become effective. Generalized cynicism abolishes (the real kernel of) the imaginary by imaginarily presenting society as being absolutely transparent—as if all structures were naked.

Cynic subjectivity assumes that it is possible to clearly see how the capitalist "world" functions, and it is this very clarity, this very transparency, which obscures, darkens, and obfuscates one's vision. In cynicism, transparency functions as new means of obscuration and obfuscation; that is to say: the very nakedness of capitalist dynamics functions as its newest disguise, which ultimately paralyzes the imaginary in such a manner that even the production of utopia seems impossible.[19] The paralyzing effect thus does not only spring from being stuck with a politically ineffective distinction that survived its own time; it also derives from this peculiar feature of late capitalist subjectivity. Since the allegedly non-naïve attitude, the "enlightened false consciousness"—that is, the cynic—assumes that he clearly sees through the functioning of capitalism, yet what he ultimately assumes to see is that one cannot change how and that capitalism works.[20] Cynicism therefore is a product of the alleged complete transparency of the functioning of capitalist dynamics (everyone knows that there are self-seeking interests behind everything, etc.), because what one

---

18 Think of the omnipresence of the "scandal" in contemporary societies. It is everywhere—although its preferred domain remains, tellingly, the competitive domain of sports. On the function of the scandal, see Alain Badiou, *A la recherché du réel perdu*, Paris: Fayard, 2015.

19 This thesis was developed in Alenka Zupančič's magnificent reading of Jean Genet's *The Balcony*: "Power in the Closet (And Its Coming Out)," podcast recording, Backdoor Broadcasting, May 21, 2015, backdoorbroadcasting.net.

20 That "knows falsehood very well . . . but still . . . does not renounce it." Slavoj Žižek, *The Sublime Object of Ideology*, London: Verso, 2008, 26.

assumes to see if one sees through this dynamics is that there is nothing left to imagine, no alternative to what is, no form of radical change. Because what one sees if one sees through its dynamics is that late capitalism is far too complex to be changed or even properly comprehended. One therefore only comprehends that one cannot comprehend it, as not even trained finance experts can (and admit it). The cynic is therefore led to assert the precise opposite of what he wanted to assert, namely that he sees through everything but ultimately he sees nothing, nothing to see, everywhere. He comprehends everything, but this in the last instance amounts to comprehending that one cannot comprehend what one sees through. It is like a twist on Hegel's famous saying that evil lies in the gaze that perceives evil everywhere: nothing (to imagine) lies in the gaze that believes to see through everything. This is why when the imaginary is paralyzed, one in a certain sense has lost one's vision.

This is why the cynic's subjectivity sees that it does not see any option to imagine a change of the system, simply because it assumes that one cannot see the system as a system. This leads to the assumption that there is no such thing as a totality of capitalism any longer, no system—for systems are those entities in which there is an ordered structure of how things, processes, and the like are related and are therefore comprehensible. Yet, if one comprehends that there is nothing to comprehend, that there is no system, this ultimately leads to the paradoxical account that there is no capitalism any longer, just disparate local phenomena. Say one assumes that the social and political situation of Congo has nothing to do with the political agendas of Western states. If one assumes to see through the dynamics of capitalism, to see capitalism with its pants down, so to speak, and at the same time that there is no comprehensible system for this very dynamic, one believes to see through capitalism's dynamics but at the same time assumes that there is no capitalism, since this very term makes no sense—as the "ism" indicates—if it is not a term related to the idea of a systematic and hence comprehensible totality.[21]

That the absence of systematicity and also comprehensibility follows from the alleged transparency of the dynamics of capitalism is the reason for transparency being directly linked to the ideology of complexity—the world is so complex that it is not comprehensible. (This results in reducing one's own experience to the locality "bodily sensation and experience," as Jameson says, a fact already observed by the early Marx.)[22] This ideology is also the reason why the majority of the people "believe that the free market actually exists"—yet they are so free that, in full animist spirit, one assumes that they can be satisfied or dissatisfied with certain political decisions or things happening in the world. That markets are free does then also mean that they are so free that they make their own decisions and laws independent human agents and in a manner that does not obey any systematic logic.[23] One may also render this in utopian terms: for the cynic there is no need for utopia anymore, simply because what she assumes to see in the world is always already a

---

21 This is another way of rendering Jameson's claim that late capitalism is a system which makes the idea of totality—an effect reinforced by postmodernity and its theory in Jameson's diagnosis—and thereby itself unthinkable and unimaginable (as a globalized *system*). For one rendering of this, see Fredric Jameson, "Cognitive Mapping," in *Marxism and the Interpretation of Culture*, ed. C. Nelson and L. Grossberg, Urbana-Champaign: University of Illinois Press, 1990, 347–60.

22 A charming and polemical criticism of this ideology can be found in Alain Badiou, *Saint Paul: The Foundation of Universalism*, Stanford, CA: Stanford University Press, 2003, 9ff. For Marx, see Frank Ruda, "Who Thinks Reductively? Capitalism's Animals," *Crisis and Critique*, Vol. 3, Issue 2, forthcoming.

23 A good example for such a position within the field of theory is Elie Ayache, *The Blank Swan: The End of Probability*, Sussex: Wiley, 2010. See also my critique of Ayache in Frank Ruda, "The Speculative Family, or: Critique of the Critical Critique of Critique," in *Filozofski Vestnik*, Vol. XXXIII, No. 2, 2012, 53–76.

utopia. And who needs utopia if one is already living in one? The disappearance of the category of totality is therefore a—representational—part of the belief that there is nothing (left) to be changed. For if capitalism disappears in and by means of its own transparency one is left with nothing to change. The cynic subject, the type of subjectivity generated by late capitalism,[24] thus assumes to (literally) see through capitalism and what it ultimately sees is the unchangeable impossibility to change it.

What is the effect this has on the production of utopias—if for this reason political programs necessarily will not seem viable any longer? Either producing utopias becomes a naïve, empty, non-enlightened, and futile exercise, and this is even the best-case scenario, or worse, it proves to be dangerous, since today "it has become fashionable to detect the seeds of the totalitarian within the utopian itself and to transform the hoary folk wisdom of the adage "the perfect is the enemy of the good" into an anti-utopian political position for which the politics of radical change . . . must inevitably lead to violence, as 'human nature' is brutally pressed into an unnatural mold and forced to take on utopian and superhuman dimensions."[25] Why should producing utopias be dangerous? Simply because if one sees through the dynamics of capitalism one also sees that the unchangeable nature of human beings makes them into self-seeking egotists, always only out for their own interest, in short: one sees that great egalitarian ideas sound nice at first but are ultimately proto-totalitarian because the human is a capitalist animal.[26] This is one of the reasons why today there is a

24 One can see how the five aspects of impossibility are here linked back to the first one: namely there is a historically specific type of subjectivity relative to the concatenation of the dimensions of impossibility.

25 Jameson, "An American Utopia."

26 This is obviously naturalizing capitalism and anchoring it in human nature. This can already be found in Adam Smith, who contended that in difference to animals humans are exchanging animals. One has never seen any dog exchange two tiny bones for a large one, but humans do such things.

"diminution in the production of new utopias" and produces the widespread *doxa* that "not only . . . the new is impossible, but also . . . utopia is just as unimaginable, its images always reflecting a kind of anthropomorphic projection which we may now limit by recognizing them as projections of our own society and its parochial obsessions."[27]

Utopia production becomes as impossible as any emancipatory political program is today. Cynicism is anti-utopianism. This is because utopias are either futile or dangerous, or, and this is the worst-case scenario, because they are nothing but reflections of the very situation—be it historical or more generally the human capitalist condition—they pretend to escape. Late capitalism thereby determines how we dream of a world beyond and after capitalism: in short, how we relate to the future in a strong sense of the term.[28] From such a perspective, communism is the ultimate (potentially totalitarian, inhuman, and violent) capitalist fantasy that we need to abandon. Here we can see the first—negative—reason for why it is fundamentally unclear if we are reading a political program or a utopia: both are equally impossible and unimaginable. Reading Jameson's text therefore means to read what cannot but take the form of an impossible political program and an impossible utopia.

Hence, exchange is in our nature—this is precisely one way of how to understand that a historically specific claim is ontologized, namely via naturalization. See Adam Smith, *The Wealth of Nations*, New York: Bantam Bell, 2003, 22–26.

27 Fredric Jameson, *Archaeologies of the Future: The Desire Called Utopia and Other Science Fictions*, London: Verso, 2005, 128.

28 An instructive elaboration of some categories, concepts, and theoretical assumptions that were produced by capitalism, yet function as if they have determined human history forever, can be found in Slavoj Žižek, *Living in the End Times*, London: Verso, 2011, 181–243.

Preliminary Talk: First as (Impossible) Utopia, Then as (Possible) Political Program

In a situation in which political program as well as utopia seems impossible, Jameson situates his own position of enunciation precisely in this impossibility. It is an *impossible position of enunciation*. But what kind of impossibility is at work here—how to further determine the sixth aspect? To answer this question it is here instructive to recall a comment by Alain Badiou apropos the psychoanalytic definition of the cure:

> Lacan said that the object of the cure is "to raise impotence to impossibility." If we are suffering from a syndrome whose worst symptom is acknowledged impotence, then we can raise this impotence to impossibility. But what does this actually mean? A number of things. It means finding a real point to hold on to, whatever the cost. It means no longer being in the vague net of impotence, historical nostalgia and the depressive component, but rather finding, constructing and holding on to a real point, which we know we are going to hold on to, precisely because it is a point uninscribable in the law of the situation . . . declared by the prevailing opinion to be both . . . absolutely deplorable and completely impracticable, but which you yourselves declare that you are going to hold on to, whatever the cost.[29]

Fredric Jameson makes this very methodological and formal move. He raises this impotence, the impotence of seeing nothing but the impotence of the system. This generates an impossible vision. This is again not an external take on Jameson's method, applying the idea of psychoanalytic cure onto it. Rather, Jameson himself argues that he proposes "the radical therapy for dystopia, its radical treatment," by means of which

29 Alain Badiou, *The Meaning of Sarkozy*, London: Verso, 2008, 34f.

"we hammer away at anti-utopianism not with arguments, but with therapy"—a therapy in the very precise sense of the Lacanian cure mentioned, which Jameson also links to what he calls "cultural revolution."[30]

The therapy of the present impotence, whose symptom is the paralysis of the collective imaginary, is to formulate an impossible proposal that can only appear deplorable and impracticable. But obviously there is more to it. This very proposal unfolds by traversing the complex course of impossibilities (from one to five) that generate the contemporary impotence to imagine radical change. It thereby produces a point of impossibility—an impossibility of a wholly different nature than the impossibilities discussed before. How to find it? First, this course tackles the historical dimension of impossibility by countering a kind of historical forgetting, and by referring to another option for how to imagine the transition out of capitalism that exceeds the classical model of revolution and reform: the "less often acknowledged, let alone discussed," seemingly forgotten option of dual power. With this emphasis, Jameson creates, secondly, a new form of thinkability that tackles not only the epistemological aspect of impossibility, but also, thirdly, its ontological repercussions. It brings about a change in the currently dominant ontology and is thereby, fourthly, able to depict new forms of collective practice that have been foreclosed. This proposal thus, fifthly, works with—better, within—the imaginary of our epoch. But why isn't this just impossible in the previous senses of the term?

The answer to this can be seen in the fact that although Jameson's proposal can be neither a political program nor a utopia (and it is both, in the sense of an impossible program and an impossible utopia), he declares it to be the latter. Jameson proposes a utopia

30 Jameson, "An American Utopia." Jameson provides an instructive contextualization of this concept in *Valences of the Dialectic*, London: Verso, 2009, 267–78.

for the age of non-utopia. Thereby he counters the alleged impossibility of utopia production; this means that with the act of proposing it, utopia again becomes imaginable. But is this not again a *Petitio Principi*, just an inverted one? It may appear so, but Jameson's text rather follows the formal structure of an act that retroactively posits its own conditions of possibility. Jameson's proposal is impossible—not only in the negative sense of the first five aspects of impossibility, but because it actually does something impossible and thereby generates the thinkability, the actuality—*Wirklichkeit*—and concrete imaginability of an "impossible possibility."[31] How does this positively relate to the present situation? How is doing something impossible related to curing anti-utopianism? Here it is important to emphasize that the sixth aspect of impossibility relevant here should not be conceived such that Jameson's text embodies a grand heroic gesture, by doing the impossible. Rather its force, its wiz as well as its wit lies in the fact that in the utopian vision the "new world will look exactly like the old one, with but a few minor modifications." This is why doing the impossible by articulating an impossible proposal ultimately is not at all different from proposing just a few minor, even modest modifications. And it is in these minor modifications (and, of course, in the fundamental consequences they will produce) where the true point of impossibility lies to which the imaginary impotence is lifted and to which one can hold on, no matter what—simply because although this is precisely what may seem impossible, it is just a modest proposal.

In a beautiful poem with the title "Communism Is the Middle Term," Bertolt Brecht once made a similar point:

> To call for the overthrow of the existing order
> May seem a terrible thing
> But what exists is no order.

---

31 Alain Badiou, *Peut-on penser la politique?* Paris: Seuil, 1985, 101.

To seek refuge in violence
May seem evil.
But what is constantly at work is violence . . .
Communism is not an extreme outlier . . .
Communism is really the most minimal demand
What is nearest, reasonable, the middle term.[32]

Radical change is nothing that especially radical and violent, rather it is just the most reasonable and minimal demand.[33] One may thus say, and this derives precisely from the modest and reasonable nature of the proposal that what one is encountering here is something which is at the same time impossible, but also modest, even necessary—as it is the reasonable thing to do. It is necessary and impossible at the same time (and one should not forget that this is one possible definition of the Real).

By suggesting such a point (or points?) of impossibility and demonstrating its necessity, the previous impotence of the collective imaginary is overcome and the impossible becomes imaginable—and it can be imagined precisely because it only takes a few minor modifications to produce it. But—and this is crucial to further determine the sixth aspect of impossibility, which is linked to the undecidability between political program and utopia at work here—as soon as the utopian proposal becomes imaginable it immediately changes its character. We find an impossible point to cling to that is nonetheless modest and starts to imagine a minimal change that has radical consequences, and in this very moment the utopia loses its utopian

32 Bertolt Brecht, "Der Kommunismus ist das Mittlere," in *Die Gedichte*, Frankfurt am Main: Suhrkamp, 2000, 182, translated and cited in Alain Badiou, "Poetry and Communism," in *The Age of the Poets and Other Writings on Twentieth-Century Poetry and Prose*, ed. and trans. Bruno Bosteels, London: Verso, 2014.

33 Walter Benjamin wrote that Brecht, in line with this, once stated: "It is not communism that is radical, it is capitalism that is radical." Cf. Walter Benjamin, *Understanding Brecht*, London: Verso, 2003, 33.

quality. Why? Because as soon as we reach this point, the proposed utopia immanently turns out to be a political program after all.

We here encounter the proper reason for the undecidability, the impossibility of distinguishing between program and utopia: in a first move, the very act of proposing an impossible utopia posits its own conditions of possibility—creates a new possible imaginary—and as soon as this act is performed there is a second retroaction involved, that leads to the fact that after the act the utopia will always have been a political program. It is a redoubled retroaction that generates the indistinguishability of utopia and political program. We can see here why treating the imaginary paralysis and impotence produced through the bundle of impossibilities opens the imaginary to something real—it reintroduces something of the Real into the imaginary. Before its articulation, it can be neither, and through its very articulation it is somehow both, utopia as well as program. The sixth aspect of impossibility is thus not only linked to the fact that program and utopia both today seem impossible, but that as soon as we treat the very imaginary constitution of their impossibility, what seems to be an impossible utopia always will have been a real, possible political program. On a formal level, the methodology of Jameson's cure for contemporary anti-utopianism operates according to the following logic: first as (impossible) utopia, then as (possible) political program.

Beginning the Cure: The Method of Embracing What One Fears

We may here raise the question of how precisely to begin the therapy envisaged thus far. How do we make the first concrete steps that enable the cultural revolution Jameson envisages if we cannot rely on what Habermas would call the "constraint-free force of the better argument"?[34]

34 Jürgen Habermas, *The Theory of Communicative Action, Vol. 1: Reason and the Rationalization of Society*, Boston: Beacon Press, 1984, 28.

Jameson contends that it is similar to "the best treatment for neurotics," which "lies in indirection." This means "*utopians* must proceed like that: they have to concentrate not on visions of future happiness"—this would be the problematic idea of a too-progressivist "cure" that solves all contemporary problems in a perfect future society—"but rather on treatments of that stubborn resistance we tend to oppose to it." He goes on to state that "every utopia today must be a psychotherapy of anti-utopian fears and a drawing of them out into the light of day . . . they must be indulged, for nothing cures a sad passion as fully as its passionate embrace, its wholehearted endorsement." How does one embrace precisely those things that are feared, or the fears themselves?

To clarify this therapeutic maneuver, a well-known joke, often used by Slavoj Žižek, can help: A worker in Stalin's Russia is sentenced to some years in the gulag. Before he leaves, assuming that all of his letters will be censored, he proposes a plan of how to get messages through anyhow. His plan is to write everything that is true in blue, everything else in red ink. When his friends receive a first letter, it states how beautiful Siberia is, how nice all the people are, especially the guards, how he feels much more healthy after long days of hard physical exercise outside in the nicely cold fresh air. Everything is perfect; there is only one thing missing. There is no red ink.

This joke illustrates that the very language, the very medium in which we articulate what is wrong can be lacking. This is why good arguments in these situations do not help. The problem then does not simply consist in not having a program of how to deal with the situation at hand; it also consists in not being able to perceive problems as problems, for example that one's anti-utopian fears are part of the alleged impossibility of utopias.[35] Therefore, the therapy also has to find the right language to recognize where

35 To be more precise here: Utopianism always suggests solutions without problems, whereas its counterpart, political theory, articulates problems without solutions. It is easy to see which to choose.

and what the problems are. Jameson's proposal therefore entails an answer to the question of how to invent a language, a red ink, to express what cannot be articulated in the present situation, and how to perceive problems as what they are. But this means that the question to be answered is: How to articulate what seems impossible?

One can see in Jameson's proposal a method that is also present in the works of thinkers like Alain Badiou or Slavoj Žižek—directly embracing what one fears. This is a peculiar strategy: Both of them resurrect concepts and ideas that seemed to be lost (forever) to the politically wrong and reactionary side. Both of them often articulate their positions by recourse to concepts that seem impossible; that is to say, the language to articulate what seems impossible is, can be, or maybe even has to be itself an *impossible language*. Recall, for example, Badiou's perpetual defense of the concept of discipline for any emancipatory conception of political subjectivity today. Even though discipline sounds to the average social democratic or liberal ears of today like a concept that is of no use for present political frameworks, the very fear it generates is an index that there is more at stake. It necessarily seems to imply authoritarianism and unegalitarian hierarchy that cannot but appear conservative or reactionary and is therefore forbidden, impossible terrain for thinking reforms and revolutions, but also utopias that want to avoid the danger of totalitarianism and the like. Yet against the widespread cynical opinion, Badiou insistently points out that there is nothing inherently reactionary in the concept of discipline. It is rather true that by branding discipline as a reactionary concept, the very fact is obscured that "those who have nothing, have only their discipline."[36]

The assumption to be countered here is that without financial assets one cannot achieve anything today. Badiou opposes this *doxa*

---

36 Alain Badiou, "'We Need a Popular Discipline': Contemporary Politics and the Crisis of the Negative," *Critical Inquiry* 34(4), 2008, 645–59.

by emphasizing that those who have no material means are not necessarily lost and impotent, since it is not impossible for them to practically organize themselves. It is rather the idea of strict discipline that provides an answer of how to overcome this alleged practical impossibility: it changes something in the imaginary. The method here is thus to take up a concept for rethinking emancipation that seemed to be impossible for doing so, as it comes with the wrong (historical, epistemological, therefore ontological and hence practical as well as imaginary) coloring. Following the same logic, Badiou recently even took up again the concept of the master, of the political leader, which Žižek also advocates in a similar vein. Žižek has also applied this methodological strategy in many cases. One of them—instructive for the Jamesonian take on cultural revolution—consisted in intervening in a debate after Angela Merkel contended the necessity of a German *Leitkultur* (dominant culture) to solve problems of "social integration of immigrants." Žižek proposed to not renounce the concept of a *Leitkultur*, although it cannot but sound reactionary to the core, but to affirm the need for a left *Leitkultur*—as the concept as such entails the dominance of a certain cultural formation and education.

In more general terms, this method of embracing what one allegedly cannot but fear is systematically linked to the very foundation of psychoanalysis—and it is thus no surprise that it comes to be an important means in Jameson's own rendering of anti-utopian therapy. Since Freud did not simply discover the unconscious, psychoanalysis as such should be understood as an invention of a new "red ink" (and hence as a "technique" truly understanding the nature of the problem at hand). Freud does provide a paradigm of this very methodological gesture, for example when he attacks the "illusion of there being such a thing as psychical freedom" and opts for complete psychical determinism.[37]

---

37 Sigmund Freud, *Introductory Lectures on Psycho-Analysis*, New York: W.W. Norton & Company, 1966, 59.

The choice between freedom and determinism—in whose regard Freud opts for the less sexy side—mirrors the logic of the famous ultimatum "Your money or your life!" In this situation, we have to choose giving away our money, as otherwise we would lose both our money and our lives. In this sense, the choice between freedom and determinism is overdetermined by one of the two sides of the choice. Speaking about a choice that is predetermined may seem intuitively wrong. However, we cannot but opt for what seems wrong, namely the determinism that occurs in the determined character of the choice itself. This situation can, of course, provoke resistance. We fear determinism, as it seems to abolish freedom, yet this fear needs to be confronted and embraced.

Freud's point is that opting for what seems to be the wrong side enables something true to emerge. In the choice between freedom and determinism, freedom ultimately implies a direct attack on rationalism, since it basically leads to the idea that some things just happen for no reason at all (recall: this is how the free markets work today) and that no rational account of them can be given. Freud avoids giving up rationalism. This implies choosing determinism, which comes with the rationalist claim that there is nothing in the human psyche which is not determined, that is, unexplainable, irrational, or irrelevant per se. There is thus nothing ephemeral in the human psyche any longer—everything is equally valid and deserves the same attention. This equality derives from opting for what seems very counterintuitive at first sight. With this peculiar reversal, we can see that allegedly ephemeral phenomena even lead more directly into the core of human subjectivity. Thereby Freud inverts not only the hierarchy between what is accidental and what is essential, but the relation between what is considered to exist (possibly) and what is impossible. This inversion is the invention of a new red ink. Inventing a new ink means to speak in an impossible language words that articulate an impossible proposal. Yet it is only from opting for something seemingly impossible that something true can emerge—and this is a rationalist position at the same time.

One can clearly see this method at work in Jameson's text: in his—nearly Badiouian—defense of discipline that privileges Trotsky's idea of disciplined army organization against "the democratic platitudes of Kautsky and the social democrats," in his rehabilitation of the idea of nationalization, in his defense of bureaucracy, in his positive revivification of the concept of cultural revolution, and most obviously in what makes the core of his proposal: his defense of the army (as national, auto-bureaucratic, culturally revolutionary tool). But this method is also at work in an inverted form in denouncing precisely those concepts, ideas, and even branches of thought that seem to be forever inscribed into any conception of political or social change and for which it seems impossible to abandon them. This is at stake in his plea for the withering away of political theory altogether (for its object is ultimately the state), in his demand to give up the idea of government as such, and in his attack on any notion of efficiency or progress. So what one encounters here is the concrete language of an impossible proposal, the very *impossible materiality of an impossible proposal*. It is made from resurrected impossible concepts and purified from all-too-possible ideas and conceptions. One could even say that the very language in which an impossible proposal is articulated is neither a possible language nor simply its negation. It is rather an un-language—it is written un-words, un-categories that enable us to formulate and bring about an impossibility that is at the same time necessary.

What are the first words, then? They emerge from a foreclosure generated by the practical inefficiency of the distinction of revolution and reform and the efficiency of cynicism. They are forgotten words that are not simply recalled by Jameson, but rather endowed with a certain force through the repetition of what was at stake with them—and one should recall that there are always things one cannot remember but can only access via repetition. These words are dual power. They neither indicate change in the classical revolutionary manner—it is not a Big Bang theory of political transformation that assumes there can be an ultimate cure—nor do they entail reformist internal modifications of the system—it is not a theory of endless approximation of a better state of things, nor a theory of constant progress. So neither no change nor absolute cure nor progress. Rather, they indicate another kind of theory of transition, a theory that is itself transitory (this is why it is first a utopia and then a political program). *A third kind of transition*—to play this pun on Spinoza's terminology—out of capitalism, produced by the method of embracing what one seeks to flee.

Where the Impossible Lies, There Also Grows That Which Makes Us Laugh: Comic Utopianism

Anyone who has read Jameson's piece knows that the third kind of transition out of capitalism, which goes under the formal name of dual power, is the universalized army, brought about by general national conscription, including both sexes and anyone from ages sixteen to sixty. The introduction of this generalized institution—a word which will receive a radically new meaning—generates a "new social structure" as it will not only be able to generate gatherings of "unmanageable crowds," but also produce the necessity of collective self-organization that would effectively make the state and any kind of government useless by universalizing bureaucracy in such a manner that anyone becomes his or her own bureaucrat.[38]

38 Jameson here makes a point in which Hegel's infamous idea of quantity turning into quality resonates—the universal army will (quantitatively) include so many people that it will qualitatively change the concept of the army such that it will become unmanageable. As admirable as this point is, I am not entirely sure why the immense quantity of people included in the universal army necessarily makes this army unmanageable—this is an important point, because from this Jameson also derives that this army will be unable to wage foreign wars or coups. This also has to do with the question of whether there could still be room for something like a political leader—a kind of Hegelian monarch, maybe?

This is, then, "a new kind of non-state." The universal army would thereby be able to deal with many, if not all contemporary problems—actually, it would provide solutions to problems that are not even perceived as problems, including that of the health care system. It would provide general public education, a universal food supply, universal housing, and universal employment and would even leave everyone with sufficient time to create cultural products, do nothing, or spend time with idiotic things. This would produce—and this is one cultural revolutionary aspect of it—new habits of living, being, and acting together; in short, it would produce a new and universal disciplined second nature. This utopian proposal does therefore not—as political theory in its history almost always did—entail the idea of a new constitution; rather, one can read in it the attempt to "rethink revolution" and to take the concept of the collective seriously. This utopia proposes a model of collective action and organization that includes an entirely new articulation of how to think of sociality. It provides a vision of a new collective fetish, which is what for Jameson provides the very cohesion of what is often called the social bond. This collective fetish, through the mediating organizational structure of the army, through the "forced association" and "experience of social promiscuity" it implies, is the collective itself: "the team as social being."[39]

This vision of a new and "different motivational system" will, through the functioning of the collective fetish, generate a new consciousness of unity, because it allows for a "collective transformation of mentalities"—and this is why there is a positive element of nationalism involved, which will even precipitate on the language used by the collective. Yet, this new sense of unity and (why not?) solidarity will not simply be unifying and level down all particularity

39 Jameson, "An American Utopia." I think that it would be interesting to attempt to imagine a nonfetishistic kind of collective political action and organization that somehow still compulsively circles around "some thing," but does not "objectify" it. But I leave this debate for another time and place.

and singularity of its members. It will certainly break the fetish of singularity so determining in late capitalism, but it will effectively function—as all society does for Jameson, only a little bit different—as a "collection of neurotics of various kinds." In the universal army we will still all be freaks, so to speak, but freaks who are forced to live together—in the very spatial sense of this expression. Here one can see how the therapy of anti-utopianism—embracing one's fears—truly structures Jameson's whole proposal, since it is precisely through the forced association of the universal army that one is also forced to embrace what Jameson sees as one of the most constitutive fears inscribed into human nature: a concept he revivifies as "strategic essentialism," "the primordial fear of the Other." In this sense, antagonisms will still result from this fear, yet these antagonisms will be independent from any class structure whatsoever.

One could assume that precisely because of this primordial fear, this proposal, if one starts imagining it, cannot but arouse a "true horror of" this military "democracy," a "terror of the collective"—in short: precisely the fear that one needs to embrace. Yet, when Jameson presented his proposal for revolutionizing society at the Graduate Center at the City University of New York, it did not cause panic or terror but laughter. Not the kind of laughter that does not take a proposal seriously and ridicules it, but rather authentic laughter. How to explain this? I want to end by arguing that this is not a displaced or false reaction to Jameson's proposal, but fully adequate, as it can be—and maybe should be—read as what I want to call a *comic utopia* (and maybe this is the first one written, maybe in a new, comic red ink). Why should this proposal be comic? For at least three reasons. The first one has to do with its origin. Jameson writes:

> It is a thought that must have first come to me many years ago, inspired by an image by one of our greatest political cartoonists . . . Ike, presumably in full military regalia, perches informally on the edge of the desk in the Oval Office and observes conversationally,

> "Well, if they want socialized medicine, they have only to join the army as I did."[40]

The origin of the utopian vision is a joke, presented in a cartoon—and if this is the case, how could not the whole vision also be of a comic nature?[41] One can add to this trivial reason a trivial second one: that some implications of Jameson's proposal are just hilarious. Recall the idea to place all pacifists in control of arms development and arms storage; the charming idea of the Psychoanalytic Placement Bureau, which will be in charge of organizing all employment as well as personal and collective therapies; and maybe even the idea (which provoked a lot of laughter when presented) that the state will wither away into some enormous group therapy where we will all constantly confront our own fear toward the others and our symptoms resulting from it—a constant therapy that is constant because we can simply not escape it.

But the most fundamental reason for the comic nature of this utopia lies, to my mind, in the very way it does something impossible. This point can be clarified by recourse to a joke with which Zupančič closes her book on comedy:

> Mujo is describing to Haso his adventures in the Sahara.—I'm walking through the desert. Nothing but sand around me, not a living soul, absolutely nothing . . . Suddenly a lion appears in front of me. What to

40 Jameson, "An American Utopia." One should here recall that Jameson already once proposed another kind of utopia with regard to a possible refunctioning of Walmart, which is comic in its own terms. See Jameson, *Valences of the Dialectic*, London: Verso, 2010, 410–34. Maybe one should read these two comic utopias together and propose the following formula: Universal militarization + refunctioned Walmart = communism?

41 I cannot discuss the difference between jokes and comedy here, but anyone working on comedy cannot but refer to one book that admirably elaborates this distinction: Alenka Zupančič, *The Odd One In: On Comedy*, Cambridge: MIT, 2008.

> do, where to hide?—I climb a tree . . . —Wait a minute, Mujo, you've just told me that there was nothing around but sand, so where did the tree come from?—My dear Haso, you don't ask such questions when a lion appears! You run away and climb the first tree.[42]

Zupančič reads this not as a joke neglecting human reality as such, but rather as "full recognition of the Real of human desire" that is able "to suddenly make a tree emerge in the middle of the desert."[43] Doesn't the anti-utopian therapy of Jameson's impossible proposal function precisely like this? Doesn't one here witness the emergence of a new universal egalitarian society in the middle of the political desert? Jameson's therapeutic method takes again into account the Real of human desire—and maybe this is what utopia here ultimately designates—and reinscribes it into the collective imaginary, whereby one actually comes to believe that it does not take much and it is possible to imagine and do the impossible. This method is similar to what Mujo does in the desert, or, to use another image, to Baron Münchhausen pulling himself out of a mire by his own hair—which, maybe not accidentally, Jameson once in passing compared to what Hegel calls *Aufhebung*.[44] To sublate the current paralysis of the collective imaginary, *comic utopianism*, the Jameson kind, may actually be the best working therapy. Its aim is to enable us to do, think, and imagine the impossible. Its slogan may be: Where the impossible lies, there also grows that which makes you laugh away your fear of change.

---

42 Zupančič, *The Odd One In*, 218.

43 Ibid.

44 Jameson, *Valences of the Dialectic*, 153.

8

After October, Before February: Figures of Dual Power

Alberto Toscano

> From now on your first imperative should be: "Imagine!" And your second, immediately connected to the first: "Fight against those who cultivate the weakening of this faculty."
>
> —Günther Anders, *The Molussian Catacomb*

1.

Reformism is our utopia.[1] That's a reasonable conclusion to draw from the discourse accompanying the recent recomposition and electoral surge of the Southern European left. Politicians who came of age in the neoliberal nineties, and whose image of

---

1 This essay incorporates, in revised form, passages from two previous attempts at tackling this issue: "Dual Power Revisited," originally published in the now-discontinued journal *Soft Targets*, and "Tragédie et transition," published in the online journal *Période*. Thanks to Sebastian Budgen for bibliographic suggestions.

antagonism was durably shaped by the so-called anti-globalization movement, now address their ideological constituencies with a simple, sober message: what constituted the policy common sense of the postwar European compact between state, capital, and labor across the social-democratic and Christian-Democrat divide—namely a welfare state driven by a regulative ideal of expansive social citizenship—is now both the "point of the impossible" (to use Badiou's formulation) of the European order, and the only basis on which to build a national popular consensus against austerity, not so much beyond but *before* left and right.[2]

In "An American Utopia," Jameson, consistent with his conviction that one must struggle indefatigably for social democracy to learn the lessons of its bankruptcy,[3] inscribes this moment of opposition not as a component of a transitional program for the present, but as a "discursive struggle" that can be waged in the representational sphere by a retooled party-political cadre—but is ultimately discontinuous with the business of materially challenging capitalist power. This predicament is a product not only of what Jameson frames as the twin implosion of the revolutionary and reformist paths, of Leninist wars of maneuver and social-democratic wars of position—which is to say, of the strategic horizons of all the Internationals of the socialist and communist movements—but of the very collapse of Gorz's framing distinction between reformist reforms and nonreformist reforms: all reformism, understood as a durable if gradual transformation of the status quo in the direction of greater equality and freedom, is stamped by neoliberalism with the mark of impossibility. The depressing pantomime of Eurogroup meetings with Greece's Syriza-led government has certainly

---

2 See Pablo Iglesias, *Politics in a Time of Crisis: Podemos and the Future of Democracy in Europe*, trans. Lorna Scott Fox, London; Verso, 2015.

3 Fredric Jameson, "Lenin and Revisionism," in *Lenin Reloaded*, ed. Sebastian Budgen, Stathis Kouvelakis, and Slavoj Žižek, Durham, NC: Duke University Press, 2007, 69.

testified to this.[4] In any instance, the fact that contemporary radicalism must articulate its mass appeal by confrontationally refunctioning the non-utopian features of reformism as the basis for a rupture with the status quo is instructive. It appears to corroborate Jameson's diagnosis of the imaginative and ideological closure of the present—a closure that, as we can currently witness, is violently reproduced, not a mere emanation of capital's religion of everyday life—even as it instantiates the very discursive struggle toward which he gestures.

2.

Though a diffuse if ineffective "anticapitalism" has been absorbed as a kind of common sense in what remains of the left and beyond (including in regressive or reactionary formations), the orientation toward reformism as a kind of *katechon* or emergency brake against neoliberal devastation is another signal that the question of *transition* remains opaque or unthinkable from within contemporary critical thought.[5] To talk of transition in these times—which may be times of riots, but are also times of stasis, reaction, and counterrevolutions-without-revolutions—may appear in bad taste, as when, to use the old situationist turn of phrase, one speaks with corpses in one's mouth. Not only does such a discussion seem out of place and out of time, considering the global balance of forces, but all the major variants of what we could call a "communist orientation" in political thought seem premised on the rejection of transition. This rejection concerns all the components of this concept: The *time* of transition, understood in terms of the linearity of stages. The *space*

4 I won't address here whether a strategic delinking from the euro could serve as a horizon of nonreformist reforms in view of a transitional project, as recently argued by Costas Lapavitsas. See S. Budgen and C. Lapavitsas, "Greece: Phase Two," *Jacobin*, March 12, 2015.

5 On reformism as *katechon*, see my "Reforming the Unreformable," in *What Are We Struggling For? A Radical Collective Manifesto*, London: Pluto, 2012.

of transition, whether a commune, state, enclave, or zone. The *political form* and *subjectivity* of transition, embodied by the party and related institutions.

Accompanying these negations, these assertions of obsolescence, is a more encompassing rejection of the "progressive" philosophy of history underlying the classical image of transition, with its analogies between the institution and the destitution of capitalism and between bourgeois and proletarian revolutions. A repudiation of the transitional imaginaries of the Internationals is present in so-called communization theory, in which the limits to capital and the termination of the notion that revolution could grow out of workers' identity and their place within the productive process ("programmatism") lead to the conclusion that only immediate communist measures could carry a revolutionary process.[6] But it is also present in talk of the commons, where it is the defense or production of nonpropertied spaces and practices of cooperation that will serve as the lived basis for emancipation, not a project of systematically disarticulating state and capital through a unified political strategy. The various species of anarchist prefigurationist activism also repudiate the very problem of transition, which appears to them as indelibly tainted with the history of state socialisms. Painting with a very broad brush, we could suggest that not only do such contemporary antagonistic perspectives reject the whole vocabulary of transition—for reasons that may be ethical, strategic, or analytical, having to do with a diagnosis of our capitalist present and its affordances—they also largely steer clear of utopian programs, preferring a negative utopian impulse or, at times, concrete utopias which join the desire for insurrection with the emergence of "communes," growing out of the collective

6 I have discussed communization in "Now and Never," in *Communization and Its Discontents*, ed. Benjamin Noys, New York: Autonomedia, 2011, and the problem of transition in "Transition Deprogrammed," *South Atlantic Quarterly* 113.4, 2014.

practice of groups without requiring—so the story goes—the prior drawing up of plans, programs, or blueprints. As negative utopias, it is often unclear whether they should be classified as utopias of *no* power, as Jameson suggests has increasingly been the case post-1968, or as utopias of *new* power.[7] To put it in other terms, whether they are anti-programmatic anti-utopias or hyperutopias of revolutionary creativity—where what is utopian is precisely the notion that the crumbling of social reproduction will give way to endemic communist cooperation, in a massively generalized "learning by doing." But for a true utopian position, the path is not entirely made by walking, to paraphrase the famous poem by Machado.

3.

It would be relatively easy, though possibly futile, to plunge into the messy archive of actual revolutions to show how the heroic stereotype of transition was openly declared by its supposed partisans to bear only a very tenuous relationship to actual revolutionary practice. It is all the more ironic that in some micro-habitats of the far left people still polish their Lenin fetishes, ignoring how Bolshevik political practice broke, at different times, with almost all the ingredients of a linear logic of transition—skipping supposedly necessary stages, acknowledging the sociological disappearance of the very working class it was meant to represent, tactically re-establishing dimensions of capitalism after its accelerated

7 I would dissent here from Jameson's association of political phobias about power with the work of Michel Foucault. Though, from the vantage points of a declining New Left, the carceral panorama of *Discipline and Punish* may have heralded a suffocating vision of power, rekindling the anarchist flame in the process, the veritable industry that has emerged around Foucault's lectures on neoliberalism, with its focus on power as a "conduct of conduct" that presupposes subjective freedom, has functioned to disperse opposition to systemic power, often alongside the capacity to even name it.

demise in war communism, and so on. Crucially, the symbolic force of linear transition was the counterpart of the conditions of unevenness and non-contemporaneity that marked all twentieth-century revolutionary experiences. Though it may have appeared as its stubborn shadow, we could say that twentieth-century revolutionary modernity was overdetermined by the persistence of non-capitalist modes of production, and of a non-capitalist peasantry. Those revolutions were all revolutions "against *Capital*," in the young Gramsci's sense. That is the truth-kernel behind the cynical statements that revolutions were but ruses of capitalist modernization—that communism, as the Eastern European joke went, was simply the longest path between capitalism and capitalism—with contemporary China as the most massive confirmation of that punch line. Conversely, what for some appears as the basis of a true revolution, the real subsumption of life by capital, the termination of all outsides and lags, has in many respects revealed itself as revolution's medusa. In Henri Lefebvre's formulation, from *The Production of Space*: "the space that contains the realized preconditions of another life is the same one as prohibits what those preconditions make possible." So it seems that transition was on the agenda when conditions were immature, and it is off the agenda in situations where capital has saturated our lifeworlds, terminating other modes of production. Beyond reflecting on this irony—which is hardly a recent discovery anyhow—are there reasons to retain the idea of transition?

4.

At the crux of Jameson's essay is the conviction, which I think is unimpeachable, that to unblock the atrophied strategic imaginary of the left a new conception of transition is necessary. It is striking nevertheless that transition is so closely associated here with the problem of *positive* utopia (and not just of the negative utopian impulse toward another future). After all, with relation to the Marxist tradition, it could even be argued that the problem of transition—as formulated in the "Critique of the Gotha Programme," *State and Revolution*, and numerous other tracts and programs—was profoundly anti-utopian in intention, delineating the strategic outlines of how the power of state and capital could be disarticulated while sidelining frameworks that would see revolution as a matter of implementing a utopian schema. (Here we would really need to reflect on how the partial Bolshevik achievement of transition led to an absolute explosion of concrete and speculative utopias, from projects of deurbanization to orchestras without conductors.[8]) This is even more the case for what Jameson presents here as the "third" transition (after revolutionary war of maneuver and reformist war of position), *dual power*. In Lenin's formulation the latter appears as an extreme anomaly or aberration, a true Russian exception that expresses the extremely unique conditions in which the deficiency of the bourgeois revolution and the premature irruption of the proletarian one overlap. There is a kind of dialectical perversity in Jameson's choice of dual power as the instrument through which to refunction both transition and utopia for a seemingly closed present. To gauge its effects, a detour through some figures of dual power is required.

5.

In 1917, during the tumultuous interregnum between the collapse of tsarism and the October revolution, Lenin stresses the unprecedented emergence of a wild anomaly in the panorama of political

---

8 See Richard Stites's wonderful *Revolutionary Dreams: Utopian Vision and Experimental Life in the Russian Revolution*, Oxford: Oxford University Press, 1991.

forms: dual power. As he remarks in *Pravda*, "alongside the Provisional Government, the government of the bourgeoisie, another government has arisen, so far weak and incipient, but undoubtedly a government that actually exists and is growing—the Soviets of Workers' and Soldiers' Deputies."[9] The often sterile disputations over the evils and virtues of the seizure of state power tend to obscure the far greater challenge posed by thinking revolutionary politics in terms of the sundering of power—not just in the guise of a face-off between two (or more) social forces in a situation of non-monopoly over violence and political authority, but in the sense of a fundamental *asymmetry* in the types of power. The power wielded by the soviets is incommensurable with that of its bourgeois counterpart, however "democratic" it may be, because its source lies in popular initiative and not parliamentary decree, because it is enforced by an armed people and not a standing army, and because it has transmuted political authority from a plaything of the bureaucracy to a situation where all officials are at the mercy of the popular will and its power of recall. The model for this power of a new type is the Paris Commune. It is the incipient, *larval* form of "a state of the type of the Paris Commune" that, in the spring and summer of 1917, coexists with the parliamentary type of state, the "dictatorship of the bourgeoisie." In the tradition that draws from Lenin's texts—yet another case in Marxism where ephemeral and exceptional categories are, for better and for worse, turned into transhistorical or at least transsituational ones—this notion of dual power as the consolidation of embryonic institutions of the "non-state state" of the proletariat is critical. Gramsci himself will speak of a state *in potentia*. From the juridical standpoint, dual power as an embryo of workers' power is also a site of legitimacy without legality, and thus the incubator or political condenser of a new legality, which is also to say new relations of

9 V. I. Lenin, "The Dual Power," April 9, 1917.

power based on the *direct* initiative of the masses.[10] But for such a preparation of new power to take place, the notion of dual power demands a deep form of pre-existent collective identity—no doubt one politically mediated and consciously intensified by these institutions, but nevertheless one that sinks its roots in class belonging. (We will return to this question of the social *basis* of dual power below.)

6.

To return to the context of interregnum, the soviets, which were not yet under Bolshevik hegemony, live in the constant menace, exacerbated by the partisans of reform, of a neutralizing absorption into a state power that in principle suffers no duality (in this sense, Lenin and Trotsky are "Weberian," and the great German sociologist will indeed return the favor by quoting Trotsky himself to back up his famous formulations on the monopoly of violence). In such a conjuncture, the only strategy is to strengthen the new type of power, "clarifying proletarian minds . . . emancipating them from the influence of the bourgeoisie," since "as long as no violence is used against the people there is no other road to [state] power." The problem of constituting a potent communist bloc and consolidating the new type of power into a force that can truly sap the dictatorship of the bourgeoisie is thus a problem of autonomy and separation, of the disciplined, painstaking constitution of a proletarian political capacity (another key sense of power) that takes its distance from the apparatus of the state precisely in order to prepare its "smashing." This process of constitution is marked by an inexorable temporal determination. The "interlocking" of

10 Riccardo Guastini, "Materiali per una teoria del doppio potere," in *I due poteri: Stato borghese e stato operaio nell'analisi marxista*, Bologna: Il mulino, 1978.

two dictatorships gives rise to an exceedingly volatile amalgam, whence the axiom: "Two powers cannot exist in a state."[11] Dual power is thus both an opportunity and a menace, the terrain where autonomy and initiative can be quashed or squandered. This is the sense in which, in June 1917, Lenin, facing a capitalist offensive in the domain of production itself, declares: "The root of the evil is in the dual power."[12] And the culprits of this crisis, the harbingers of the "evil," are precisely those subjects who seek to serve as hinges between the two powers, the "Narodniks and Mensheviks" who lead the soviets (the power of the majority) in the interests of the bourgeoisie (the dictatorship of the minority). In any case, "this dual power cannot last long." This merely transitory *kairos* that dual power represents, founded on the lethal contest between the two dictatorships—the two types of power—means that Lenin cannot accept the "fetishism" of the soviet as an organ of self-government (which might even be compatible with certain bourgeois parliamentary forms) but will seek, through the fundamental instance of the party, in Antonio Negri's gloss, to "fix in the Soviets the immediate expression and political form of class insubordination to the general experience of exploitation" and to maintain the dyad "autonomy-organization."[13] Without class autonomy there is no organization and without organization, class autonomy—independent proletarian political capacity—dissipates. In this context, dual power, as Negri notes—and contrary to the Menshevik vision of incorporating the soviets within the state as a "regional" instance of workers' self-government and self-management—is "not an institutionalizable juridical relationship" (we will return to the seeming paradox of an institutionalization of

11 V. I. Lenin, "The Tasks of the Proletariat in Our Revolution [Draft Platform for the Proletarian Party]," September 1917.

12 V. I. Lenin, "Has Dual Power Disappeared?"

13 Antonio Negri, *Factory of Strategy: 33 Lessons on Lenin*, trans. Arianna Bove, New York: Columbia University Press, 2014, 123–4.

civil war, or *stasis*). For Negri, the ambiguity of dual power "must be confronted and resolved from the workers' perspective: first of all, its intensification must be advocated, then the proletarian moment of antithesis must be exalted until the foundation of the dictatorship of the proletariat in its Soviet form."

7.

While Jameson enlists dual power in the critique of political theory, of the political as a theoretical and practical chimera, it could be argued that in Lenin's work, precisely as an anomaly, aberration, or exception—albeit one that demands to be seized upon strategically—dual power marks out the space for a specifically Marxist political thought. This is not a thought of transhistorical normativity or of the state and its antinomies, but a thought of the necessary invention, in situations of crisis, of political forms oriented toward the abolition of capital. In his *Dual Power in Latin America*, the Bolivian theorist René Zavaleta Mercado, writing through the unraveling of the incomplete experiences of dual power in Bolivia and Chile in the early seventies, signaled this singularity of the notion of dual power while attending to the conceptual and political history of the notion in Russia and the Southern Cone by referring to it as "a Marxist metaphor that designates a special type of state contradiction or a state conjuncture of transition."[14] I take this to suggest that *unlike the concepts of classical political theory*, dual power, as a term trying to approximate the uniqueness of a social and state crisis, does not clearly subsume its cases. In stressing (and indeed, perhaps overstressing) the difference between Lenin and Trotsky on this matter, Zavaleta Mercado argues that while, in Lenin, the phenomenon of dual power *between* February

14 René Zavaleta Mercado, *El poder dual en América Latina: Estudio de los casos de Bolivia y Chile*, México: Siglo XXI, 1974, 18.

and October is an extremely singular exception to antecedent theories of revolution, an overdetermined *fact* that demands the invention of an organization and strategic response, for Trotsky's later systematization of the notion of dual power in his history of the Russian Revolution, dual power is a *regularity*, a *social law* of revolution that can find its instances in conjunctures as different as the opposition of parliament and king in prerevolutionary England or of the Constituent Assembly and the monarchy in prerevolutionary France. Notwithstanding the brilliance of Trotsky's play of historical analogies, for Zavaleta Mercado, turning dual power into a social law ultimately dissolves the singularity of Lenin's proposal, which is to name as dual power a phase of *qualitative contemporaneity and antagonistic development* of two asymmetrical, incommensurable powers, and even more precisely, of *two revolutions*, a congenitally malformed bourgeois one and a larval but powerful proletarian one. There is a qualitative asymmetry of powers as well as a quantitative conflict. Of this *political* unevenness there isn't really any "law," but only, I would suggest, *figures*. It is one of the extreme weaknesses of "Leninism" as a *forma mentis* and fetish that it has tried to turn the extremely exceptional circumstances of 1917, and the Bolsheviks' forced choices, into a cookbook for revolutions and insurrections to come. In this respect, dual power—like, in a different vein, transition itself—is a *problem* (or a metaphor, in Zavaleta Mercado's sense), not a concept or a theory.

8.

As Negri presents it in his *Factory of Strategy*, Lenin's is a constant struggle against the "constitutional mummification" of dual power, the transmutation of the soviets into organs of democratic representation and not of class dictatorship, inserted into the international process of revolution. Communists must always reject this transformation; the movement must continue, it must surpass itself. Indeed, some of Negri's most interesting pages in his lessons on Lenin bear on the manner in which capital, in its high reformist moments (e.g., the New Deal), inoculated itself with the soviet form; how it institutionalized the apparatus of self-government in the guise of workers' self-management and their collaborative insertion into the mechanisms and the ideology of industrial work. Against this recuperative dialectic, the autonomist imperative is that of an institutionalization of antagonism, the creation of "class institutions, for the class, in the class," the

> institutionalizations inside capital of what capitalism can only institutionalize for the purposes of domination, the consolidation of struggle for the purposes of power, and the irreversibility of struggles from the standpoint of struggle itself, of the process of destruction of the existing.[15]

Negri's wager, then, is that the task of repeating Lenin must pass through a reckoning with the transformation in class composition (that is, both in the subjective capacity of the class and its insertion into the dynamics of capitalist development) as well as in the very meaning of power. Dual power retains its pertinence, but it is no longer thought exclusively in terms of the state as separate apex and possessor of power but in view of a "tendential identification of capital and the State (a total fusion of organization and command)." Under these conditions of real subsumption, there is a plenitude of power, a fullness of capitalist power and a fullness of workers' power: the capitalist unification of society and its totalizing organization reproduce over the entirety of the social fabric the full potency of class antagonism, which is essential to the definition of capital. (It is obvious that in Jameson's reflections on the present, this fullness is rather

15 Negri, *Factory of Strategy*, 142.

unilateral instead, and understandably so.) But if the overall concept of power under conditions of the real subsumption of society under capital cannot be identified with the seizure of state power per se, then, following Negri's argument, we could say that there emerges yet another "new type" of (proletarian) power. Lenin's vision of dual power as a critical and explosive but still transitory stage depended on a certain conception of power that Negri calls a "non-dialectical absolute," not so distant from the bourgeois theories of power *qua* monopoly exemplified by Weber and presaged in classic doctrines of sovereign *raison d'état*. On the contrary, the workers' struggles of the '60s and '70s, according to Negri (who does not flinch, in these pages, from invoking Mao as a distant witness), determine a new experience and a new concept of power, understood as a "dialectical absolute" allowing "dual power to spread over a long period, as a struggle that upsets the capital relation by introducing into it the worker variable as the conscious will of destruction." This newer type of proletarian power is paradoxically qualified as a form of *extremist gradualism*, a "gradualness of power and its management which is the gradualness of the destruction of capitalist power, of the capital relation." Whence the thesis that underlies the new sovietism which Negri, at the time immersed in the experience of Potere Operaio, proclaims to be "the transformation of the concept of insurrection into that of permanent civil war." Without entering into the virtues of such a provocative proposal, or indeed how it might relate to a strategic (mis) calculation of class forces and class composition, it is worth remarking that the vision of this permanent civil war, and of its new type of prolonged, gradual/destructive dual power, led to an attempt to appropriate and defend physical areas of autonomy and "self-valorization"—"red bases" or liberated zones. The presence of these Maoist concepts points to a key aspect of the autonomist theorization of dual power under conditions of real subsumption, namely its fusion of two models and practices of dual power: first, the intensive and metropolitan "general strike scenario" (the model of urban insurrection present in the Paris Commune, the Petrograd Soviet, or the uprisings in Hamburg, Canton, and Barcelona), which might lead us to interrogate Jameson's distinction between dual power and uprising; second, the extensive and territorial prolonged "popular war scenario," for which the Chinese revolution serves as a paragon, and which might lead us to qualify Jameson's separation of dual power from the figure of the *enclave*.[16] On the basis of the conviction of the full (and irreversible?) power of the metropolitan proletariat in its new class composition, the long duration of the people's war is injected into the fabric of the city.

9.

In his more recent work with Michael Hardt, Negri has given a biopolitical twist to these earlier reflections on dual power. Writing of the legacy of guerrilla warfare, he notes that as it

> increasingly adopted the characteristics of biopolitical production and spread throughout the entire fabric of society, it more directly posed as its goal the production of subjectivity—economic and cultural subjectivity, both material and immaterial. It was not just a matter of "winning hearts and minds," in other words, but rather of creating new hearts and minds through the construction of new circuits of communication, new forms of social collaboration, and new modes of interaction. In this process we can discern a tendency

16 See Daniel Bensaïd, "On the Return of the Politico-Strategic Question," August 2006, marxists.org, originally published in English as "The Return of Strategy," *International Socialism* 113, January 2007; *La politique comme art stratégique*, Paris: Syllepse, 2010. Also Ben Brewster's reflections on the Comintern's manual on *Armed Insurrection*, signed "Neuberg," in "Armed Insurrection and Dual Power," *New Left Review* 66, 1971.

> toward moving beyond the modern guerrilla model toward more democratic network forms of organization.[17]

Is the contemporary horizon for a recovery and recasting of the theme of dual power a "biopolitical" one? It is difficult to ignore that whether we are talking about the nonantagonistic forms of participatory dual power in the Porto Alegre model, the Zapatista attempt to defend zones for the self-organization of "civil society" against oligarchic repression, or the attempts to articulate forms of democracy from below with national popular projects in Bolivia and Venezuela, the biopolitical element (understood both in the sophisticated sense of Hardt and Negri, but also in the simpler sense of welfare) is prominent.[18] The Lebanese Hezbollah is a significant figure in this respect, representing the rise of a kind of "biopolitical Islamism" in a context of dual power. Determined by a very unique historical and political constellation—which combines the anti-Israeli national resistance struggle, a Khomeneist party ideology profoundly modulated by the conditions of a multi-confessional Lebanon permanently threatened by relapse into bloody sectarianism, the contradictory support of Syria and Iran, and a wide proletarian Shi'a social base—Hezbollah has thrived in the systematic use of the duality power (military, territorial, moral) and represents a variant of this political form which is irreducible both to the model of the Leninist *kairos* as well as to that of the people's war. This variant of dual power instead functions within something like a *permanent interregnum*, where its power is wielded forcefully but not in the sense of a unilateral seizure.

Within this volatile geometry of forces, the "biopolitical" element provides much of the substance of dual power. In the

---

17 Michael Hardt and Antonio Negri, *Multitude: War and Democracy in the Age of Empire*, New York: Penguin, 2005, 81.

18 For "civil society," see the Second Declaration of the Selva Lacandona, 1994.

"planet of slums" anatomized by Mike Davis, we could even say that the "biopolitical supplement" to the neoliberal evacuation of services and solidarity is inextricable and primary vis-à-vis any mere military strategy. Much of Hezbollah's hegemonic trajectory depends on addressing key questions of the government of life, adopting a "process of advocacy based on extensive fact-finding and teamed with grassroots support." In these Islamist inquiries of sorts, issues such as water problems are addressed through scientific-academic methods (Hezbollah's Center for Developmental Studies) and by encouraging "the formation of residential and professional groups" that can provide the territorial rooting for these welfare ventures.[19] In a situation of prolonged dual power where the stakes, contrary to those Negri envisions, are precisely based on averting civil war while gaining relative hegemony over a population sidelined by a fragmented, unequal, and threadbare state (what Judith Palmer Harik simply calls "the abandoned"), dual power is biopower, and daily garbage collection, large-scale health service delivery, and emergency water delivery are weapons of the first order. Though little if anything can be directly extrapolated from a unique situation in which the notion of "balance of power" takes on an intense and tragic if quotidian connotation, Hezbollah's important variant of "biopolitical Islam" hints at some of the contemporary conditions for the rethinking and exercise of dual power, where the separation of an autonomous political capacity and the generation of new types of power (whether revolutionary, conservative, or reactionary) cannot bypass the dimension of the production and reproduction of social life—in short, the question of survival. These interstitial, secessionist, or parallel figures of para-state power are in turn bound to the mutations in the state form itself, which increasingly, especially as concerns territories targeted by neocolonial and neoimperial

---

19 Judith Palmer Harik, *Hezbollah: The Changing Face of Terrorism*, London: I.B. Tauris, 2005.

operations, no longer posit an overlay of state, territory, and population, but instead propose violent governance by "zones," indexed to the shifting requirements of extraction and security.[20] It is this context of neoliberalism which is shifting the link between capital and spaces of government and jurisdiction and allowing for a proliferation, in certain parts of the world, of violently overlapping authorities and enclaves in conjunctures of incomplete sovereignty.

10.

A possible foothold for beginning to think transition concretely would then be to consider the crucial phenomenon of what we could call a kind of dual biopower—which is to say the collective attempt to appropriate politically aspects of social reproduction that state and capital have abandoned or rendered unbearably exclusionary, from housing to medicine. These aspects—which, incidentally, are also the privileged sites for any nonreformist reforms one could propose in the current moment—are today the principal organizing bases of successful popular movements, whether progressive or reactionary. But they have also been the fulcrums from which to think the dismantling of capitalist social forms and relations without relying on the premise of a political break in the operations of power, without waiting for "the day after," the seizure or "evaporation" of the repressive apparatus. Though they could be read in a merely ameliorative lens, I think the brutally repressed experiments of the Black Panthers with breakfast programs, sickle-cell anemia screening, and an alternative health service for the black "lumpen"—to use their own terminology—are one such example, and their articulation with a

20 Badiou stresses this question of zones in his lecture course *Images du temps présent (2001–2004)*, Paris: Fayard, 2014.

conception of self-defense not irrelevant to our own time.[21] The "epidemiological dual structure" of which Jameson beguilingly speaks resonates with this, and we should remark the centrality of health to transitional imaginaries in a phase plagued by the crisis of social reproduction (the critical and rational core, to my mind, of discussions on biopolitics): from the ongoing Solidarity for All initiatives that accompanied Syriza's rise in Greece to Hazan and Kamo's utopian speculations on how health could be a prominent locus of "first revolutionary measures."[22] As we begin to see spatial and temporal "dualities," or sheer fragmentation and "zoning," in the domain of social reproduction and the formations of collectivities through the very uneven time and space of crisis, we could also start to think which of these experiences can be propagated or scaled up—not in fantasies of secession, and not in the illusion that post-capitalism is really possible now, but as ways of rooting the need to undo capitalist relations in the real, if partial, experience of attempts to limit its powers and repurpose its (our) dead labors.

11.

Even if, following Zavaleta Mercado, we treat dual power as a metaphor or problem rather than a universal whose particulars we can inventory, it is still possible to identify some of its elements. In

21 Alondra Nelson, *Body and Soul: The Black Panther Party and the Fight against Medical Discrimination*, Minneapolis: University of Minnesota Press, 2013; Joshua Bloom and Waldo E. Martin, *Black Against Empire: The History and Politics of the Black Panther Party*, Berkeley: University of California Press, 2014.

22 Eric Hazan and Kamo, *Prèmieres mesures révolutionnaires*, Paris: La Fabrique, 2013. See the extremely perspicuous critical comments in Jason E. Smith's extended review of this pamphlet, "The Day after the Insurrection: On *First Revolutionary Measures*," *Radical Philosophy* 189, 2015.

light of these, I want to address Jameson's anchoring of his utopian speculation in the "universal army" as a concrete institution of dual power. Whether we identify the space-time of dual power as that of a punctual, if uneven, crisis of the state or in the protracted or "permanent" (if also uneven) crisis of social reproduction, the great majority of invocations of dual power follow Lenin's lead in seeing it as inextricable from *crisis*. While war is certainly on the horizon, mediate or immediate, of these debates, to the extent that it is the crisis of the state and its functions that they address, we could say that all the figures of dual power surveyed above already, to different degrees, respond to Jameson's important entreaty: "We must invent better temporal models of crisis, long- and short-term, than those afforded by war." Whether they throw up psychic analogues of war at the level of popular unity is a somewhat different matter, though we might already suggest that total mobilization is perhaps not where the lessons of dual power are to be sought. The second element, along with crisis, is obviously the *state*: whether they are shadowed, as Bolshevik debates certainly were, by a conception of the state as a unified monopoly of violence that cannot tolerate duality, or whether they conceive the duality (or multiplicity) of powers in terms of a waning or fragmentation of the state, shedding areas of control or reproduction, the image of dual power is intimately bound to the extant modalities of state power. It is, to quote Zavaleta Mercado again, "a special type of state contradiction or a state conjuncture of transition." This contradiction is exacerbated by the third element I'd like to stress, that of dual power as determined by the emergence of an *embryo of alternative power*, a *qualitatively different* power (and state), which shares and shapes the space-time of the official and legitimate power and which sinks its roots in the *capacity* of an emergent class, so that—at least in "classical" theories of this ultimately nonclassical notion—dual power as a political term is foreshadowed by a dual power transpiring from the domain of production itself.

12.

Jameson's American utopia of dual power appears to foreground this third element, the identification of an institutional embryo of a power other than that of the capitalist state, to the detriment of the other two. Against the "classic"—i.e., Leninist—figure of dual power, which links this hopeful but unstable strategic aberration to the specificity of a general crisis of the state, Jameson stages his search for a candidate for dual power in terms of the apparent impossibility of the very break in the structures of the state that was the condition of possibility for classic dual power in the first instance. Where the latter signaled an uneven qualitative interlocking of bourgeois and proletarian revolution, war of position and war of maneuver, dual power as speculative utopia is occasioned by the seeming occlusion of the very horizon in which these distinctions were possible. Crisis, both in the sense of a more or less punctual political rupture and of the aforementioned implosion of social reproduction, certainly shadows this valiant speculative effort, but it is not as such integrated into the concept of dual power, save in the form of an indispensable symbolic ingredient, an analogue of war as mobilizing "fetish" for a collective. Jameson's communist fabulation shares with many of the utopias he's so brilliantly analyzed elsewhere a curious relation to political time, which the terminology of dual power exacerbates: on the one hand, the turn to a revised notion of dual power is required by the absence of a prospect of revolutionary crisis, and thus suggests itself as a mechanism to unblock a situation of cognitive and practical paralysis; on the other, as the reference to Bisson's splendid *Fire on the Mountain* intimates, such a dual power in real "competition" with the state could only be envisaged *after* a rupture (and it is telling that the greatest twentieth-century proliferation of utopian texts, projects, and experiences took place *after* the Bolshevik revolution and not as its preparation). No doubt, classic dual power itself was both *after* a rupture (February) and *before* the decisive one (October), but dual power as speculative utopia shifts from this determinate indeterminacy—which binds dual power to the conjuncture of the interregnum—to a rather different scenario, in which the background conditions of the classic form seem missing. Today, we are after October—still dragging along shards of the Bolshevik explosion, some as futile relics, others as potential weapons—but we remain, in most of the world, before February, without a rupture in state domination yet in sight (the Arab Februaries have grimly demonstrated that the incompleteness of revolution in no way moderates the brutality of counterrevolution).

13.

This displacement or black-boxing of dual power as a state crisis of transition can be approached through the debates and shifts the concept has undergone from its initial formulations—in particular its resurgence in the 1970s in Latin American and European debates on dual power and democratic roads to socialism, and the series of theories and practices already alluded to that stress a duality or plurality of powers surfacing out of the state's abdication of many of its social reproduction functions. In both of these historical and conceptual clusters, we could speak of something like *diffuse* dual power, while recognizing, in the wake of Zavaleta Mercado's warnings, that any such diffusion, or indeed generalization, of dual power risks fatally *dissolving* the notion, watering down its *anomaly*. While maintaining a classic emphasis on the institutional duality of powers in the "same" space-time (namely against the enclave and the "riot-commune" as potential candidates of dual power), Jameson's American utopia inherits from the post-Leninist mutations of dual power the problem of how to think transitional institutions outside of a decisive rupture. In this respect, despite opting to retain the terminology of dual power, Jameson's proposal seems to share more with the strategic horizon of Poulantzas's democratic socialism—which envisaged a kind of erosion of the bonds between the bourgeoisie and the state—than with the Trotskyist vision of dual power advanced against the Greek philosopher by the young Henri Weber, for whom a military-political rupture was indispensable to retain any conception of revolution—a rupture that would be precipitated by the consolidation of diffuse social dual powers (the plurality of embryos of self-organization and popular power emerging in a protracted situation of social crisis) into a *frontal* challenge to the capitalist state.[23] Weber thus reasserts the classic perspective that a clash, a decisive rupture with some military dimension, cannot be circumvented, and suggests *contra* Poulantzas that without full-blown dual power, no rupture is possible. Viewed from the vantage point of the 1970s debates on transition and dual power, Jameson's speculative utopia is somewhat of a centaur—trying to articulate the duration of a long march *of* the institution (in this case the universal army) with a firm commitment to duality (against Poulantzas's much more "molecular" conception of democratic struggles)—and, no doubt due to its US vantage point, which quickly puts paid to any parliamentary illusion, it entirely sidelines the problematic of representation and the party form that dominated these debates.[24]

14.

What then of the provocation of seeking the site of dual power in the army? Set against the often disavowed anarcho-individualist or radical-liberal tendencies of much *soi-disant* anticapitalism

---

23 See their 1977 debate on "The State and the Transition to Socialism," now in *The Poulantzas Reader: Marxism, Law and the State*, ed. James Martin, London: Verso, 2008.

24 The party is, of course, the element of the classical Leninist theory of dual power that serves as a kind of Lacanian *point de capiton* or 'quilting point' for the other three elements: the situation of crisis, the challenge to the state, and the embryos of power.

today, this provocation is of course, as Jameson eventually concedes, the very *point* of the exercise, serving as a kind of *reactant* to reveal our deep-seated *fear of the collective*. Yet Jameson has anchored his utopia in a *fact of revolutionary analysis and strategy*, so we can be excused for also approaching it in that register. The first comment to make in that respect is that Jameson's search in *existing* institutions for his experimental subject of dual power goes against the grain of many of the debates we've already surveyed. Whether in the *cordones industriales* or the Asemblea Popular of Chile, the Panthers' health programs, the *shura* councils of the Iranian Revolution, or indeed the Petrograd Council of Workers' and Soldiers' Deputies, this embryonic revolutionary power is organized around *new* institutions that from the start assert their asymmetry and incommensurability with the extant institutions of the state. Not that the refunctioning of existing institutions is a theme absent from revolutionary theory—far from it, as, notwithstanding *de rigueur* nods to the *smashing* of the state, most revolutionary practice is nothing but such a refunctioning, with all the contradictions, setbacks, and counterfinalities that entails. And yet that is not the unique problem that dual power has generally been invoked to articulate, or rather not so much to solve as to describe.

Now, and this is the second comment I want to make on the universal army, Jameson's utopia turns the classic problem of dual power—in a nutshell, there are but there cannot be two repressive apparatuses in one state, which is also to say two states in one state—into its own solution, by transmuting the army into the dual power itself. Yet in his own description of this utopian army, which emerges in a situation of dual power, and

> which begins life as a parallel force alongside the state *and its official army* [my emphasis] and finds its first tasks and indeed its vocation in the fulfillment of neglected social services and in a coexistence with the population of a wholly different type,

we sense that the figure of the *situation* of dual power is wholly unlike that faced by Lenin, for whom *by definition* an army couldn't be a locus of dual power. A *parallel* force (rather than one embroiled in a frontal struggle) could only emerge once a rupture had taken place, be it only in the rise of the kind of *governmental* power that could decree universal conscription as a first transitional measure. But we are arguably here in a rather different terrain than "classic" dual power; more, perhaps, a contradictory polity in which the duality of powers is experimented with both from above and from below, in which (parts of) the state and (parts of) society are involved in a transitional effort that does not take the form of a frontal conflict (which would be *immediate* given the existence of two armies representing different social and political imperatives in the same territory). Whether we want to call this an expanded or diffuse dual power or abandon the terminology altogether (as Poulantzas urged), it is nevertheless evident that we are very much in a post- or non-Leninist horizon. It is a horizon in which the state is neither an instrument nor a fortress, but a field of struggle (and whatever Jameson's universal army might be, it still remains in many ways of the state, even or especially as it is envisaged as sapping the anti-emancipatory features of US *states*).[25] This diffusion (and potential dissolution) of the problematic of dual power can be located in many disparate moments across the twentieth century: Korsch's councilist proposals for socialization from above and from below; the debate on *poder popular* in the last months of Allende's Unidad Popular government in Chile[26]; Negri's speculations about "permanent dual power" quoted above; but also theoretical efforts by the likes of Sartre or Althusser to think how the

25 See Panagiotis Sotiris, "Neither an Instrument nor a Fortress: Poulantzas's Theory of the State and His Dialogue with Gramsci," *Historical Materialism* 22.2, 2014, 135–57.

26 See Franck Gaudichaud, ed., *¡Venceremos! Analyses et documents sur le pouvoir populaire au Chili (1970–1973)*, Paris: Syllepse, 2013.

party could be reimagined no longer as the monopolist of power, in a different articulation with mass initiatives and forms of self-organization that would allow us to envisage a non-Leninist politics that would still remain resolutely antiliberal, not allowing dual power to devolve into the balance of powers.[27] In our own century, this is how some have sought to theorize the institutional experiments of the Bolivarian revolution in Venezuela.[28] Another way to pose this question, which perhaps resonates with Jameson's bracing reflections on envy, is whether *stasis*, the division fracturing a polity, can somehow be institutionalized. Though post-Marxists have unconvincingly interpreted late liberalism as bearing this agonistic politics within it, surely it would be a task of any transition to communism to invent modalities of antagonism not steeped in belonging, identity, or class. One might take inspiration here from Solon's stunning decree providing for punishment for any citizen who had not taken sides in a civil war. Of course, Solon's proposal depended on the politically reproduced identity of citizen, and one of the questions we need to ask ourselves in gauging

---

27 Responding to Rossana Rossanda, also Althusser's interlocutor in the interview on "Marxism as a Finite Theory," in which he advanced strangely similar views, Sartre says: "At any rate, what seems to me interesting in your schema is the duality of power which it foreshadows. This means an open and irreducible relation between the *unitary* moment, which falls to the political organization of the class, and the moments of self-government, the councils, the fused groups. I insist on that word 'irreducible' because there can only be a permanent tension between the two moments. The party will always try, to the degree that it wants to see itself as 'in the service' of the movement, to reduce it to its own schema of interpretation and development; while the moments of self-government will always try to project their living partiality upon the contradictory complex of the social tissue. It is in this struggle, maybe, that can be expressed the beginning of a reciprocal transformation." Jean-Paul Sartre, "Masses, Spontaneity, Party," *Socialist Register*, 1970.

28 See especially the stimulating analysis in George Ciccariello-Maher, "Dual Power in the Venezuelan Revolution," *Monthly Review* 59.4, 2007.

the pertinence of dual power today is whether the link between the emergence of an embryonic power and a pre-existing identity—be it of class, *ethnos*, or community—can be broken. After all, another point in which Jameson's proposal moves beyond revolutionary classicism is by seeing the function of the universal army not only in undoing class distinction but in making possible a dual power that is not itself grounded on class difference—*unlike* most of those we can encounter in both classical and diffuse figures of dual power. This question is even more urgent inasmuch as what I've called dual biopower very often—though certainly not always, as anti-austerity examples from Europe illustrate, from the Spanish Platform for those Affected by Mortgages (PAH) to Solidarity for All in Greece—roots itself in ethnic, religious, or racialized communities, distant from the modernity of nation-state identity formation that still appears to serve as the background of Jameson's reflections.

15.

It is of course the US context of Jameson's utopia that lends the seemingly classical modernity of a national popular army its antisystemic charge, as though a kind of anticipatory nostalgia for a Jacobinism pre-empted by US federalism pervaded Jameson's vision. Here Jameson's violent excision of a whole welter of American utopias of secession should not go unremarked upon. The abrogation of any radical reference to the Constitution or the Declaration of Independence that preceded it doesn't just cut off the problematic tendency among some US progressives to echo Hannah Arendt's positioning of a US revolutionary tradition against the supposed trap of an exquisitely French "social question." It also distances the persistence of these references among practitioners of embryos of dual power in the United States—not least the Black Panther Party, whose Ten-Point Program concludes with an acute *détournement* of the Declaration of Independence:

> When a long train of abuses and usurpations, pursuing invariably the same object, evinces a design to reduce them under absolute despotism, it is their right, it is their duty, to throw off such government, and to provide new guards for their future security.

There is an even stronger opposition in Jameson—and I would argue a salutary one—to the *frontier anarcho-communism* (contaminated with settler-colonialism) that serves as the political unconscious of much of the US extreme left, and which can be traced back not so much to the militia ideal that is most active on fringes of the white supremacist right, but to that whole host of experiments, often promoted by the escapees of the failed European revolutions of the nineteenth century, but also permeated by the sectarian exuberance of American Christianity, which we find inventoried in Charles Nordhoff's classic volume *The Communistic Societies of the United States*.

16.

Though it is a utopia that tries to refunction against political theory one of the key notions around which Marxists have tried to invent a *sui generis* Marxist politics (one breaking with political theory or philosophy as classically construed, by posing the very problem of a "non-state state"), the heart of Jameson's proposal is evidently not strategic in any customary understanding of that term. The bold attempt to refashion a Fourierism for our time, largely autonomous from the willfully paradoxical hypothesis of a dual-power army, shows that the core of this "therapeutic" utopia is *cultural revolution*, a theme that punctuates Jameson's work but is here encapsulated in the idea of the "programming and retransformation of subjects trained in one society for functioning in a different one." The terms—like the long quote from Trotsky's bleak directives on militarization, which in turn hark back to Engels's bluntly "realist" "On Authority"—are precisely selected to elicit a libertarian reaction that Jameson rightly connects, in the US context, to the deep tendrils that anticommunist discourse has projected into the very mental habits of progressives. We can extract from this essay a salutary antidote to what has almost become common sense in contemporary far-left discourse, to wit, that today's struggles, all the everyday ruptures, all the cracks in capitalism, are already presaging the sloughing off of the whole integument of alienated life. We might thus wish to balance the consoling notion that "we are the change we were waiting for" with Franco Fortini's poetic counsel: "Among the enemies' names / write your own too."[29] Whether because of a (partially justified) horror of the specter of the state or a kind of ontological optimism about the human condition (which Jameson nicely punctures), today's "communisms" (of the commons, communization, or the commune) largely reject this very problem, that of what we could call an *anthropological transition*. In the end Jameson has refunctioned the strategic singularity of dual power into a speculative tool to pose this very question, repressed along with the Stalinist nightmare of the New Man (but also the Fanonian discourse of a new humanity). This is a vital contribution for which no amount of pseudo-iconoclastic invocations of communism as the imageless movement of the destruction of the status quo can substitute—for the destruction of the status quo will also need to be the destruction, the "programming and retransformation," of ourselves, of our own status.

---

29 Franco Fortini, "Translating Brecht," trans. Michael Hamburger, in *Poems*, Todmorden: Arc, 1978.

17.

I can't exhaust the wealth of speculative suggestions in Jameson's piece—from the tantalizing invention of the Psychoanalytic Placement Bureau to the problematic bracketing of the self-management of *producers* (surely not an insignificant question given the vastness of today's global proletariat)—but, to conclude, I will touch on two of its features that I think deserve further . . . speculation. The first is the theme of a "utopia of the double life." Here I think Jameson is right to eschew the fusional imaginaries that would see freedom and necessity merge into a seamless socialization of play. Not only should a utopia for today fully assume and mobilize negativity (as the theme of "envy" hammers home), it should also attend to what we may term, echoing Marcuse, necessary as opposed to surplus alienation. Yet the double life needs to take into account the tragic, shattering duality that has often accompanied revolutionary efforts, none perhaps more so than the Bolshevik one. As Robert Linhart showed in his incisive *Lenin, the Peasants and Taylor*, the political pedagogy and emancipation of workers *qua* administrators of the new state went hand in hand in Lenin and Trotsky's position with an exceptional, extreme regimentation of production. How would the double life not revive the punishing schizophrenia where the worker is politically (or libidinally) liberated only to be productively shackled (no matter for how few hours) by an agency that speaks in his or her name? No Leninist "habit" is going to happily square this circle, nor answer the psycho-political question of the persistence of the state, of its transcendence not only as an institution but as a super-egoic entity in the transitional period. I fear that Jameson's animus against politics and the political—despite serving as a healthy bending of the stick—might make it difficult indeed to pose these questions, or to address the fact that a thinking of transition, as Lenin himself showed in coining this weird and unstable "metaphor" of dual power, demands the *invention* of a communist politics that, like dual power itself, must be asymmetrical from its bourgeois counterpart. Such an invention can, I think, take inspiration, and this is my second point, from a theme that pervades "An American Utopia," and this is Jameson's attempt to imagine various modalities for *disactivating* political (and we could say sovereign) power, linked to his attention to the enduring need for *fetishes* (or in Badiou's parlance, *ideas*) even "after" the transition. Our anthropology of transition will need to face not just the bond of the state with fear, but another Hobbesian theme, the persistence of politics as a *desire for domination* and a related drive toward conflict. Will this require politics in its classical acceptation to continue in the mode of the "as if"? Doesn't this slip toward a cynical reason that is hardly conducive to the efficacy of these rituals and fetishes? The horizon of Jameson's utopia would thus be not that of a constituent power (which his objections to the US Constitution make clear) but, to echo Giorgio Agamben's most recent investigations, that of a *destituent* power, where what is to be destituted, hollowed out, sapped, is politics itself. I would argue however—and here a reading of Agamben is instructive—that destitution is not just an antipolitical but an antistrategic concept, a messianic one. In order to retain the fecund tension between the utopian and the strategic that traverses Jameson's American utopia, I think, to borrow from Zavaleta Mercado's *El poder dual* one last time, that what we need to turn our speculative and practical attentions toward is forging a *disorganizing power*, a power to disorganize not just the institutions of the capitalist state but, as Jameson rightly notes, the manner in which they pervade the very structure of our desires, including our desires for revolution—or the lack thereof.

9

Utopian Therapy: Work, Nonwork, and the Political Imagination

Kathi Weeks

Fredric Jameson's "An American Utopia" is a meditation on what the Marxist tradition calls the problem of the transition, or more specifically the eventual transition to what some continue to name communism. Refusing more familiar templates for change, including the enclave, the uprising, reform, and revolution, Jameson settles instead on the model of dual power. He nominates the army for that position, the parallel institution with the potential to serve as the organizational vehicle for the transition beyond capitalism. There are two parts to the exercise: first, a practical proposal for universal military conscription; this is then converted into the material base for a utopian vision of a new society upon which collective and individual freedom can flourish.

But the *army*? As part of a utopian vision? "Military democracy" sounds more like a contribution to a popular game played to pass the time on long road trips—alongside "jumbo shrimp" and "vacation Bible school"—than a description of a better future. I am surely not the only reader to find this disconcerting. My immediate reactions, although no doubt predictable objections from a feminist political theorist, are probably not uncommon. The first stems from my difficulty imagining a gender-neutral military, that is, a military culture and organization that is somehow shorn of its long historical entanglements with certain iconic constructions of sexual difference. One need not resort to essentialist metaphysics to recognize the gendering of the institution. Given the weight of this gendered history, the universalization of conscription seems in itself inadequate to break the bonds that have knit together models of militarized masculinity with masculinist militarization. The absence of politics is my other stumbling block to thinking along this utopian trajectory. Here I refer not to politics as the art and power of the state, as Jameson defines it, but politics as processes of collective decision-making and sites for the mediation of social antagonism; politics in this sense refers to venues where conflicts are staged and the processes by which relations of cooperation are forged. The figure of the army I think functions to deflect these questions about its internal structures and relational dynamics because it is equated with the very essence of order: because organization, especially hierarchical organization, is considered somehow inherent to or definitive of the institution. As a gendered machine for the production of leaders and subordinates, it is difficult for me to imagine the army, even a universal army, one that is itself transformed over time, as capable of coexisting with, let alone as a school for, the development of democratic capacities and egalitarian values.

Utopian hermeneutics

There are, however, many more promising points of the proposal to consider, as well as more fruitful ways to approach the points addressed above. To see beyond these initial objections and recognize the potential power of Jameson's thought experiment, it helps to situate it in relationship to his longstanding interest in utopia. In contrast to others in the Marxist tradition—occasionally including Marx himself—who refer to the utopian with disdain, Jameson approaches it as a richly complex and continually relevant form of praxis. In a departure from more conventional views of utopian literature as representations of alternatives, Jameson has long emphasized the way they operate as forms of critique. His signature contribution to utopian studies involves a shift in focus from the positive content of a utopian vision to its negative function of producing an estrangement from and neutralization of the present order of things. From this angle, even the failures of speculative thinking can be effective as critical tools for the present. In his most famous formulation of this thesis, Jameson advances the marvelously provocative claim that the "deepest vocation" of utopias "is to bring home, in local and determinate ways, and with a fullness of concrete detail, our constitutional inability to imagine utopia itself, and this, not owing to any individual failure of imagination but as the result of the systemic, cultural, and ideological closure of which we are all in one way or another prisoners."[1]

One could read "An American Utopia" as a dramatic departure from this earlier approach. Here Jameson offers a concrete political proposal followed by the outline of a substantive alternative. In a seeming reversal of his previous commitments, content takes precedence over form; inspiration displaces critique. Whereas he had once memorably claimed that "utopia as a form is not the representation of radical alternatives; it is rather simply the imperative to imagine them,"[2] in the recent text he wonders if "perhaps, then, the task of utopianism today is rather to propose more

---

1 Fredric Jameson, "Progress versus Utopia; or, Can We Imagine the Future?" *Science Fiction Studies* 9(2), 1982, 153.

2 Fredric Jameson, "'If I Find One Good City I Will Spare the Man': Realism and Utopia in Kim Stanley Robinson's Mars Trilogy," in *Learning from Other Worlds: Estrangement, Cognition, and the Politics of Science Fiction and Utopia*, ed. Patrick Parrinder, Durham: Duke University Press, 2001, 231.

elaborated versions of an alternate social system than simply to argue the need for one." But I think that would be to overstate the shift in direction. In "An American Utopia" Jameson also affirms the critical function of utopian thinking and the efficacies of the form itself. Here too he insists that the fundamental function of utopias is to revive a sense of the future, which requires taking aim at the forces that prevent us from venturing out from the comfortingly familiar confines of the present. Thus "utopianism is at one with this therapy of the anti-utopian," and, for this dual task, form and content must operate both together and in tandem such that form can still be approached also as its own content. To put it another way, "An American Utopia" is best read not quite, or not only, literally. To borrow from an earlier, often cited critique that Jameson has leveled, when we approach utopias only in terms of their literal content, "there results an impoverishment which is due to the reduction of the multiple levels of the Utopian idea to the single, relatively abstract field of social planning."[3]

Rather than merely a series of arguments to evaluate, Jameson also presents the exercise as something to undergo, a form of political and ideological therapy. Let me offer two quick examples of this kind of formal effectivity of a text that exceeds its content. Although I remain more hopeful about the political utility of some of those mechanisms of transition that Jameson was willing to discard, the model of dual power and the proposal for a universal army both pose a provocative challenge to certain left dispositions. First, as an exercise in thinking the transition, the strategy of dual power—irrespective of the model's substantive specificities—obliges us to think on a larger social scale and along a longer temporal trajectory than most seem willing to entertain these days. With its goal of fundamental and systemic change, the model forces us to scale up a political imagination more accustomed to

3 Fredric Jameson, *Marxism and Form: Twentieth-Century Dialectic Theories of Literature*, Princeton, NJ: Princeton University Press, 1971, 145–6.

partial and immediate reform so that it can operate on the level of the social totality, with its network of institutions and ecosystem of structures and subjectivities; it compels us to expand our historical capacity further into the future so that we can think along the longer timeframe necessary for radical transformation and contemplate a transition that is still only a transition to another transition. In these ways, Jameson's program of dual power, regardless of its specific qualities, usefully exposes at least two forms of what he refers to elsewhere as our "difficulties in thinking quantity positively."[4]

The proposal for the universal army poses a second set of challenges for the typical reader. Jameson is well aware of the reactions his scheme can trigger: the horror that the prospect of the existing military assuming power can inspire. To nominate the army for this revolutionary position is to throw down the gauntlet to the anti-institutional left, to force its resistances out into the open where they can be critically examined. More specifically, in order to begin to consider the army as a revolutionary form, we must first confront any lingering attachments we might have to a model of revolutionary transition as complete rupture, whereby the future is imagined to spring forth from the ashes of which it never bears the stain. Like Marx and Engels in the *Manifesto*, the path to Jameson's utopian future passes through what is for many of us an exemplar of the dystopian present. The analysis thus models in exceptionally unambiguous terms a rigorously immanent logic of transitional thinking; whatever one might think of the universal army, one of the things Jameson's defense does quite effectively is to drive to the surface and force us to confront any longings we might harbor for the purity of clean breaks and

4 Fredric Jameson, "Utopia as Method, or, the Uses of the Future," in *Utopia/Dystopia: Conditions of Historical Possibility*, ed. Michael D. Gordin, Helen Tilley, and Gvan Prakash, Princeton, NJ: Princeton University Press, 2010, 29.

aversions we might hold for the messiness of complex complicities and protracted struggles. In this respect, the exercise bears some kinship to a number of notable precedents, including Marx's interest in the joint-stock company as the potential seed or sign of a postcapitalist future; Jameson's earlier speculations about the utopian lessons of Walmart; and Donna Haraway's affirmation of the cyborg as at once the product of militarized technoscience and a way to conceive a better future.[5] By designating the army as a means by which to build a different future, Jameson is clearly, dare I say even didactically, playing the cards we were dealt.

Work Unbound

This brings me to one of the most intriguing elements of "An American Utopia" and the focus of the remainder of the essay: namely, the place of work in this template of a possible future. The vision is organized around a rough distinction between base and superstructure that maps onto divisions between economy and culture, necessity and freedom, and work and leisure. The first realm designated by these oppositions is narrowly delimited so as to create the conditions for the sphere of life with which it is paired to expand and flourish. By far the most appealing and—to borrow Jameson's term—therapeutic element of this schema is the strict separation that he maintains between work and nonwork. Work is reduced to the equivalent of a few hours a day of necessary social reproduction, performed in work clothes and in teams, and while he insists—unnecessarily, it seems to me—on full employment, a generous guaranteed wage weakens the coercive force of the link

5 Karl Marx, *Capital*, Vol. III, trans. David Fernbach, London: Penguin, 1981; Jameson, "Utopia as Method"; Donna Haraway, "A Manifesto for Cyborgs: Science, Technology, and Socialist Feminism in the 1980s," *Socialist Review*, 80 1985, 65–107.

between work and income with which we are now forced to contend. Work is hardly glorified in this account, relegated as it is to "ordinary drudgery, the necessary tasks, and the like." Instead of dressing it up and calling it freedom, as in so many utopian dreams of nonalienated labor, Jameson names it (mere) work, reduces the hours of its operatives, and dresses them down in uniforms.[6] By these means, the borders around the work of economic (re)production are tightly drawn to make ample room for a vision of free—unscripted and unaccountable—time to develop on its basis.

This carefully circumscribed vision of work—confined to shorter shifts and restricted to the execution of necessary tasks—can serve as an effective counter to and treatment for the present hegemony of work and its values. By calling out and into question the present unbounded and overvalued status of work, this utopia of a double life, of work and nonwork strictly cordoned off from one another, forces us to imagine freedom not in work but in the spaces and times outside work. This careful partitioning of base and superstructure, which Jameson likens in some respects to the older separation between church and state, functions like a secularizing tonic to help wean us of our almost religious devotion to the metaphysics of labor and the productivist gospel of work.

To appreciate the value of this dimension of Jameson's exercise in utopian thinking, one must grasp the enormity of the current problem it serves to redress. Work has come to so dominate our existence that we have trouble imagining a life not subordinated to it. The utopia of the double life that Jameson depicts offers both a diagnosis of and a remedy for our addiction to work, our reverence for its values, and our inability to imagine a life outside it. There are a number of reasons why it is difficult both to put work

6 To fans of utopian fiction: in its conception of work, both in itself and in relation to leisure, "An American Utopia" sides more with Team Bellamy than Team Morris.

in its place and to imagine nonwork as something other than more work. The general obstacle to thinking beyond work could be described in Marxist terms as the move from the formal to the real subsumption of reproduction into production, or of life into work. The traditional division between economy and society is made ever more tenuous as the chief warrant of social institutions like the family, school, army, prison, and clinic becomes reduced to the production or restoration of employability. As cultures and socialities are absorbed into economic production as both inputs and outputs, the borders between work and nonwork times, spaces, relations, and activities become ever more blurred, giving work free rein to define our existence. For one minor but telling symptom of the subsumption of life into work: the dubious concept of "work/life balance" is being replaced in some human-resource management circles with the more ominous goal of "work/life integration."[7]

Another obstacle to imagining the contents of work and the relationship between work and nonwork differently is the contemporary hegemony of the work ethic. In elevating work over other activities as highest calling and moral duty, as an end in itself and rightful center of our identities and socialities, the work ethic is a kind of glue that fastens us to the status quo, something that synchronizes so many of our desires for individual achievement and social contribution—desires for personal growth and social solidarity—to the paltry terms of the wage relation. The work ethic binds us to the job by hailing us not only as desiring consumers but, perhaps more important, as would-be producers, as subjects too often willing to serve capital's purposes by living for and through work.

The hegemony of this ethos of work extends broadly across the social fabric and bores deeply into the individual psyche. The

---

7 Matt Richtel, "Housecleaning, then Dinner? Silicon Valley Perks Come Home," *New York Times*, October 19, 2012.

ethical mandate to dedicate our lives to work is fundamental to the social contract; it is the essence of what we owe one another, the major currency of social reciprocity. The liability to labor becomes the single most significant measure of a worthy citizen; indeed, the productive citizen has somehow become the moral equivalent of the socially responsible and responsive citizen. The steadfast commitment to work and principled commitment to productivity that the work ethic preaches stand today as fundamental mechanisms of social articulation, the connective tissues of the social order.

This ethic of work penetrates deeply into the fibers of our being. Indeed, neoliberal subjectivities are defined by their entrepreneurial enthusiasm for work and their fidelity to the productivist ethos. Melissa Gregg describes one consequence of this as the ever more intimate relationship that many workers have to work and the romance narratives they use to describe their love for and devotion to it.[8] Having internalized the value of efficiency, these neoliberal worker-subjects find pleasure and confirmation above all in the *feeling* of productivity.[9] This is not a collective pleasure, or pleasure in the collective. Rather, it is a deeply individualized and individualizing ethic of work, in accordance with, to borrow Nietzsche's quietly snide description, "virtue has come to consist in doing something in a shorter time than another person."[10] The Krisis-Group's "Manifesto against Labor" explains the hegemony of work values this way: whenever we want to signal the seriousness and value of an activity, they observe, we add the word *work* to it; and the list they provide includes some of our most intimate activities, including dream work, relationship work, and grieving

8 Melissa Gregg, *Work's Intimacy*, Cambridge: Polity, 2011.

9 Melissa Gregg, "Getting Things Done: Productivity, Self-Management, and the Order of Things," in *Networked Affect*, ed. Ken Hillis, Susanna Paasonen and Michael Petit, Boston: MIT Press, 2015, 187–202.

10 Friedrich Nietzsche, *The Gay Science*, trans. Walter Kaufmann, New York: Vintage Books, 1974, 259.

work. But it is not just laudable activity that merits the label of work; activity itself becomes understood through the rubric of work and is shaped by its priorities. "As soon our contemporary rises from the TV chair," they write, "every action is transformed into an act similar to labour."[11] Again, these values go deep, structuring not only our conscious but also our unconscious lives. In one particularly telling example, Rob Lucas recounts in a recent essay how, as an IT worker, he found himself dreaming in code. It was not that he dreamt about the job; rather, he dreamt within its rationale. "It is as if," he reports, "the repetitive thought patterns and the particular logic I employ when going about my work are becoming hardwired; are becoming the default logic that I use to think with."[12] This is "alienation entirely swallowing that which it alienates," alienation that penetrates the depths of subjectivity. It is, among other things, work's intimacy—to borrow Gregg's term—that allows it to burrow so deeply into our minds where it can impede the achievement of critical distance and colonize the political imaginary.

The Krisis-Group describes the consequences of this intimate relationship to work in eloquent terms:

> After centuries of domestication, the modern human being can not even imagine a life without labour. As a social imperative, labour not only dominates the sphere of the economy in the narrow sense, but also pervades social existence as a whole, creeping into everyday life and deep under the skin of everybody.[13]

As a result, to adapt a claim that Jameson, among others, has recounted about how it is easier to imagine the end of the world

---

11 Krisis-Group, "Manifesto against Labour," 1999, www.krisis.org/1999/manifesto-against-labour.

12 Rob Lucas, "Dreaming in Code," *New Left Review* 62, 2010, 125.

13 Krisis-Group, "Manifesto against Labour."

than the end of capitalism, at this point it may be easier to imagine the end of capitalism than to imagine the end of work.

Failed Visions of Nonwork

Given the breadth and depth of our attachments to work, the relationships that hinge upon it, and the identities we are encouraged to invent and invest there, it is no easy task to envision how, to use one of Jameson's formulations, we might "disintoxicate ourselves from the older system's powerful addictions." The utopia of the double life, the larger part of which exists free of work, poses a compelling critique of and treatment for those who suffer today from the ever more capacious and intimate world of work. But that said, I think it remains more powerful as a critical pedagogy for the present subsumption of life into work than an inspiring vision of a substantive alternative to it, a conclusion that simply places this aspect of "An American Utopia" firmly within the tradition of Jameson's larger utopian oeuvre. If that is the case, then the problem of imagining the positive content of nonwork continues unresolved. But how can we dream outside the code of work when work and its values know no bounds? For further evidence of the profound obstacles we face in thinking differently about work, I want to turn briefly to another archive, one comprised of deficient attempts to conceive life beyond work.

This very partial chronicle of the failed imagination of nonwork will be organized around three headings.[14] The first of these conceives nonwork through an oppositional logic of imagination such that, if work is productive activity, nonwork is understood as unproductive. This is perhaps most clear when the only imagined existence of nonwork is defined by sloth, as in the frequently

14 The discussion expands on an argument I outlined in an earlier essay: Kathi Weeks, "Imagining Non-Work," *Social Text Periscope*, March 28, 2013.

voiced fear that if it were not for work there would be no reason to get out of bed or off the couch. If activity itself is so strictly identified with and reduced to work, then nonwork is defined by its absence as *pure indolence*. I think this same logic of imagination animates Franco Berardi's recent defense of a mode of "radical passivity" to oppose the neoliberal mandate of "relentless productivity" and Ivor Southwood's endorsement of the estranging capacity of critical negativity as an antidote to a culture of compulsory positivity.[15] Jonathan Crary's claim in his book *24/7* that sleep can both pose a limit to capitalism as well as the template of an alternative also fits within this general rubric. As in the previously cited examples, one reason Crary likes sleep is that value cannot be extracted from it. But more promising are two additional qualities of sleep that he develops. One is his argument that while we think of sleep as a private and individual experience, it is more accurately characterized as "one of the few remaining experiences where we abandon ourselves to the care of others," a state of vulnerability and hence of dependence on others and even a temporary "release from individuation."[16] The second virtue of sleep as part of an alternative imaginary is the way that the category is, for Crary, inclusive of dreaming in both its forms. In contrast to the ways that the 24/7 temporality of late capitalism represents for him the triumph of the present over both the past and the future, night dreams allow us to access the past and daydreams to entertain the possibility of better futures. Lucas's less hopeful story about dreaming in the code of work notwithstanding, Crary offers an intriguing account of what sleep is and what it can do. Nonetheless, I would still maintain that sleep—as

15 Franco "Bifo" Berardi, *After the Future*, ed. Gary Genesko and Nicholas Thoburn, Oakland, CA: AK Press, 2011, 138; Ivor Southwood, *Non-Stop Inertia*, Winchester, UK: Zero Books, 2011, 84, 88.

16 Jonathan Crary, *24/7: Late Capitalism and the End of Sleep*, London: Verso, 2013, 25, 126.

the opposite of active wakefulness and paradigm of nonproductivity and as, despite Crary's claim to the contrary, something posited as a natural outside to capitalist culture—remains more of a reactive reversal of the work society than a way to imagine a future beyond it.

In a second formulation, nonwork is conceived not as work's flip side but as its mirror image, as when it is described in terms of doing the same things for the same long hours we now do at the job or at home, but under different conditions: that is, time for *industrious creativity*. This nonwork imaginary is governed not by an oppositional logic but by a continuist one. Here I am thinking in particular about any number of earnest efforts on the left to distance nonwork from both the sin of sloth and the degrading amusements of consumption. Work as it is transformed under communism, authors like Jon Elster and Michael Walzer have assured us, will involve goal-oriented, rule-governed, purposive action, not passive, trivial, hedonistic pastimes and indulgences.[17] So the limitation of this second notion of nonwork—as creative industry—is that it is often described in terms of the kind of single-minded focus, self-discipline, and worthy outcomes that the work ethic celebrates as the essence of work. Thus in some Marxist accounts, the achievement of nonexploited and unalienated labor is more a matter of changing the relations of production than the labor process itself and the role of work in our lives. In that case, its vision of "not working as we now know it" looks very much like work as we know it only too well. I would include in this second category of industrious creativity another notable alternative to work, namely play, at least insofar as it is often offered up as

---

17 Jon Elster, "Self-Realisation in Work and Politics: The Marxist Conception of the Good Life," in *Alternatives to Capitalism*, ed. Jon Elster and Karl Ove Moene, Cambridge: Cambridge University Press, 1989, 127–58; Michael Walzer, "A Day in the Life of a Socialist Citizen," in *Radical Principles: Reflections of an Unreconstructed Democrat*, New York: Basic Books, 1980, 128–38.

yet another stand-in for rule-bound and fruitful creativity. Although it may have functioned as an Other to the model of industrial work, today the way that play—even the sad copy of it marketed to employers by "funsultants"—has been incorporated into managerial regimes and retooled as part of work undermines its ability to generate an alternative imaginary. Today it is quite routine to see employers of (presumably) high-value employees encouraging them to work hard but play harder as a way to stimulate, and legitimate their own harnessing of, their employees' creative powers. In these respects, play is more continuous with the way work is conceived today than transformative of it.

A third set of attempts to conceive nonwork are limited because of the way they mistake the inside for the outside: that is, because what they offer as a standpoint outside the existing world of work remains firmly ensconced within it. Consumption, typically posed as a negative alternative to production, as in the often repeated warning that with more time off work we will fill our time with shopping, thus descending further into commodity fetishism, fits within this rubric: though they are imagined here as an opposition, production and consumption are only two sides of the same system. What Marx characterizes as the submerging of our passions and activities in greed is central to the construction of the subject as worker.[18] Current needs for consumer gratification are the kinds of needs that, in his words, "lead the fly to the gluepot," needs that are functional to and complicit with the very system that demands that we work our lives away in order to live.[19] In this third group we could also include *leisure time*, traditionally understood as time to recover from or prepare for work. This connection to work is particularly clear in the notion of the vacation, constructed as a reward for, and a way to renew, waged workers and family

---

18 Karl Marx, *The Economic and Philosophic Manuscripts of 1844*, trans. Martin Milligan, New York: International Publishers, 1964, 150.

19 Ibid., 148.

members by allowing them to escape both job and home for a time. This nonwork for the sake of work includes the leisure time to upgrade our labor, as in the nineteenth-century call for more "vigorous leisure time" for the working class to cultivate the moral virtues, or acknowledgment in the twenty-first century that workers need time to grow their networks or colleague sets and work on their employability.[20] Like consumption, leisure in this traditional sense functions to reproduce the existing systems of economic production and subject construction. Finally, those who propose family time as an alternative to work time are also imagining an outside that is inside, as if the institution of the family was not a mechanism for the organization and distribution of the reproductive work necessary for productive work; as if the family did not serve as a supplement to the income allocation function of work; as if the ideology of the family was not intimately bound up with the ascetic ideal of the work ethic; as if, in short, the home was not a place of work. In these examples the model of nonwork is already folded into work.

To summarize: in the first case nonwork is cast as *unproductive*, in the second it is posed as differently *productive*, and in the third it is figured as *reproductive* of the subject as a worker. In one nonwork is the other of work; in the second it is its twin; and in the third it is work's complement. The first employs an oppositional logic of imagination, the second a continuist one, and the third an imagination that is drawn from what it seeks to overcome. Although they may appear to be categories of nonwork, they fail to escape the

---

20 On nonwork for the sake of work, see Bob Black, "The Abolition of Work," in *Reinventing Anarchy, Again*, ed. Howard J. Ehrlich, Oakland CA: AK Press, 1996, 237. For a critical account of the nineteenth-century call for productive leisure time activities, see Benjamin Hunnicutt, *Free Time: The Forgotten American Dream*, Philadelphia: Temple University Press, 2013. For an uncritical contribution to the more recent discourse about leisure-time networking, see Tom Peters, "The Brand Called You," *Fast Company* 10, 1997, 83–94.

imaginary of productivity or the models of the subject that would deliver it. My point is that because these notions of work's refusal are still under the sway of its ethics, the models of nonwork they generate are too locked within the orbit of work as we now know it to push us very far beyond its gravity.

To return again to Jameson's earlier thesis, there is a good case to be made that these failures of imagination are themselves instructive. Our encounter with the failed political imagination, he claims, can help us better to recognize the true extent of our affective attachments to, and ideological complicity within, the present. To borrow this insight for my purposes here, it may be that the failure of our imagination of nonwork can help to deepen our critical understanding of work and provide an opportunity to confront not only our incapacity for imagining nonwork, but also our fear of and resistance to the utopian imagination of a postwork future, a fear that the specters of individual idleness and collective indiscipline are especially adept at generating.

I am more sympathetic to that response to the dilemma of imagining nonwork than I am to the idea that our problems could be overcome with the aid of empirical examples, glimpses of existing practices that might help us to imagine the possibilities of nonwork time in more concrete terms. Because the difficulties in imagining beyond work as we know it are not only due to the ways we are overwhelmed by the present practical, ideological, and subjective demands of work; we are also hampered in locating promising examples of nonwork by a lack of knowledge of the existing world of employment. Our cognitive mappings of the work society are woefully incapable of orienting us. We may know more than we want to about our own jobs, but our knowledge of the experience and conditions of other jobs is severely limited. The abstraction of labor that folds the heterogeneity of concrete labor into labor in general renders us inattentive to the specific qualities of different forms of work. The work ethic teaches us to value any job at any wage; any employment is considered productive employment and a sign of one's moral rectitude. This is why government job-creation initiatives rarely mention what kinds of jobs will be created. In the absence of viable diagrams of the work society, our navigable coordinates are reduced to the narrow range of jobs of which we have first- or secondhand knowledge, a tiny subset of the larger pool of employment that is typically reserved for one's own class fraction. We can hardly imagine a future beyond something we presently know so little about.

The possibility of coming up with living examples of nonwork is also hindered by the way history can often obscure our view of the present. We are also haunted by work's past, something that is revealed in the backward-looking and nostalgic content of many of the examples that have been offered as representatives of the larger world of work. Consider the famous Marxist example of the description of a day under communism spent hunting in the morning, fishing in the afternoon, rearing cattle in the evening, and criticizing after dinner. Terrell Carver claims that the original draft of this passage in the *German Ideology* suggests that Engels wrote the section and then Marx inserted some additions designed to flag it as a sarcastic sendup of the bygone pastoral visions advanced by the utopian socialists.[21] Outdated examples persist in the later industrial period, when images of artisanal and crafts labor were still used to represent workers, and today under post-Fordism, when the figure of the Fordist company man is still often evoked when work is addressed or when the newspaper help-wanted ads are offered as the way for the chronically unemployed and underemployed to better themselves.

In light of these obstacles to envisaging a radically new relationship to work and to imagining nonwork on a different model, rather than searching for nonwork in the past or the present, it is perhaps more helpful to tether our imagination of it to the future

---

21 Terrell Carver, *The Postmodern Marx*, University Park: Pennsylvania State University Press, 1998, 106.

so that we conceive it not as something to recover or defend but rather to invent. But this brings us face to face with what is perhaps the greatest obstacle to postwork speculation: the fear of our own extinction as individuals. Jameson has written about this elsewhere, describing this particular fear of utopia as the fear of becoming otherwise: "a thoroughgoing anxiety in the face of everything we stand to lose in the course of so momentous a transformation that—even in the imagination—it can be thought to leave little intact of current passions, habits, practices, and values."[22] We would not survive a radical transformation of the conditions of our own construction as subjects. This form of anti-utopian resistance stems from a desire for self-preservation in the most literal sense, as the commitment to the continuation of our individual selves. Given the intimate relationship to work and its values that we are today expected to forge, the prospect of a post-work society can generate some particularly strong resistance along these lines.

Postwork Therapies

"We hammer away at anti-utopianism not with arguments," Jameson maintains, "but with therapy: every utopia today must be a psychotherapy of anti-utopian fears and draw them out into the light of day, where the sad passions like blinded snakes writhe and twist in the open air." This final section draws on Jameson's larger project, including this most recent installment, to construct another exercise in utopian envisioning. This far less practically minded exercise is designed, following Jameson's instructions, as therapy for anti-utopian fear and anxiety. This course of treatment focuses in particular on exposing and indulging our anxiety about the

---

22 Fredric Jameson, *The Seeds of Time*, New York: Columbia University Press, 1994, 60.

prospect of a future that could not sustain us as individuals, the fear of becoming undone as a subject. Although the therapeutic capacity of utopian thinking derives from the intermixture of the critical and inspirational qualities of both the utopian form and its substantive content, in keeping with the interpretive practices employed to read "An American Utopia," I will be less concerned with the literal representation of utopian content than with the potential effects of the form that the exercise takes. To construct this contribution to postwork speculation, I will return to the Marxist tradition and briefly explore two of its utopian texts, one from the early Marx and the other by second-wave feminist Shulamith Firestone.

In a section of the *Economic and Philosophic Manuscripts of 1844* with the title "The Meaning of Human Requirements," Marx offers some suggestive ideas about how we might begin to think about how to spend nonwork time and produce postwork selves. He does this by casting nonwork not as a time within which we can meet our existing needs, but in relation to the possibility of new needs. In his indictment of bourgeois political economy, Marx describes it as a moral doctrine parading as if it were value-free science, a "science of *asceticism*" that shapes the worker in accordance with its own moral ideal: "Self-denial, the denial of life and of all human needs, is its cardinal doctrine."[23] This is how these political economists make workers out of human beings: by reducing our needs—from needs for food and shelter, to needs for activity, pleasure, and sociality—to a specific functional minimum.

Marx's characterization of who we become as workers in this model of the work society includes references to the impoverishment of our senses and "a dulled capacity for pleasure."[24] Our affective capacities and modes of sociality are equally diminished, since if we "want to be economical," we should spare ourselves

23 Marx, *Economic and Philosophic Manuscripts*, 95.

24 Ibid., 94.

"all sharing of general interest, all sympathy, all trust, etc.," leaving self-interest free rein. Becoming an economic subject means managing what today is referred to as our employability: according to this economic ethic, "you must make everything that is yours *saleable*, i.e., useful."[25] By this estimation the problem is not that we need and want too much, as those who preach the ethics of hard work and decry our "entitlement attitudes" would have it, but that we have too few needs and too little desire.

It is worth noting here that Marx's critique in this text is not an example of the usual ascetic diatribe against the pleasures of consumption. Consider his mocking description of the teachings by which we are made into the ethical subjects of a capitalist work society:

> The less you eat, drink and read books; the less you go to the theatre, the dance hall, the public-house; the less you think, love, theorize, sing, paint, fence etc., the more you *save*—the *greater* becomes your treasure which neither moths nor dust will devour—your *capital*.[26]

In this way, multiple modes of doing, being, and communing are subordinated to having: as Marx summarizes this advice, "the less you *are*, the more you *have*."[27] But note that the kinds of things we are counseled to minimize, which he lists in that passage, are not necessarily what we would characterize as unproductive indolence, or productive creativity, or reproductive leisure (to recall my three earlier examples of the failed imagination of nonwork). Rather, by framing his critical analysis in terms of our needs—their qualities and quantities, their expansion and contraction—he sidesteps the question of whether such activities or experiences are

25 Ibid., 96.

26 Ibid., 95–6.

27 Ibid.

productive or unproductive and poses the problem on an ontological register, emphasizing instead the question of what their impact on our subjectivity might be, on who it is we are encouraged—and able—to become.

I want to emphasize that it is not precisely the content of nonproductive and nonreproductive pastimes, which the political economists warn us against and Marx affirms, that I want to take away from this reading. (Perhaps fencing offers a case in point.) In addition to the above list, Marx offers one more glimpse of an alternative later in the section, in the form of an example of how we might create new needs. There he describes how, as proletarian activists come together *as workers* to do political work, a different mode of being emerges as a new "need for society" develops—a need for a form of sociality quite different from that orchestrated through the capitalist division of labor and even different than the kind of sociality that initially brought them together as workers in their opposition to capitalism. As they come together, their process, their means or methods of organizing—he lists "company, association, and conversation"—become ends in themselves.[28] In contrast to the ethical subject constituted in relation to the ascetic ideals of "acquisition, work, thrift, sobriety," we are invited by such examples to think about nonwork on a future trajectory, as an opportunity to cultivate a new wealth of human needs.[29]

Just as I drew on Marx to think beyond the empirical example, to conceive nonwork not as content to recover but as possibilities to invent, I want to look to Firestone for an additional point of instruction. I am particularly interested in the final chapter of her iconoclastic masterpiece from 1970, *The Dialectic of Sex: The Case for Feminist Revolution*, wherein Firestone explicitly defends speculation about what she mockingly calls "dangerously utopian" proposals and offers, for her contribution to that project, a vision

28 Ibid., 99.

29 Ibid., 97.

of cybernetic, postfamilial communism. Firestone does not offer anything approaching a blueprint; her deliberately "sketchy" propositions are meant to "stimulate thinking in fresh areas rather than to dictate the action."[30] Insisting that we need a "qualitative change in humanity's basic relationships to both its production and its reproduction," she advances two proposals: a guaranteed basic income as a step towards postwork communism and a variety of options for postfamilial household formation.[31] Here too it is not the examples that interest me most. Like other utopias, this one is both prescient and dated, and it is worth noting that Firestone is at her least provocative when she resorts to an example from her own present, a seed she thought could be, or develop into, an alternative to the family: an example that she calls—complete with quotation marks every time she refers to it—"living together."

Instead I want to spotlight a third element of her exercise in utopian speculation: a vision of a world beyond gender and sexual identities as we now know them. "The end goal of feminist revolution must be," she declares, "not just the elimination of male *privilege* but of the sex *distinction* itself: genital differences between human beings would no longer matter culturally."[32] This particular form of feminist anti-identitarianism is now rare in feminist theory, which is another reason to return here to Firestone. While one may or may not find the content of this genderless utopia attractive, and may or may not find instruction in Firestone's deep commitment to her gender together with a call for its withering away, the form of the exercise is I think nonetheless important. Even more than Marx, Firestone understood that this radical transformation of subjectivity was not about us. So as I read them, Marx helps us to think about nonwork along a future trajectory as

30 Shulamith Firestone, *The Dialectic of Sex: The Case for Feminist Revolution*, New York: Farrar, Straus and Giroux, 2003, 203.

31 Ibid., 183, 207.

32 Ibid., 11.

something to invent over time; Firestone then adds to this the insight that this future of nonwork will not be our future. Thinking the future requires that we think beyond ourselves, within a long enough temporal frame to imagine the extinction of our current structures of desire, subjectivity, and sociality. As part of her affirmation of a postindividual temporality, Firestone also cautions against a prescriptivist politics of personal change, insisting instead on collective and structural rather than individual change. "It is unrealistic," she argues,

> to impose theories of what ought to be on a psyche already fundamentally organized around specific emotional needs . . . We would do much better to concentrate on overthrowing the institutions that have produced this psychical organization, making possible the eventual—if not in our lifetime—fundamental restructuring (or should I say destructuring?) of our psychosexuality.[33]

We are not the targets of this change, not the subjects of this future, even if we might be among its agents. It is a difficult thing she asks of us: to think, want, and struggle for a future that will not be our future. On the one hand, to engage in political action requires some longing for and imagination of a different future, one that we might want; on the other hand, we must also appreciate that we will not be, and perhaps could not be, the subjects of that world.

This, then, is how the form of the exercise asks us to begin to imagine the contents of a postwork future. Against the economic and emotional asceticism of work ethic, we think about how to cultivate a wealth of needs for care, sociality, pleasure, activity, desire, and affect that exceed the world of work, and that we learn how to be willing to imagine such a future as simultaneously our own and not for us.

33 Ibid., 216.

10

The Seeds of Imagination

Slavoj Žižek

Contemporary literary and cinema theory has elaborated the notion of the "seed of imagination," the germ out of which the fictional universe of a work of art grows.[1] This fantasmatic core is not simply the basic plot, the figure of a central hero, or any of the similar obvious candidates—it is, as a rule, an element that is unrecognizable in the final product. For example, Henry James's masterpiece *The Ambassadors* grows out of the idea of an American returning from Europe to the United States after he learns that his father has died. The "seed of imagination" of Hitchcock films is usually not even a narrative element but the formal motif of a scene, a shot, or a gesture. Perhaps philosophical revolutions evolve in a similar way: their "seed of imagination," the particular topic or deadlock that triggers the process out of which the revolution grows, is as a rule something unrecognizable in the new edifice that results from it. The "seed" of Kant's transcendental turn was his preoccupation with ghosts, his attempt to reject Swedenborg's

1 See, among others, Kim Jong Il, *On the Art of the Cinema*, Honolulu: University Press of the Pacific, 2001, 13–23.

theosophy; the seed of Hegel's mature dialectics was English political economy (as Georg Lukács demonstrated in his *Young Hegel*). Such "seeds" are sometimes accidental, and indifferent starting points which are *aufgehoben* (sublated) can be forgotten once the new form of thought is here; sometimes they are crucial and have symptomal value of indicating a "repressed" dimension of a theoretical edifice; sometimes they are both—their contingent origin *is* their symptomal point. What today's radical left needs are such "seeds of imagination" that would enable it not only to provide a new vision of a Communist society, but also to break out of the terrifying impoverishment of our power of imagination in our late capitalist society.

When it was announced that, from July till September 2015, "Jade Helm 15"—large military exercises—would take place in the southwestern United States, the news immediately gave rise to a suspicion that the exercises were part of a federal plot to place Texas under martial law, in direct violation of the Constitution. We find all the usual suspects participating in this conspiracy paranoia, up to Chuck Norris; the craziest among them is the website All News Pipeline, which linked the exercises to the closure of several Walmart megastores in Texas:

> Will these massive stores soon be used as "food distribution centers" and to house the headquarters of invading troops from China, here to disarm Americans one by one as promised by Michelle Obama to the Chinese prior to Obama leaving the White House?[2]

What makes the affair more ominous is the ambiguous reaction of the leading Texas Republicans. Governor Greg Abbott ordered the Texas National Guard to monitor the exercise, while Senator

---

2 Stefan Stanford, "Are the Wal-Mart Closings in Jade Helm 15 States a Sign We've Sold Them the Rope They'll Use to Hang Us with by Shopping at Wal-Mart All These Years?" *All News Pipeline*, April 14, 2015, allnewspipeline.com.

Ted Cruz demanded details from the Pentagon. How can something so openly "irrational" take place? For Ezra Klein, the ultimate reason is that partisanship is increasingly driven by hatred and fear of the other guy rather than love of your team. Texas conservatives are so much driven by hatred of Obama that they are ready to believe he actually wants to facilitate a Chinese takeover of the US Southwest. While the leading Texas Republicans are of course not ready to publicly embrace such crazy conspiracy theories, they nonetheless want to signal their solidarity with the anti-Obama fanatics among their voters.[3]

How are we to read this weird, paranoiac construct? Its ideological investment is clearly ambiguous. In a first approach, we are clearly dealing with the populist distortion of a fully justified distrust of the oppressive state apparatuses. However, one can also read it as the elaboration of a correct insight into an unexpected emancipatory potential in the US Army—the topic of Jameson's essay, debated in the present volume. The fact that such an idea cannot but appear to us as an ominous eccentricity bears witness to the fateful limitation of our ability to imagine alternatives. A recent scientific report describes how future biotechnology could be used to trick a prisoner's mind into thinking they have served a thousand-year sentence. Drugs could be developed to distort prisoners' minds into thinking time was passing more slowly. According to Rebecca Roache,

> There are a number of psychoactive drugs that distort people's sense of time, so you could imagine developing a pill or a liquid that made someone feel like they were serving a 1,000-year sentence. A second scenario would be to upload human minds to computers to speed up the rate at which the mind works. If the speed-up were a factor of a million, a millennium of thinking would be accomplished

3 Matthew Yglesias, "The Amazing Jade Helm Conspiracy Theory, Explained," *Vox*, May 6, 2015, vox.com.

> in eight and a half hours. Uploading the mind of a convicted criminal and running it a million times faster than normal would enable the uploaded criminal to serve a 1,000-year sentence in eight and a half hours. This would, obviously, be much cheaper for the taxpayer than extending criminals' lifespans to enable them to serve 1,000 years in real time.[4]

An ethical twist is then added to the argumentation:

> Is it really OK to lock someone up for the best part of the only life they will ever have, or might it be more humane to tinker with their brains and set them free? When we ask that question, the goal isn't simply to imagine a bunch of futuristic punishments—the goal is to look at today's punishments through the lens of the future.[5]

But what about the opposite intervention, which would enable us to make love for ten minutes and experience it hundreds of years? What about a life whose temporality could be totally manipulated in both directions, so that one can also make someone experience a ten-year prison sentence as something that lasts only ten minutes? How would such temporarily manipulated life look, and how would it be experienced? In short, does imagining the consequences of the manipulability of our perception of time only along the lines of how it could render serving a prison sentence more productive not provide an extreme example of the misery and limitations of our imagination of the future? This limitation is clearly perceptible even when we are dealing with critical dystopias: Jameson is right to emphasize how dystopias that abound in recent blockbuster movies and novels (*Elysium*,

4 Rhiannon Williams, "Prisoners 'Could Serve 1,000 Year Sentence in Eight Hours,'" *Telegraph*, March 14, 2014. Incidentally, this was also the plot of a *Star Trek: Deep Space Nine* episode.

5 Ibid.

The Hunger Games), although apparently leftist (presenting a postapocalyptic society of extreme class divisions), are unimaginative, monotonous, and also politically wrong. Here is another extreme case of this misery of imagination: the German, pro-Zionist *anti-Deutsche* leftists wrote in one of their programmatic texts that, because of their extreme suffering, when communism arrives and with it the dissolution of national identities, Jews would be allowed to be the last to abandon their national identity. Can we even imagine a more perverted line of thought? Its underlying premise is that communism will entail the sacrifice of our most precious features, so that a special favor should be granted to the Jews and they should be allowed to enjoy their ethnic identity a little bit longer.

The bleak picture of the total triumph of global capitalism, which immediately appropriates all attempts to subvert it, is itself the product of ideological imagination. It makes us blind for the signs of the New that abound in the very heart of global capitalism. For example, in his *The Zero Marginal Cost Society*, Jeremy Rifkin develops how, with the emerging Internet of Things, we are entering the era of nearly free goods and services: the rise of a global Collaborative Commons entails the eclipse of capitalism. There is a paradox at the heart of capitalism that has propelled it to greatness but is now taking it to its death: the inherent entrepreneurial dynamism of competitive markets that drives productivity up and marginal costs down, enabling businesses to reduce the price of their goods and services in order to win over consumers and market share. (Marginal cost is the cost of producing additional units of a good or service, if fixed costs are not counted.) While economists have always welcomed a reduction in marginal cost, they never anticipated the possibility of a technological revolution that might bring marginal costs to near zero, making goods and services priceless, nearly free, abundant, and no longer subject to market forces.

Now, a formidable new technology infrastructure is emerging with the potential of pushing large segments of economic life to near-zero marginal cost in the years ahead. The communication Internet is converging with a nascent energy Internet and logistics Internet to create a new technology platform that connects everything and everyone. Billions of sensors are being attached to natural resources, production lines, the electricity grid, logistics networks, and recycling flows and implanted in homes, offices, stores, vehicles, and even human beings, feeding Big Data into a global neural network. People can connect to the network and use Big Data, analytics, and algorithms to accelerate efficiency, dramatically increase productivity, and lower the marginal cost of producing and sharing a wide range of products and services to near zero, just like they now do with information goods. This plummeting of marginal costs is spawning a hybrid economy, part capitalist market and part Collaborative Commons: people are making and sharing their own information, entertainment, green energy, and 3D-printed products at near-zero marginal cost; they are sharing cars, homes, clothes, and other items via social media sites, rentals, redistribution clubs, and cooperatives at low or near-zero marginal cost; students are enrolling in free open online courses that operate at near-zero marginal cost; entrepreneurs are bypassing the banking establishment and using "crowdfunding" to finance startup businesses as well as creating alternative currencies in the fledgling sharing economy. In this new world, social capital is as important as financial capital, access trumps ownership, sustainability supersedes consumerism, cooperation ousts competition, and "exchange value" in the capitalist marketplace is increasingly replaced by "sharable value" on the Collaborative Commons. Capitalism will remain, but primarily as an aggregator of network services and solutions—a powerful niche player in the coming world beyond markets, where we are learning how to live together in an increasingly interdependent global Collaborative Commons (a term that effectively sounds like a clumsy translation of "communism").

Here, however, we encounter one of the great antagonisms of our digital age: the very feature that sustains utopian hopes also sustains new forms of alienation. The catch resides in the infinitesimal temporal gap between the pure synchronicity of the web (we appear to be all simultaneously connected, so that it doesn't matter where we are located in physical reality) and the minimal temporality that remains as a trace of the materiality of the web. This minimal gap is mobilized by high-frequency traders (HFTs) to earn billions, as Michael Lewis exposed in *Flash Boys*.[6] Using fiberoptic cables that link superfast computers to brokers, HFTs intercept and buy orders, sell the shares back to the buyer at a higher price, and pocket the margin. Here, then, is how it works from the standpoint of a broker buying stocks: he sits in front of a screen, sees an offer that he considers acceptable, presses the "YES" button, and the deal is instantly concluded, albeit at a minimally higher price. What he doesn't know is that in the milliseconds between his pressing "YES" and the conclusion of the deal (which appeared to him instantly), the HFT's computer (operating on a special algorithm) has detected his "YES," bought itself the stock for the offered price, and then sold them back to him for a slightly higher price—the time gap is so small that the whole operation is unnoticed. This is why HFTs built, in secrecy, an 827-mile cable running through mountains and under rivers from Chicago to New Jersey: it reduces the journey of data from 17 to 13 milliseconds. There is also a transatlantic cable still under construction that will give a 5.2-millisecond advantage to those looking to profit from trade between New York and London.

After the book was launched, several regulatory agencies took action: the Justice Department, the FBI, the Securities and Exchange Commission, and the Financial Industry Regulatory Authority had been investigating HFT firms and exchanges for violations of insider trading and other Wall Street rules. Why such an outcry when receiving trading data a few milliseconds ahead of someone

6 I rely here on Andrew Ross's review of *Flash Boys* in the *Guardian* (May 16, 2014).

else—the *raison d'être* of HFT—is technically legal? The reason is obvious: what HFTs are doing is proof that the stock market is rigged in favor of front-running traders while other players are screwed for having slower connections, so that the all-important image of the stock market as open and transparent is ruined. But there is another reason. The HFT scandal is only the latest evidence that the stock market's clubby insiders have always enjoyed an advantage for getting better and faster information. Yet the fiction of equal access is necessary to draw the punters into the casino and to ensure that the market escapes heavy regulation. Books like Matt Taibbi's *The Divide* attracted much less attention than Lewis's, although Taibbi fully details the record of bankers' malfeasance and extortion: predatory lenders, crooked collection agents, illegal foreclosures, PPI rip-offs, and other swindles that are considered business as usual by the finance industry, so that, as Andrew Ross put it succinctly, the dupes in Lewis's story are the Wall Street brokers and hedge-fund managers who were outrun by flash boys; the victims in Taibbi's book are the rest of us. Focusing on HFTs thus brings forward a marginal phenomenon that appears as a specific distortion, thereby allowing us to adhere to the myth that the market is in itself a balanced and open mechanism.

But there is yet a third, more fundamental, "metaphysical" even, reason. Franco Berardi locates the origin of today's uneasiness and impotence in the exploding speed of the functioning of the big Other (the symbolic substance of our lives) and the slowness of human reactivity (due to culture, corporeality, diseases, etc.): "The long-lasting neoliberal rule has eroded the cultural bases of social civilization, which was the progressive core of modernity. And this is irreversible. We have to face it."[7] Are HFTs not an exemplary case of how our brains, our mental abilities, are no longer synchronous with the functioning of the social-symbolic system? What happens in those milliseconds is simply beyond the

7 Franco Berardi, *After the Future*, Oakland: AK Press, 2011, 177.

scope of our normal perception; agents don't know what goes on primarily not because of the immense complexity of the process, but because what gets enacted there is a kind of minimal self-reflexivity: my own act (my reaction to the offer, my pressing "YES") is inscribed, taken into account, into what I perceive as the state of things (the price which I pay)—I decide (to buy), and my decision changes the price of what I buy. Furthermore, far from relying on some kind of mysterious synchronicity, the HFTs' operation mobilizes precisely the minimal gap between the virtual digital space and its material embodiment: our spontaneous illusion, while we surf on the web, is that we are in the domain of pure synchronicity where the contact between all participants is direct. As the saying goes, when I communicate on the web, it doesn't matter where I am; my partner can sit in the next room or stand on some Himalayan peak. The HFTs' operation demonstrates that it *does* matter where I am; it is a kind of revenge of materialism against the spontaneous idealist illusion that pertains to the digital space.

There is a kind of twisted emancipatory potential in what HFTs are doing: to quote Marx, what happens in their operation is a minimal "expropriation of the expropriators" (stock-market speculators, rich investors), who are getting their comeuppance—perhaps *this* is why *Flash Boys* created such a fuss. With HFTs, financial speculation reaches its meaningless pinnacle, bringing out the nonsense that sustains the entire edifice of financial speculations—in this sense, one can say that HFTs are too bright for their own good.

The German weekly magazine *Der Spiegel* reported, among the greatest recorded stupidities and blunders of 1998, the case of a German robber who grabbed an old woman's purse while she was taking a photo of herself in the automatic photo booth at a railway station. Unfortunately for him, one of the usual four photos was taken at exactly the moment he leaned in to snatch the purse, so that his face and hand were clearly discernible on the photo, delivering to the police the direct proof of the crime plus who committed it. Don't we encounter something similar with HFTs? Do we not see there the direct proof of how the crime is committed?

But there is an even deeper and properly uncanny dimension in what HFTs are doing. The way they demonstrate how markets are rigged points toward a more fundamental ontological deadlock in which (what we experience as) *reality itself is "rigged"* in the sense that we don't perceive it "objectively," since our act is already inscribed into what we perceive. So it is as if HFTs do not simply operate in our reality, but intervene into the very mechanism of how we perceive/constitute (what we experience as) reality: the most spontaneous link between action and reaction (I press the "YES" button to a deal, the deal is immediately confirmed) is already manipulated. And does quantum physics not entertain the same "riggedness" of reality itself? At its most daring, it seems to allow the momentarily suspension, "forgetting," of the knowledge of the real. Imagine that you have to take a flight on day X to pick up a fortune the next day, but do not have the money to buy the ticket; then you discover that the accounting system of the airline is such that if you wire the ticket payment within twenty-four hours of arrival at your destination, no one will ever know it was not paid prior to departure. In a homologous way,

> the energy a particle has can wildly fluctuate so long as this fluctuation is over a short enough time scale. So, just as the accounting system of the airline "allows" you to "borrow" the money for a plane ticket provided you pay it back quickly enough, quantum mechanics allows a particle to "borrow" energy so long as it can relinquish it within a time frame determined by Heisenberg's uncertainty principle . . . But quantum mechanics forces us to take the analogy one important step further. Imagine someone who is a compulsive borrower and goes from friend to friend asking for money . . . Borrow and return, borrow and return—over and over

> again with unflagging intensity he takes in money only to give it back in short order . . . a similar frantic shifting back and forth of energy and momentum is occurring perpetually in the universe of microscopic distance and time intervals.[8]

This is how, even in an empty region of space, a particle emerges out of nothing, "borrowing" its energy from the future and paying for it (with its annihilation) before the system notices this borrowing. The whole network can function like this, in a rhythm of borrowing and annihilation, one borrowing from the other, displacing the debt onto the other, postponing the payment of the debt—it is really like the subparticle domain is playing Wall Street games with the futures. What this presupposes is a minimal gap between things in their immediate brute reality and the registration of this reality in some medium (of the big Other): one can cheat insofar as the second is in a delay with regard to the first. So, like with HFTs, reality itself (the way we perceive it) is "rigged" because of things taking place in the imperceptible interstices of time.

The most important lesson of the latest technological progress and its social impact is therefore its radical ambiguity. During a debate with Jameson at the City University of New York (CUNY), Stanley Aronowitz claimed that the main reason of the decline of social utopia in the last decades is that, due to technological progress, we no longer need to resort to utopias, since in our reality itself (almost) everything is now possible. However, this sense of unlimited possibilities is accompanied by a set of impossibilities: today the very idea of a radical social transformation appears to be an impossible dream—and the term "impossible" should make us stop and think. Impossibility and possibility are distributed in a strange way, both simultaneously exploding into an excess. On the one hand, in the domains of personal freedoms and scientific

8 Brian Greene, *The Elegant Universe*, New York: Norton, 1999, 116–9.

technology, the impossible is more and more possible (or so we are told): "Nothing is impossible." We can enjoy sex in all its perverse versions, entire archives of music, films, and TV series are available for downloading, going to space is available to everyone (with money), there is the prospect of enhancing our physical and psychic abilities, of manipulating our basic properties through interventions into the genome, up to the tech-gnostic dream of achieving immortality by way of fully transforming our identity into software that can be downloaded from one hardware to another. On the other hand, especially in the domain of socioeconomic relations, our era perceives itself as the era of maturity in which, with the collapse of Communist states, humanity has abandoned the old millenarian utopian dreams and accepted the constraints of reality (read: the capitalist socioeconomic reality) with all its impossibilities: *you cannot* engage in large collective acts (which necessarily end in totalitarian terror), cling to the old welfare state (it makes you uncompetitive and leads to economic crisis), isolate yourself from the global market, etc. (In its ideological version, ecology also adds its own list of impossibilities, so-called threshold values—no more global warming than 2 degrees Celsius, etc.—based on "expert opinions."[9]) The reason is that we live in the postpolitical era of the naturalization of economy: political decisions are as a rule presented as matters of pure economic necessity, so that when austerity measures are imposed, we are repeatedly told that this is simply what has to be done. In such postpolitical conditions, the exercise of power no longer primarily relies on censorship, but on unconstrained permissiveness, or, as Alain Badiou put it in thesis fourteen of his "Fifteen Theses on Contemporary Art":

> Since it is sure of its ability to control the entire domain of the visible and the audible via the laws governing commercial circulation

9 I owe this idea to Alenka Zupančič.

> and democratic communication, Empire no longer censures anything. All art, and all thought, is ruined when we accept this permission to consume, to communicate and to enjoy. We should become pitiless censors of ourselves.[10]

Effectively, today, we seem to be at the opposite point of the ideology of 1960s: the mottos of spontaneity, creative self-expression, etc., are taken over by the system, i.e., the old logic of the system reproducing itself through repressing and rigidly channeling the subject's spontaneous impetuses is left behind. Nonalienated spontaneity, self-expression, self-realization—they all directly serve the system, which is why pitiless self-censorship is a *sine qua non* of emancipatory politics. Especially in the domain of poetic art, this means that one should totally reject any attitude of self-expression, of displaying one's innermost emotional turmoil, desires, dreams. True art has *nothing whatsoever* to do with disgusting emotional exhibitionism—insofar as the standard notion of "poetic spirit" is the ability to display one's intimate turmoil, what Mayakovsky said about his turn from personal poetry to political propaganda in verses ("I had to step on the throat of my Muse") is the constitutive gesture of a true poet. If there is a thing that provokes disgust in a true poet, it is the scene when a close friend opens up his heart, spilling out all the dirt of his inner life.

The two lines from Kipling's "If"—"If you can wait and not be tired of waiting, if you can dream—and not make dreams your master"—seem quite an appropriate guide for those who want to remain faithful to communism. I see Jameson's "American Utopia" as a big step in this direction of censoring our dreams. His achievement in imagining the future outside the constraints of the existing order and in mercilessly breaking old taboos is (at least) triple. These taboos arise from the fact that every historical situation

10 Alain Badiou, "Fifteen Theses on Contemporary Art," *Lacanian Ink* 22, 2003, lacan.com.

contains its own unique utopian perspective, an immanent vision of what is wrong with it, an ideal representation of how, with some changes, the situation could be rendered much better. When the desire for a radical social change emerges, it is thus logical that it first endeavors to actualize this immanent utopian vision, which is why it has to end in a catastrophe.

A voluptuous lady from Portugal once told me a wonderful anecdote: When her most recent lover had first seen her fully naked, he told her that, if she lost just one or two kilos, her body would be perfect. The truth was, of course, that had she lost the kilos, she would probably have looked more ordinary—the very element that seems to disturb perfection itself creates the illusion of the perfection it disturbs: if we take away the excessive element, we lose the perfection itself. It is at this level that we should also discern the mistake of Marx: he perceived how capitalism unleashed the breathtaking dynamics of self-enhancing productivity—see his fascinated descriptions of how, in capitalism, "all things solid melt into thin air," of how capitalism is the greatest revolutionizer in the entire history of humanity. On the other hand, he also clearly perceived how this capitalist dynamics is propelled by its own inner obstacle or antagonism—the ultimate limit of capitalism (of self-propelling capitalist productivity) is capital itself, that is, capitalism's incessant development and revolutionizing of its own material conditions, the mad dance of its unconditional spiral of productivity, is ultimately nothing but a desperate flight forward to escape its own debilitating inherent contradiction. Marx's fundamental mistake was to conclude, from these insights, that a new, higher social order (communism) is possible, an order that would not only maintain but even raise to a higher degree and effectively fully release the potential of the self-increasing spiral of productivity which, in capitalism, on account of its inherent obstacle (contradiction), is again and again thwarted by socially destructive economic crises. Which, then, are the taboos Jameson breaks?

First, he dismisses not only the two main forms of the

twentieth-century state socialism (the social democratic welfare state and the Stalinist party dictatorship) but also the very standard by which the radical left usually measures the failure of the first two, the libertarian vision of communism as association, multitude, councils, anti-representationist direct democracy based on citizens' permanent engagement. This aspect is unacceptable for our ordinary democratic stance—no wonder that, in his debate with Jameson, Aronowitz desperately tried to reduce Jameson's utopian idea of universal conscription back to the anti-representationist direct democracy where people (soldiers) organize themselves in councils, like they do in rebellious people's armies. Such direct democracy is the extreme point of the politicization of the entire society, while Jameson repeatedly emphasizes that his idea of universal conscription aims at the disappearance of the political dimension as such: all that remains in Jameson's utopian society is a militarily (i.e., nonpolitically) organized economy with no need for the permanent engagement of the people, and the immense, also nonpolitical, domain of cultural pleasures, from sex to art. (The truth we have to embrace is that, if we want to move out of representation toward direct democracy, this direct democracy has always to be supplemented with a non-representational higher power, say, of an "authoritarian" leader—in Venezuela, Chavez's leadership was the necessary obverse of his attempts to mobilize direct democracy in barrios.)

For Toni Negri, the dream to be censored is his idea of the goal of emancipatory movements: the state in which the "dual power" shared between multitude and state organs is overcome and the self-organized multitude takes over completely the entire social reproduction and regulation. It is as if, in the recent Brazilian revolts and mass protests, Negri, a longtime sympathizer of the Lula government, got his own message back in its true form—the government of Dilma Rousseff, Lula's successor, spectacularly failed to contain and integrate the protesting multitude. Although life of the poor and the middle classes improved considerably, it was as if this improvement, and the very attempt of the government to involve excluded minorities in a dialogue and empower them as autonomous political agents, backfired and strengthened acts of resistance—here is Hugo Albuquerque's concise description of this process in Negri's terms:

> The central issue is less that people *objectively* "improved their lives," as the economists, sociologists, and statisticians . . . would have us believe, but rather that they feel authorized to desire and, therefore, now desire without authorization.
>
> This class has no name because it does not need one; it is the very expression of many minorities—the poor, blacks, women, etc.—that are sufficient in themselves, that go beyond labels and labeling and simply live. Without a name, this class is in some sense not orderable, since only a subject that has a name, and is thus subject to a regime, is capable of receiving orders.[11]

The future of this nameless class thus

> depends on positively embracing its own internal plenitude and differences. Carnival, with its masks and its lawlessness, not the normalization of bureaucratic seriousness . . . will allow a future for these lands . . . no repressive formula is capable of containing the intense investment of desire—at least not for long.[12]

There is undoubtedly a moment of truth in this description: it renders the reality of how the protesters experience their situation, and the despair of the state power that fails to contain protests through "rational" measures of material improvement. The dimension that prevents the protesting multitude from satisfactory,

---

11 Hugo Albuquerque, "Becoming-Brazil: The Savage Rise of the Class without Name," *South Atlantic Quarterly* 113–4, Fall 2014, 856–7.

12 Ibid., 861.

nonantagonistic collaboration with a "progressive" power is correctly characterized as *desire*—and to discern the problem, one should give to this term all its Lacanian weight. Desire is always a desire for its own nonsatisfaction: its ultimate aim is always to reproduce itself as desire, which is why its basic formula is always something like "I demand this from you, but if you give it to me, I will reject it because this is not really *that* (what I really want)"—i.e., desire is a gap, a void, in the heart of every demand. Is not an exemplary case of this dialectic of demand and desire the case of a protest movement that demands from the government a measure X (say, to repeal a new law or to abolish a new tax), and if the government immediately concedes, protesters feel frustrated and somehow cheated?

But there is another paradox that defines the protesting multitude: the quoted text that talks about the awakened desire in multitudes also claims that they are "sufficient in themselves," that they "go beyond labels and labeling and simply live"—how can multitudes be "sufficient in themselves" while engaged in continuous protesting, provoking the state power, bombarding it with demands?

> Maybe, one should render problematic the very basic coordinates of this view, and turn around the opposition between fluid life of multitudes and the regulating oppressive power of the state apparatuses: what if the notion of power as the agency which regulates the de-territorialized flux of multitudes should be turned around? What if the basic units of social life, "sufficient in themselves," tend to "simply live" in their secluded groups, in their stable territorialized bases, and what if the de-territorializing agency is the state apparatus itself? The destabilizing logic of desire belongs to the fluid political superstructure—it is this superstructure which is in excess with regard to the base . . . No wonder, then, that, in an interview from January 2015, Negri made two "general propositions," announcing a change in his position: The first one is that after 2011 horizontality

> must be criticized and overcome, clearly and unambiguously . . . Secondly, the situation is probably ripe enough to attempt once again that most political of passages: the seizure of power. We have understood the question of power for too long in an excessively negative manner.

The critique of political representation as a passivizing alienation (instead of allowing others to speak for them, people should directly organize themselves into associations) reaches here its limit. The idea to organize society in its entirety as a network of associations is a utopia that obfuscates a triple impossibility:[13]

(1) There are numerous cases in which representing (speaking for) others is a necessity—it is cynical to say that victims of mass violence from Auschwitz to Rwanda (and the mentally ill, children, etc., not to mention the suffering animals) should organize themselves and speak for themselves.

(2) When we effectively get a mass mobilization of hundreds of thousands of people organizing themselves horizontally (Tahrir Square, Gezi Square), we should never forget that they remain a minority and that the silent majority remains outside, unrepresented. (This is why, in Egypt, this silent majority defeated the Tahrir Square crowd and elected the Muslim Brotherhood.)

(3) Political engagement has a limited timespan: After a couple of weeks or, rarely, months, the majority disengages. The problem is to safeguard the results of the uprising at this moment, when things return to normal. No—there is nothing inherently "conservative" in being tired of the usual radical leftist demands for permanent mobilization and active participation, demands that follow the superego's logic—the more we obey them, the more we are guilty. The battle has to be won *here*, in the domain of citizens'

---

13 I rely here on Rowan Williams's "On Representation," presented at the colloquium *The Actuality of the Theologico-Political*, Birkbeck School of Law, London, May 24, 2014.

passivity, when things return back to normal the morning after the ecstatic revolts. It is (relatively) easy to have a big ecstatic spectacle of sublime unity, but how will ordinary people feel the difference in their ordinary daily lives? No wonder conservatives like to see sublime explosions from time to time—they remind people that nothing can really change, that the day after, things return to normal. In the final scene of *V for Vendetta*, thousands of unarmed Londoners wearing Guy Fawkes masks march toward Parliament; without orders, the military allows the crowd to pass the Parliament and the people take over. When Finch asks Evey for V's identity, she replies: "He was all of us." OK, a nice ecstatic moment, but I was ready to sell my mother into slavery to see *V for Vendetta 2.* What would have happened the day after the victory of the people? How would they (re)organize daily life?

One should thus abandon ("deconstruct," even) the topic of the opposition between the "normal" run of things and the "state of exception" characterized by fidelity to an Event that disrupts the "normal" run of things. In the "normal" run of things, life just goes on, following its inertia; we are immersed in our daily cares and rituals and then something happens, and there is an evental Awakening, a secular version of a miracle (a social emancipatory explosion, a traumatic love encounter). If we opt for fidelity to this Event, our entire life changes; we are engaged in the "work of love" and endeavor to inscribe the Event into our reality. At some point, then, the evental sequence is exhausted and we return to the "normal" flow of things. But what if the true power of an Event should be measured precisely by its disappearance: by the change in "normal" life when the Event is erased in its result? Let's take a sociopolitical Event: what remains of it in its aftermath when its ecstatic energy is exhausted and things return to "normal"? How is this "normality" different?

Jameson's second achievement concerns the problem of resentment: He totally rejects the predominant optimist view according to which, in communism, envy will be left behind as a remainder of capitalist competition, to be replaced by solidary collaboration and pleasure in others' pleasures. Dismissing this myth, Jameson emphasizes that in communism, precisely insofar as it will be a more just society, envy and resentment will explode. He refers here to Lacan, whose thesis is that human desire is always desire of the Other in all the senses of that term: desire for the Other, desire to be desired by the Other, and, especially, desire for what the Other desires.[14] This last makes envy, which includes resentment, both constitutive components of human desire, something Augustine knew well—recall the passage from his *Confessions*, often quoted by Lacan, the scene of a baby jealous of his brother sucking at the mother's breast: "I myself have seen and known an infant to be jealous though it could not speak. It became pale, and cast bitter looks on its foster-brother."

The Soviet writer Yuri Olesha published in the late 1920 a short novel, *Envy*, which deserves to be reread from the later experience of the failure of Soviet communism. Its main character is Nikolai Kavalerov, who, shaped by the vanishing nineteeth century, when the imagination was king and art had no other purpose than being art, cannot but find repulsive the world in which he lives, the rapidly industrializing USSR. After getting booted out of a bar, he is found in the gutter by Andrei Babichev, a Soviet industrialist who is developing a sausage that will be inexpensive yet delicious and thus affordable for workers. Although Babichev offers Kavalerov a place to stay in his villa and finds him a little work to do (editing food-processing manuals), Kavalerov loathes Babichev for his vulgar utilitarianism. The second part shifts the focus onto the sexual comedy, but what makes the novel interesting is the ambiguity of its satire: should we read it as a satiric portrait of the old bourgeois individualists who cannot accommodate themselves to the new society (on account of this reading, the novel was popular in the USSR), or as the satiric condemnation of the new vulgar

14 Jacques Lacan, *Ecrits*, Paris: Editions du Seuil, 1966, 689–98.

utilitarian spirit? In other words, who envies whom? Does Kavalerov envy the social and sexual success of the new Soviet men, or does Babichev secretly envy Kavalerov's sensitive imagination, which is beyond the grasp of their narrow minds?

Based on this insight, Jean-Pierre Dupuy proposes a convincing critique of John Rawls's theory of justice: in Rawls's model of a just society, social inequalities are tolerated only insofar as they also help those at the bottom of the social ladder, and insofar as they are not based on inherited hierarchies but on natural inequalities, which are considered contingent, not merits.[15] Even the British Conservatives seem now to be prepared to endorse Rawls's notion of justice: in December 2005, David Cameron, the newly elected leader, signaled his intention of turning the Conservative Party into a defender of the underprivileged, declaring, "I think the test of all our policies should be: what does it do for the people who have the least, the people on the bottom rung of the ladder?" But what Rawls doesn't see is how such a society would create conditions for an uncontrolled explosion of *ressentiment*: in it, I would know that my lower status is fully "justified" and would thus be deprived of the ploy of excusing my failure as the result of social injustice. Rawls thus proposes a terrifying model of a society in which hierarchy is directly legitimized in natural properties, thereby missing the simple lesson an anecdote about a Slovene peasant makes palpably clear. The peasant is given a choice by a good witch. She will either give him one cow and his neighbor two cows, or she'll take one cow from him and two from his neighbor. The peasant immediately chooses the second option. Gore Vidal demonstrates the point succinctly: "It is not enough for me to win—the other must lose." The catch of envy/resentment is that it not only endorses the zero-sum game principle, where my

15 Jean-Pierre Dupuy, *Avions-nous oublie le mal? Penser la politique après le 11 septembre*, Paris: Bayard, 2002; John Rawls, *A Theory of Justice*, revised edition, Cambridge, MA: Harvard University Press, 1999.

victory equals the other's loss, it also implies a gap between the two, which is not the positive gap (we can all win with no losers at all), but a negative one. If I have to choose between my victory and my opponent's loss, I prefer the opponent's loss, even if it means also my own loss. It is as if my eventual gain from the opponent's loss functions as a kind of pathological element that stains the purity of my victory.

Friedrich Hayek knew that it was much easier to accept inequalities if one can claim that they result from an impersonal blind force: The good thing about the "irrationality" of the market and success or failure in capitalism is that it allows me precisely to perceive my failure or success as "undeserved," contingent.[16] Remember the old motif of the market as the modern version of an imponderable Fate. The fact that capitalism is not "just" is thus a key feature of what makes it acceptable to the majority. I can live with my failure much more easily if I know that it is not due to my inferior qualities, but to chance.

What Nietzsche and Freud share is the idea that justice as equality is founded on envy—on the envy of the Other, who has what we do not have and enjoys it. The demand for justice is thus ultimately the demand that the excessive enjoyment of the Other should be curtailed so that everyone's access to *jouissance* is equal. The necessary outcome of this demand, of course, is asceticism. Since it is not possible to impose equal *jouissance*, what is imposed instead to be equally shared is *prohibition*. Today, however, in our allegedly permissive society, this asceticism assumes the form of its opposite, a *generalized* superego injunction, the command "Enjoy!" We are all under the spell of this injunction. The outcome is that our enjoyment is more hindered than ever. Take the yuppie who combines narcissistic "self-fulfillment" with those utterly ascetic disciplines of jogging, eating health food, and so on.

16 Friedrich Hayek, *The Road to Serfdom*, Chicago: University of Chicago Press, 1994.

Perhaps this is what Nietzsche had in mind with his notion of the Last Man, though it is only today that we can really discern his contours in the guise of the hedonistic asceticism of yuppies. Nietzsche wasn't simply urging life-assertion against asceticism: He was well aware that a kind of asceticism is the obverse of a decadent excessive sensuality. His criticism of Wagner's *Parsifal*, and more generally of late Romantic decadence, which oscillates between damp sensuality and obscure spiritualism, makes a very pertinent and valid point.[17]

How, then, should communism deal with this problem? Perhaps Kojin Karatani indicates one possible way with his apparently eccentric idea of combining elections with lottery in the procedure of determining who will rule us. This idea is more traditional than it may appear (he mentions ancient Greece)—paradoxically, it fulfills the same task as Hegel's theory of monarchy. Karatani takes a heroic risk in proposing a crazy-sounding definition of the difference between the dictatorship of the bourgeoisie and the dictatorship of the proletariat: "If universal suffrage by secret ballot, namely, parliamentary democracy, is the dictatorship of the bourgeoisie, the introduction of lottery should be deemed the dictatorship of the proletariat."[18]

At this point, we have to confront the question of democracy. When Badiou claims that democracy is our fetish, this statement is to be taken literally, in the precise Freudian sense, not just in the vague sense that we elevate democracy into our untouchable absolute: "Democracy" is the last thing we see before confronting the "lack" constitutive of the social field, the fact that "there is no class relationship," the trauma of social antagonism. It is as if, when confronted with the reality of domination and exploitation, of

---

17 Alenka Zupančič, *The Shortest Shadow*, Cambridge, MA: MIT Press, 2006.

18 Kojin Karatani, *Transcritique: On Kant and Marx*, Cambridge, MA: MIT Press, 2003, 183.

brutal social struggles, we can always add: Yes, but *we have democracy*, which gives us hope to resolve or at least regulate struggles, preventing their destructive explosion. Exemplary cases of democracy as fetish are provided by bestsellers and Hollywood blockbusters, from *All the President's Men* to *The Pelican Brief*, in which a couple of ordinary guys discover a scandal that reaches up to the president, who is forced to step down. Even if the corruption is shown to reach the very top, ideology resides in the upbeat final message of such works: What a great democratic country is ours, where a couple of ordinary guys like you and me can bring down the president, the mightiest man on earth!

This is why the most inappropriate, stupid even, names for a new radical political movement that one can imagine are those that combine "socialism" and "democracy." It effectively combines the ultimate fetish of the existing world order with a term that blurs the key distinctions. Everyone can be a socialist today, up to Bill Gates—it suffices to profess the need for some kind of harmonious unity of society, for the common good, for the care of the poor and downtrodden—or, as Otto Weininger put it succinctly more than a century ago, socialism is Aryan and communism is Jewish.

An exemplary case of today's "socialism" is China, where the Communist Party is now engaged in an ideological campaign of self-legitimization which promotes three theses: (1) only Communist Party rule can guarantee successful capitalism; (2) only the rule of the atheist Communist Party can guarantee authentic religious freedom; and, most surprising, (3) only continuing Communist Party rule can guarantee that China will be a society of Confucian conservative values (social harmony, patriotism, moral order). Instead of dismissing these claims as nonsensical paradoxes, we should discern their reasons: Without the stabilizing power of the Party, (1) capitalist development would explode into chaos of riots and protests, (2) religious factional struggles would disturb social stability, and (3) unbridled hedonist individualism would corrode social harmony. The third point is crucial, since what lies in the background is the fear of the corroding influence of Western "universal values" of freedom, democracy, human rights, and hedonist individualism. The ultimate enemy is not capitalism as such but rootless Western culture, which invades China through the free flow of the Internet, and one has to fight it with Chinese patriotism—even religion should be "Sinicized" to ensure social stability. Xinjiang's Communist Party secretary, Zhang Chunxian, recently said that, while "hostile forces" are stepping up their infiltration, religions must work under socialism to serve economic development, social harmony, ethnic unity, and the unification of the country: "Only when one is a good citizen [can] one be a good believer."[19]

But even this "Sinicization" of religion is not enough: any religion, no matter how "Sinicized," is incompatible with membership in the Communist Party. An article in the newsletter of the party's Central Commission for Discipline Inspection claims that since "the founding ideological principle that Communist Party members cannot be religious," party members don't enjoy any right to religious freedom: "Chinese citizens have the freedom of religious belief, but Communist Party members aren't the same as regular citizens; they are fighters in the vanguard for a communist consciousness."[20] But how does this exclusion of believers from the Party help religious freedom? Marx's analysis of the political imbroglio of the French Revolution of 1848 comes to mind here. The ruling Party of Order was a coalition of the two royalist wings, the Bourbons and the Orleanists. The two parties were, by definition, unable to find a common denominator at the level of royalism, since one cannot be a royalist in general, only support a

---

19 Josh Rudolph, "Xinjiang Party Chief Calls for the 'Sinicization' of Religion," *China Digital Times*, June 15, 2015, http://chinadigitaltimes.net/2015/06/xinjiang-official-sinicize-religion-to-combat-hostile-forces/.

20 Xin Lin and Hai Nan, "Warning over Religious Believers in Chinese Communist Party Ranks," trans. Luisetta Mudie, *Radio Free Asia*, May 25, 2015, rfa.org.

determinate royal house, so the only way for the two to unite was under the banner of the "anonymous kingdom of the Republic"—in other words, the only way to be a royalist in general is to be a republican.[21] The same holds true for religion: one cannot be religious in general, one can only believe in some god(s) to the detriment of others, and the failure of all the efforts to unite religions proves that the only way to be religious in general is under the banner of the "anonymous religion of atheism." Effectively, only an atheist regime can guarantee religious tolerance: the moment this neutral atheist frame disappears, factional struggle among different religions has to explode. This is why, although fundamentalist Islamists attack the godless West, the worst struggle goes on among them (ISIS focuses on killing Shi'a Muslims).

There is, however, a much deeper fear at work in this exclusion of religious believers from membership in the Communist Party:

> It would have been the best for the Chinese Communist Party if its members were not to believe in anything, not even in Communism, since numerous party members joined some of the churches (most of them the Protestant one) precisely because of their disappointment at how even the smallest trace of their Communist ideals disappeared from today's Chinese politics.[22]

In short, the biggest opposition to the Chinese Party leadership consists today precisely of truly convinced Communists, a group composed of old, mostly retired cadres who feel betrayed by the unbridled capitalist corruption, and of the proletarian losers of the "Chinese miracle": farmers who have lost their land, workers who have lost their jobs and wander around in search of means of

---

21 Karl Marx and Friedrich Engels, *Collected Works*, Vol. 10, London: Lawrence and Wishart, 1978, 95.

22 Zorana Baković, "Kako bo bog postal Kitajec?" *Delo*, June 17, 2015 (in Slovene).

survival, workers exploited at FoxConn and similar companies, all those who suffer injustices and humiliations and have no one to turn to. They often participate in mass protests wearing posters with Mao quotes, and one can imagine how potentially explosive such a combination of experienced cadres and the poor who have nothing to lose is. China is not a stable country with an authoritarian regime guaranteeing harmony and thus keeping under control the capitalist dynamics. Every year, thousands, tens of thousands even, of chaotic rebellions of workers, farmers, minorities, etc., have to be squashed by the police and army. No wonder the official propaganda obsessively insists on the motif of harmonious society: this very insistence bears witness to the opposite, to the threat of chaos and disorder. One should apply here the basic rule of Stalinist hermeneutics: since official media do not openly report on troubles, the most reliable way to detect them is to search for the positive excesses in the state propaganda—the more harmony is celebrated, the more chaos and antagonisms there are likely to be. China is full of antagonisms and barely controlled instabilities that threaten to explode.

It is only against this background that one can understand the religious politics of the Chinese Party: the fear of belief is effectively the fear of the *Communist* "belief," the fear of those who remain faithful to the universal emancipatory message of Communism. Significantly, one looks in vain in the ongoing ideological campaign for any mention of this basic class antagonism which is exploding daily in workers' protests. There is no talk about the threat of "proletarian Communism"—all the fury is directed against the foreign enemy:

> Certain countries in the West advertise their own values as "universal values," and claim that their interpretations of freedom, democracy, and human rights are the standard by which all others must be measured. They spare no expense when it comes to hawking their goods and peddling their wares to every corner of the planet, and stir up

> "color revolutions" both before and behind the curtain. Their goal is to infiltrate, break down, and overthrow other regimes. At home and abroad certain enemy forces make use of the term "universal values" to smear the Chinese Communist Party, socialism with Chinese characteristics, and China's mainstream ideology. They scheme to use Western value systems to change China, with the goal of letting Chinese people renounce the Chinese Communist Party's leadership and socialism with Chinese characteristics, and allow China to once again become a colony of some developed capitalist country.[23]

There are some true points in the quoted passage, but they function as particular truths covering up a global lie. It is of course true that one cannot and should not naïvely trust the "universal values" of freedom, democracy, and human rights promoted by Western powers, that their universality is a false one, hiding a specific ideological bias. However, if Western universal values are false, is it enough to oppose them with a particular way of life like the Confucian "China's mainstream ideology"? Don't we need a different universalism, a different project of universal emancipation? The ultimate irony here is that "socialism with Chinese characteristics" effectively means *socialism with a market economy (with capitalist characteristics)*, i.e., socialism that fully integrates China into the global market. The universality of global capitalism is left intact, it is silently accepted as the only possible frame, and the project of Confucian harmony is mobilized only in order to keep under control the antagonisms that come from global capitalist dynamics. All that remains of socialism are the Confucian "national colors," which should enable the Party to keep in check the antagonisms engendered by capitalist globalization. Such a socialism with national colors—a national socialism—is a socialism whose social horizon is the patriotic

23 Samuel Wade, "Unraveling China's Campaign Against Western Values," *China Digital Times*, March 5, 2015.

promotion of one's own nation, and the immanent antagonisms generated by capitalist development are projected onto a foreign enemy that poses a threat to our social harmony. What the Chinese Party aims at in its patriotic propaganda, what it calls "socialism with Chinese characteristics," is yet another version of "alternate modernity": capitalism without class struggle.

If what goes on in China today can be characterized as "capitalist socialism," what, then, to do with fundamentalist movements like Boko Haram? From the perspective of a traditional communal life, women's education is a key moment of the devastating effect of Western modernization; it "liberates" women from family ties and trains them for becoming a part of the Third World's cheap labor force. The struggle against women's education is thus a new form of what Marx and Engels, in *The Communist Manifesto*, called "reactionary (feudal) socialism," the rejection of the capitalist modernity on behalf of traditional forms of communal life. However, with a closer look, we can clearly see the limitation of this view: Whatever Boko Haram is, it does not practice a return to premodern communal life, since it is (in its organizational form) an extremely modern organization that brutally imposes its universal model on traditional communal life in the territory it occupies. Boko Haram is run like a modern centralized terrorist/revolutionary organization with leaders exerting total control, not as a tribal network where paternal chiefs meet to deliberate and decide on communal matters. It is thoroughly internationalist: It pursues a universal model, ignoring particular ways of life or particular ethnic identities. In short, Boko Haram is itself a form of perverted modernization. It obliterates traditional communal forms of life even more brutally than Western capitalist modernization does.

Back to Jameson, what this means is that we should reject not only all attempts of "alternate modernity" (which amount to a "capitalism without capitalism," without its destructive aspect), but also all attempts to rely on particular traditional life-worlds (local cultures) as potential "sites of resistance" against global capitalism.

Jameson's third achievement is to reject the notion of communism as a higher unity of production and pleasure (or work and Eros), a society in which this most basic opposition, the zero-level of alienation, is overcome, so that work becomes pleasure, etc. It will be only in communism that the gap that separates production from pleasure (inclusive of culture, art, etc., up to social work and private life) will be thoroughly asserted—in contrast to capitalism, in which even the most intimate pleasures are commodified, made into a moment of capitalist self-reproduction. Do we not find a trace of this assertion of a gap already in early Bolshevism? From what we know about love among the Bolshevik revolutionaries, something unique took place there, a new form of love-couple emerged: a couple living in a permanent emergency state, totally dedicated to the revolutionary cause, ready to sacrifice all personal sexual fulfillment to it, even ready to abandon and betray each other if revolution demanded it, but simultaneously totally dedicated to each other, enjoying rare moments together with extreme intensity. The lovers' passion was tolerated, even silently respected, but ignored in the public discourse as something of no concern to others. (There are traces of this even in what we know of Lenin's affair with Inessa Armand.)

Jameson posits as the basic feature of his utopian society a radical division between the domain of economy (production, goods and services) and the domain of cultural pleasures, endorsing universal conscription, i.e., the model of the army, as the organizational mode for the sphere of production. When he looks for the organizational model for the sphere of cultural pleasures, he of course cannot avoid the obvious candidate, the church or a similar religious organization, which imposes itself the moment we remember Freud's famous example of two artificial crowds, army and church. Freud fails to clearly distinguish between the church model and the army model of the artificial crowd: while "church" stands for the hierarchic social order, which tries to maintain peace and balance by way of necessary compromises, "army" stands for an egalitarian collective of struggle, defined not by its internal hierarchy but by the opposition to its enemy, trying to destroy it—radical emancipatory movements are always modeled on the army, not on the church, while millenarian churches are really structured like armies.

Jameson engages in a complex argument against the church as a regulating mechanism of pleasures, preferring some kind of psychoanalytic institute that will educate people not to succumb to envy (by way of, among other things, teaching them to recognize pleasure in their very envy). But do these arguments really hold? Is the ultimate function of religion not precisely to regulate pleasures? And can we really imagine a psychoanalytic institution to meet the requirements of a body destined to educate people in the art of pleasure?

Furthermore, what disappears in Jameson's utopian vision—as he is well aware, and that's his point—is politics as such, the properly political process of making and enacting decisions that concern communal life. The clear-cut division between production and pleasure is here to guarantee this disappearance of the political, and the price Jameson pays for this disappearance is that he ignores basic questions like who will command the army and how, who will allocate jobs and how, how the psychoanalytic institutions regulating pleasures will be empowered, and so on. His dream is one of apolitical invention and regulation—no wonder he refers with great sympathy to apolitical neoliberal speculations about how to organize the economy efficiently, claiming that we should agree with everything there except the essential (capitalist private property).

Jameson's vision is not so much utopia as fantasy proper, "having a cake and eating it": Its main premise is the clear division between the kingdom of necessity and the kingdom of freedom, between production and culture/pleasure. Production is militarized and everyone is allocated a job, while outside this kingdom of necessity total freedom reigns supreme, with the wildest diversity of freaks organizing their weird pleasures. (Do we not have today almost the obverse of this fantasy: liberalization of market economy, militarization of pleasures, in the guise of the duty to enjoy which demands discipline and training, conquest, and the battle of the sexes?) Can this be done? Does obscene pleasure not always-already contaminate obligatory disciplined activity, so that we find pleasure in it? And does militarization-discipline not always-already contaminate pleasure—pleasure as a duty, done as a task?

The basic enigma here is: why the army? Jameson's army is, of course, a "barred army," an army with no wars—wars and heroes are just celebrated in empty rituals (here we encounter pleasure in the kingdom of necessity). (And how would this army operate in an actual war, which is becoming more and more likely in today's multicentric world?) What instigated this role of the army in Jameson's utopia is clear: in the United States the army is the last big institution with full free health care, free education, job security, etc. But still: why the army, why not just a centrally organized economy that allocates jobs and guarantees full employment? What surplus aspect is added by the army? It is the aspect of struggle, the emergency state, fighting the enemy. When, at the aforementioned debate at CUNY, Jameson was asked how he imagines the eventual implementation of his utopia of universal militarization, he evoked an emergency state caused by a large ecological catastrophe (to which we could also add a major financial meltdown, large-scale unrest, etc.). One can mention here the tradition of catastrophe movies in which, as Jameson noticed, the threat to humanity creates a sense of solidarity and collaboration in which the old hierarchical and other differences become irrelevant. Does, however, this reply not rely on the sad prospect that only a great catastrophe can save the radical left? This surplus element is enigmatic and crucial: what if the militarized form is the very form in which the excluded politics and its obscene pleasures return in the pragmatic domain of production, of servicing the goods?

There is, however, a moment of truth in Jameson's rejection of politics: the ultimate horizon of emancipatory politics is what Badiou posits as the basic premise of the idea of communism, the "axiom of equality"—in stark contrast to Marx, for whom equality is

> an exclusively *political* notion, and, as a political value, that it is a distinctively *bourgeois* value (often associated with the French revolutionary slogan: *liberté, égalité, fraternité*). Far from being a value that can be used to thwart class oppression, Marx thinks the idea of equality is actually a vehicle for bourgeois class oppression, and something quite distinct from the communist goal of the abolition of classes.[24]

Or, as Engels put it:

> The idea of socialist society as the realm of *equality* is a one-sided French idea resting upon the old "liberty, equality, fraternity"—an idea which was justified as *stage of development* in its own time and place but which, like all the one-sided ideas of the earlier socialist schools, should now be overcome, for it produces only confusion in people's heads and more precise modes of presentation of the matter have been found.[25]

Does this not hold even for today's French political theory, from Balibar's *égaliberté* to Badiou? Back to Marx, he unequivocally rejects what Allen Wood calls "egalitarian intuition"—egalitarian justice is unsatisfactory *precisely because* it applies an equal standard to unequal cases:

---

24 Allen Wood, "Karl Marx on Equality," n.d., http://philosophy.as.nyu.edu/docs/IO/19808/Allen-Wood-Marx-on-Equality.pdf.

25 Karl Marx and Friedrich Engels, *Collected Works*, Vol. 24, London: Lawrence and Wishart, 1978, 73.

> Right by its very nature can consist only in the application of an equal standard; but unequal individuals (and they would not be different individuals if they were not unequal) are measurable by an equal standard only insofar as they are brought under an equal point of view, are taken from one definite side only, for instance, in the present case, are regarded *only as workers* and nothing else is seen in them, everything else being ignored. Further, one worker is married, another is not; one has more children than another, and so on and so forth. Thus with an equal performance of labor, and hence an equal share in the social consumption fund, one will receive more than another. To avoid all these defects, right instead of being equal would have to be unequal.[26]

In claiming that it is not just to apply equal criteria to unequal people, Marx may appear to repeat the old conservative argument for the legitimization of hierarchy. However, there is a subtle distinction that has to be taken into account here: this argument is false when we are in a class society in which class oppression overdetermines inequality, but in a post-class society it is a legitimate one, since inequality is there independent of class hierarchy and oppression. This is why Marx proposes as the axiom of communism "to each according to his needs, from each according to his abilities." Wood points out that this maxim, although popularly associated with Marx, originated from Louis Blanc (who wrote, in 1851, "De chacun selon ses moyens, à chacun selon ses besoins") and can even be traced back to the New Testament: "And all that believed were together, and had all things common; and sold their possessions and goods, and parted them to all men, as every man had need" (Acts 2:44–5).

So we have to qualify Badiou's thesis that "equality is the point of the impossible proper to capitalism"[27]—yes, but this impossible

26 Ibid., 86.

27 Alain Badiou, *A la recherché du reel perdu*, Paris: Fayard, 2015, 55.

point is *immanent to the capitalist universe*, it is its immanent contradiction: Capitalism advocates democratic equality, but the legal form of this equality is the very form of inequality. In other words, equality, the immanent ideal-norm of capitalism, is necessarily undermined by the process of its actualization. For this reason, Marx did not demand "real equality"—his idea is not that equality as the real-impossible of capitalism should become possible; what he advocated was a move beyond the very horizon of equality.

Furthermore, the "point of the impossible" of a certain field should not be elevated into a radical utopian Other. The great art of politics is to detect it locally, in a series of modest demands that are not simply impossible but appear as possible although they are de facto impossible. The situation is like the one in science-fiction stories where the hero opens the wrong door (or presses the wrong button) and all of a sudden the entire reality around him or her disintegrates. In the United States, universal health care is obviously such a point of the impossible; in Europe, it seems to be the cancellation of the Greek debt, for example. It is something you can (in principle) do but, de facto, cannot or should not do—you are free to choose it *on condition you do not actually choose it*. Therein resides the touchy point of democracy, of democratic elections: The result of a vote is sacred, the highest expression of popular sovereignty—but what if people vote "wrongly," demanding measures that pose a threat to the basic coordinates of the capitalist system? This is why the ideal that emerged from the European establishment's reaction to the threat of a Syriza victory in Greece was best rendered by a headline in the *Financial Times*: "Eurozone's weakest link is the voters."[28] In this ideal world, Europe gets rid of this "weakest link" and experts gain the power to directly impose necessary economic measures—if elections take place at all, their function is just to confirm the consensus of experts. (Incidentally,

---

28 Gideon Rachman, "Eurozone's Weakest Link Is the Voters," *Financial Times*, December 12, 2014.

the same feature characterized Communist regimes in Eastern Europe: an apparently modest demand, totally consistent with the official ideology and the existing legal order—like the demand to repeal a certain law or replace some top politician—threw the *nomenklatura* into a much greater panic than direct calls for the overthrow of the system. Back in the early 1970s, the so-called "affair of the twenty-five members of Parliament" caused a scandal in Slovenia. Twenty-five MPs proposed to replace the unpopular official Slovene candidate for a high federal post with another name, and although the entire action was totally legal and this other person was also a high-ranking member of the *nomenklatura*, the reaction was extremely brutal. All twenty-five MPs were forced to resign their posts.

On account of necessary inconsistencies of global capitalism, this paradox of the "point of the impossible" goes up to self-reference: the point of the impossible of global market could well be (and are) "free" market relations themselves. A couple of years ago, a CNN report on Mali described the reality of the international "free market." The two pillars of Mali's economy are cotton in the south and cattle in the north, and both are in trouble because of the way Western powers violate the very rules they try to impose brutally onto the impoverished Third World nations. Mali produces cotton of top quality, but the problem is that the US government spends more money on the financial support of its cotton farmers than the entire state budget of Mali; no wonder Malians cannot compete with US cotton. In the north, the European Union is the culprit: Malian beef cannot compete with the heavily subsidized European milk and beef—European Union subsidizes every single cow with about 500 euros per year, more than the per capita gross national product in Mali. No wonder the minister of economy commented: We don't need your help or advice or lectures on the beneficial effects of abolishing excessive state regulations, just, please, stick to your own rules about the free market and our troubles will be basically over.

Advocates of capitalism often point out that, in spite of all the critical prophecies, capitalism is, overall, from a global perspective, not in crisis but progressing more than ever—and one cannot but agree with them. Capitalism thrives all around the world (more or less), from China to Africa, it is definitely not in crisis—it is just the people caught in this explosive development that are in crisis. This tension between overall explosive development and local crises and misery (which from time to time vacillate the entire system) is part of capitalism's normal functioning: capitalism renews itself through crises.

Let's take the case of slavery. While capitalism legitimizes itself as the economic system that implies and furthers personal freedom (as a condition of market exchange), it generated slavery on its own, as a part of its own dynamics: although slavery was almost extinct at the end of the Middle Ages, it exploded in colonies from early modernity till the American Civil War. One can risk the hypothesis that today, with the new epoch of global capitalism, a new era of slavery is also arising. Although it is no longer a direct legal status of enslaved persons, slavery acquires a multitude of new forms: millions of immigrant workers in the Saudi peninsula (United Arab Emirates, Qatar, etc.) who are de facto deprived of elementary civil rights and freedoms; total control over millions of workers in Asian sweatshops often directly organized as concentration camps; massive use of forced labor in the exploitation of natural resources in many central African states (Congo, etc.). But we don't have to look so far. On December 1, 2013, at least seven people died when a Chinese-owned clothing factory in an industrial zone in the Italian town of Prato, ten kilometers from the center of Firenze, burned down, killing workers trapped in an improvised cardboard dormitory built onsite. The accident occurred in the Macrolotto industrial district of the town, known for its large number of garment factories. Riberto Pistonina, a local trade unionist, commented: "No one can say they are surprised at this because everyone has known for years that, in the area between Florence and Prato, hundreds if not thousands of people are living and working in conditions of near-slavery."[29] Only Prato has at least 15,000 legally registered immigrant workers in a total population of under 200,000, with more than 4,000 Chinese-owned businesses. Thousands more Chinese immigrants are believed to be living in the city illegally, working up to sixteen hours per day for a network of wholesalers and workshops turning out cheap clothing. We thus do not have to look for the miserable life of new slaves far away in the suburbs of Shanghai (or Dubai or Qatar) and hypocritically criticize China—slavery can be right here, within our house: we just don't see it (or, rather, we pretend not to see it). This new de facto apartheid, this systematic explosion of the number of different forms of de facto slavery, is not a deplorable accident but a structural necessity of today's global capitalism, so a consequent struggle against it can trigger a global change.

There is what appears to be a strong counterargument against this strategy. Many times, the left has engaged in the battle against a particular feature of capitalism with the presupposition that this feature is crucial for the reproduction of the entire capitalist system, and has been proven wrong. Marx's support of the North in the American Civil War was based on the premise that cheap cotton produced by slaves in the South and then exported to England was crucial for the smooth functioning of the British capitalism, so that the abolition of slavery in the United States would bring crisis and class war into England. The premise of feminists and sexual-liberation partisans was that the patriarchal family is crucial for the reproduction and transmission of private property, so that the fall of patriarchal order would undermine the very roots of capitalist reproduction. In both cases, capitalism was able to integrate this change without any serious problems . . . But

29 James MacKenzie, "At Least Seven Dead in Italian Textile Factory Fire," Reuters, December 1, 2013, reuters.com.

does this counterargument really work? It certainly doesn't work today, when global capitalism not only cannot afford any widening of workers' rights but even has to abolish many traditional social democratic achievements and gains.

This brings us back to Jameson's utopia of militarization. One can argue that, while the deadlocks of global capitalism are more and more palpable, all the imagined democratic-multitude-grassroots changes "from below" are ultimately doomed to fail—the only way to effectively break the vicious cycle of global capitalism is some kind of "militarization," which is another name for suspending the power of self-regulating economy. An obvious counterargument to this project of militarization is that even if we concede its need, we can conditionally endorse it only for a short period of transition: fully developed communism can in no way be imagined along these lines. However, things get very problematic here. In traditional Marxism, the predominant name for this transitional period was the "dictatorship of the proletariat," a notion which has always caused a lot of discontent. Etienne Balibar drew attention to the tendency in official Marxism to "multiply the 'intermediary stages' in order to resolve theoretical difficulties: stages between capitalism and communism, but also between imperialism and the passage to socialism"—such a "fetishism of the formal number of these stages" is always symptomatic of a disavowed deadlock.[30] What if, then, the way to subvert the logic of the "stages of development" is to perceive this logic itself as the sign that we are at a lower stage, since every imagining of higher stages (to be reached through the sacrifices and sufferings of the present lower stage) is distorted by the perspective of the lower stage? In a properly Hegelian way, we effectively reach the higher stage not when we overcome the lower stage but when we realize that what we have to get rid of is the very idea that there is a higher

30 Etienne Balibar, *Sur la dictature du proletariat*, Paris: Maspero, 1976, 148, 147.

stage to follow what we are doing now and that the prospect of this higher stage can legitimize what we are doing now, in our lower stage. In short, the "lower stage" is all we have and all we will ever get.

Jameson goes far in this direction, breaking many taboos—but it seems that one taboo remains: his anti-statal vision, his traditional Marxist idea of dismantling the state apparatus. Perhaps the army as the model for organizing social production is ultimately an ersatz state; perhaps this last taboo should also fall, and the big task that lies ahead is how to rethink the state. Let's return briefly to China. Another feature of how Chinese power functions today has to be noted: the state apparatus and legal system are redoubled by the Party institutions, which are literally illegal. As He Weifang, a law professor from Beijing, puts it succinctly:

> As an organization, the Party sits outside, and above the law. It should have a legal identity, in other words, a person to sue, but it is not even registered as an organization. The Party exists outside the legal system altogether.[31]

It is as if, in Walter Benjamin's words, the state-founding violence remains present, embodied in an organization with an unclear legal status:

> It would seem difficult to hide an organization as large as the Chinese Communist Party, but it cultivates its backstage role with care. The big party departments controlling personnel and the media keep a purposely low public profile. The party committees (known as "leading small groups") which guide and dictate policy to ministries, which in turn have the job of executing them, work out of

31 Quoted in Richard McGregor, *The Party*, London: Allen Lane, 2010, 22.

> sight. The make-up of all these committees, and in many cases even their existence, is rarely referred to in the state-controlled media, let alone any discussion of how they arrive at decisions.[32]

The front stage is occupied by "the government and other state organs, which ostensibly behave much like they do in many countries": the Ministry of Finance proposes the budget, courts deliver verdicts, universities teach and deliver degrees, even priests lead rituals.[33] So, on the one hand, we have the legal system, government, elected national assembly, judiciary, rule of law, etc. But—as the officially used term, "party and state leadership," indicates, with its precise hierarchy of who comes first and who comes second—this state power structure is redoubled by the Party, which is omnipresent while remaining in the background. Is this redoubling not yet another case of diffraction, of the gap between the "two vacuums": the "false" summit of state power and the "true" summit of the Party? There are, of course, many states, some even formally democratic, in which a half-secret exclusive club or sect de facto controls the government; in apartheid South Africa, for example, it was the exclusive Boer Brotherhood. However, what makes the Chinese case unique is that this redoubling of power into public and hidden is itself institutionalized, done openly.

All decisions on nominating people to key posts (party and state organs, but also top managers in large companies) are first made by a Party body, the Central Organization Department, whose large headquarters building in Beijing has no listed phone number and no sign indicating the tenant inside. Once the decision is made, legal organs (state assemblies, manager boards) are informed and go through the ritual of confirming it by a vote. The same double procedure—first in the Party, then in the state—is reproduced at

32 Ibid., 21.

33 Ibid., 14.

all levels, up to basic economic policy decisions, which are first debated in the Party organs and, once the decision is reached, formally enacted by government bodies. This brings us to the crucial idea of Jameson's utopia: his rehabilitation of the old Leninist idea of dual power. Is what we find in today's China not also an unexpected kind of dual power? Does the same not also hold for Stalinism? Perhaps it is time to take seriously Stalin's obsessive critique of "bureaucracy," and to appreciate in a new (Hegelian) way the necessary work done by the state bureaucracy. The standard characterization of Stalinist regimes as "bureaucratic socialism" is totally misleading and (self-)mystifying: it is the way the Stalinist regime itself perceives its problem, the cause of its failures and troubles—if there are not enough products in the stores, if authorities do not respond to people's demands, etc., what is easier than to blame the "bureaucratic" attitude of indifference and petty arrogance? No wonder that, from the late 1920s onward, Stalin was writing attacks on bureaucracy and bureaucratic attitudes. "Bureaucratism" was nothing but an effect of the functioning of Stalinist regimes, and the paradox is that it is the ultimate misnomer: what Stalinist regimes really lacked was precisely an efficient "bureaucracy": a depoliticized and competent administrative apparatus. In other words, the problem of Stalinism was not that it was too "statist," implying the full identification of party and state, but, on the contrary, that party and state were forever kept at a distance. The reason was that Stalinism (and, in general, all communist attempts until now) was not really able to transform the basic functioning of the state apparatus, so the only way to keep it under control was to supplement state power with "illegal" party power. The only way to break out of this deadlock . . . here a new "seed of imagination" is desperately needed.

An America Utopia: Epilogue

Fredric Jameson

Old clothes in the morning. Or work clothes, if you prefer, remembering that blue jeans—their pastiche—is one of America's greatest cultural exports. Perhaps the vision of everyone trudging to work in the morning is something of a nostalgia film, but after all the nostalgic or postmodern aesthetic is a new way of handling and aestheticizing necessity—nothing wrong with it. The consensus is that no one likes work; the political question, then, seems to be pleasure and how work can be made pleasurable (in all the psychoanalytic senses). Fourier reflected deeply on it; Hegel preferred to call it *Befriedigung*, or satisfaction, a concept that had something to do, surely, with whether the work was yours or not: identification, choice, compulsion, working for yourself or working for the Spaniards and the Greeks (as the Germans like to put it), or better still (from a left standpoint) for those who don't work because they don't have to. The psychology runs like this: if everyone has to work, then you don't feel quite so resentful. In his great East German Utopia, Rudolf Bahro insisted that Politburo members themselves do some manual labor every week, garbage collection for example, and perhaps do a little more than just to be seen at it (he also thought that everyone, at whatever level, should be paid the same salary, which in a situation of universal labor is tantamount to a guaranteed minimum annual wage). This is the window dressing of necessity, whose true limits are to be found in the three or four hours a day we are told will be required of the planetary species.

When you think of it that way, then the matter of agriculture inevitably raises its head, ugly or not: the stumbling block for every mode of production in history. Can peasants change jobs at will like everybody else? Will postcontemporary versions of the Green Revolution and agribusiness abolish agriculture as such? Or do you prefer to fantasize all this in terms of technology and robots? What about experts, job training, seniority, learning to labor, management, bad backs, natural endowment, innate skill, manual versus intellectual labor? Will the drill sergeant take a few hours to train his team for the rice paddies? Will job fatigue become the new version of post-traumatic stress disorder?

In *Almanac of the Dead*, Leslie Marmon Silko has one of her characters observe that the real crime, the only true crime, is starvation. This is what utopia, and everything else, is all about. It is what socialism is all about, and I feel it may not have been clear enough in the original proposal that work, production, the base, is what the universal army is also all about—your three or four hours in the morning. After that, change your clothes and, as they used to say in Rabelais's old monastic Utopia, do what you like.

To be sure, the superstructure, culture, begins when we then have to confront this new problem, which has no natural solution. The organic species had one task, to reproduce itself; after that, nature has done with it and casts it aside like an old shoe. But not only is this nihilism, it explains the deeper rejection by modern philosophy of philosophy itself in its traditional form of the desire for a system of truths and universals, now stigmatized as metaphysics. But the critique of metaphysics was also philosophy, just as the critiques of the centered subject and of representation were.

All these conceptual positions—to call them beliefs would be to revert to an older, now outmoded Enlightenment polemic—are in fact what it is urgent and alone meaningful to call ideologies. Pragmatism, vitalism, the philosophy of as-if, negative dialectics, the deconstructive renunciation of any truth position, non- or anti-philosophy, the "philosophy" of language games as a "theory" of meaning, theory itself—all these posttraditional, postsystematic, or post-Hegelian attempts to square the circle amount to little more than new philosophies in their own right, which is to say, so many ideologies. For *ideology*—one of those words so profoundly saturated with truth that everyone instinctively wants to avoid using it—is how you designate the situation-specificity of all thought and all positions (no matter how universally articulated). Ideology is what comes naturally to a species made up of individuals as we are: namely, that we can never reach "the universal," that everything we think is slanted and conditioned by the situation in which we are formed, from the existential and psychoanalytic all the way to class, nation, race, gender, and so forth. This is the deeper sense of "metaphysics" and indeed of "meaning" itself, and why all modern philosophies have been designed to avoid, to elude, and to denounce those seemingly affirmative positions and to find some suitably negative standpoint from which to project what we perhaps no longer dare to call truth. Marxism came the closest to squaring this circle, insofar as it included the very theory of ideology within its own system—which has, however, been as prone to philosophizing as all the others, as the quantity of Marxisms available today readily testifies. If the upshot of this "death of philosophy" is nihilism, why, then it only remains to point out that nihilism itself is also philosophy, just another philosophy, an ideology, a metaphysic in its own right as well. "Meaning" is always ideological, in the sense in which Heidegger tells us that existence and death are always my own, always personal.

In this situation, what one can say, as Giambattista Vico seems to have been one of the first to do, is that while nature is meaningless, history has a meaning; even if there is no meaning, the project and the future produce it, on the individual as well as the collective basis. The great collective project has a meaning and it is that of utopia. But the problem of utopia, of collective meaning, is to find an individual meaning.

Having secured the reproduction of the species, the organism, then—whether you want to call it "naked life" or the Lacanian death drive, the problem of leisure time, or the nature of the Good—has to find something else to do with itself, and human history has developed a whole shopping mall full of solutions, beginning with religion and art and running the gamut, not excluding asceticism, renunciation, self-mutilation, and a whole array of other pleasurable non- or anti-pleasures which it is the duty of every self-respecting utopia to take into account and to provide for. Presumably other people, the big Other, collectivity are always part of the scheme, a part that cannot be theorized or predicted in advance but that affects everyone. Heidegger's great ethic—let the Other be in its being!—has always seemed to me as detestable as it is comprehensible and even attractive, but impossible.

So it is that utopian reflection—of which political reflection is necessarily a subset—however venal or otiose—finds itself drawn apart in two directions: the practical and technical details of the impossible thing and its plans for our subjectivities. I want to clarify some of the former.

Any discussion of the "base" today will probably have less to do with the construction of socialism than with the deconstruction of advanced capitalism. The conversion of the great monopolies into state-owned institutions—in this case, branches of the army—is a topic already widely discussed in the literature, and probably needs augmentation in three areas: information technology, the elimination of the profit-oriented dimensions of finance capitalism, and the hygienic surveillance of bureaucracy. But eliminating the intolerable proliferation of commodities like toothpaste has a more direct impact on contemporary daily life, while the place for start-ups, however chastened by treatment of American get-rich-quick fantasies (and those of wealth in general), has to be preserved, not only for the practices of innovation but even more urgently for the investment of those tremendous youthful energies now currently engaged in everything from youth gangs and sport to computer games and business schools. The army was once a generally second-class repository for a fraction of those energies: it now has to absorb and encourage them all in ways that are both materially productive and psychically exciting. The production of new desires, Marx called it, but he could not have had in mind the metastasis of commodity fetishism, whose symptoms perplex visitors to drugstores and manipulators of television remotes alike. Peace Corps–type altruisms are not for everybody, and certainly the Aristotelian ideal of the life of the mind today at best arouses little more than images of academic specialization. But it is important to eschew the puritanical solutions of the image cures proposed by Baudrillard or Sontag in their aesthetic "diets": Nothing good ever comes from repression, which can also, as Marcuse taught us, take the form of desublimation. Let the superstructures take care of themselves (exchange, consumption), and insist only, but rigidly and sternly, on production and distribution. As for money—always the central obsession of utopian fantasy and for serious capitalist power struggles—assign its interminable discussion to the philosophers and limit its use to a coinage so heavy and cumbersome it can only be deployed on special occasions. The topic is otherwise the symbolic substitute for the twin problems of the transfer of raw materials in the production process and of redistribution to ecologically poorer or impoverished regions (the central dilemma of federalism). Is population movement an infrastructural or a superstructural problem? No utopia will want everyone living on the beaches; nor will it probably want to require some system of official permits to move to the city. The problem of land tenure is the reason for the emergence of political theory in the first place and, unfortunately, it may not have a conceptual solution, let alone a practical one. The grid of army bases was the one offered here; let's hear some better ones! In any case, socialism will not be possible without an influx of just such new fantasy images, capable of overcoming those of present-day late capitalism.

Right now, only religion seems to be mining that vein with any diligence, and this is where psychoanalysis is supposed to help us out. It is clear that the drawing power of religion today does not lie in its impoverished promises of gratification, which are scarcely even wish fulfillments, but rather in its offer of discipline and repression. I was impressed, in the waning years of the 1980s, by the meritorious arguments of a non-Marxist, Robert Heilbroner, for the continuing validity of Marxism and its socialism; he gave up after 1989 like so many others, but in his final effort he was only able to point to the attractions, for some, of the monastery and the religious commonwealth (which was also, to be sure, the fantasy origin of Thomas More's own *Utopia*). Yet monastic discipline, Max Weber showed us, was also the original proving ground for the "spirit of capitalism"; the Jesuits certainly still hold many valuable lessons for those who speculate on the possibilities for the creation of some new kind of (communist) party. But surely we will not wish to return to religion as the only alternative. The church or the army, said Freud in his analysis of collectivities: in that case, the army by all means! (But remember that capitalism is not a form of collectivity!)

These are not, however, names for "organic" groups (ethnicities, peasants, class types, etc.) but rather for institutional organizations (which, to be sure, tend to produce their own professional psychologies over time). Just as structural modifications in the religious orders can generate very different and sometimes more progressive psychologies, as with the worker priests, so also a universal army structure is likely to strengthen egalitarian tendencies (and prejudices).

What must be insisted on, however, is a radical separation between the systems of psychological analysis available to describe individuals and the theoretical proposals advanced for collectivities. Both are, to be sure, ideological, but systems of collective analysis are far more directly political and instrumental, inasmuch as all our named conceptions of groups and collectivities are inevitably and necessarily flawed and slanted. Collectivities cannot be represented, and therefore it is desirable that we evoke them in the most neutral terms available. For one thing, any materialist approach to collectivities will wish to identify the structures—social or biological—in which they are formed. But even such materialist accounts will carry a political charge: thus a concept like "the people"—populist in formation, as the cognate suggests—carries a historical and class content that is finally not more theoretically acceptable than the more overtly reactionary notions of the crowd or the mob utilized by LeBon, Canetti, or even Freud himself. Rousseau's tour de force—the General Will—is a unique theoretical and philosophical attempt to name a collectivity while positing its physical impossibility as a social entity: all the rest is empirical sociology, while only the concept of class manages to include its own material determination within itself, at the price of also including history (the distinction between the class-in-itself and the class-for-itself).

Meanwhile, the notion of "antagonism," as it has become popular since Laclau and Mouffe's pathbreaking book on "socialist strategy," is unacceptable for the opposite reason, namely that it extends observations about individual psychology to collective societies at large. That all otherness is fundamentally conflict would be a healthy conviction to share; when applied to the social, however, it becomes an anti-utopian weapon designed to discourage revolutionary strategies or, at best, to limit radical politics to local issues. The popularity of a pop-psychological concept of this kind inclines one to believe that the excesses and failures of earlier revolutions have led their sympathizers not to understand and correct those defects, but rather to flee ideals of radical and systemic social change altogether: so it is that the psychic rewards of late capitalism combine with historical images of revolutionary defeat to encourage the conviction that history is over and that nothing further can be changed (except for natural disaster).

As for specific named groups, it may be worthwhile to recapitulate my earlier "defense" of bureaucracy, inasmuch as, sociologically, the army itself no doubt falls under this category. To be sure, the most powerful and minimally functionally bureaucratic structures today are not those associated with the hated state or government but with the great corporations, where indeed they transcend the various state apparatuses on a worldwide scale. Much of the force of contemporary anarchism derives from its unconscious assimilation of the monopoly of physical violence and repression by the state to the omnipresence of our bureaucratized societies. It is more satisfying to denounce totalitarianism than it is to complain about the officials who turn you away on account of an incomplete form or lack of one, who are surly and take their own kind of pleasure in enforcing impossible rules and regulations, who make no exceptions, who are not interested in listening to your problems or personal stories, who hang up the closed sign and cut off a lengthy queue of no longer very patient petitioners. It is less easy to arouse enthusiasm for the heroic moments of bureaucracy—the social workers, the parish priests, the teachers who established the first lay schools of the Republic in an era of clerical domination, the union organizers, the inspectors and whistleblowers, the canvassers for voting registration or party membership.

Would the attack on bureaucracy be politically useful? The answer is dual and contradictory: Yes, it would, under socialism, inasmuch as one of the watchwords of socialism is the avoidance of the formation of groups (the founding fathers called them "factions") of this kind; no, under capitalism, inasmuch as bureaucracy is not a class and such attacks contribute little enough to any genuine class politics.

I have already said that I prefer the word *socialism* to *communism* in discussions today, because it is more practical than the latter and actually raises questions of party formation as well as transitions, privatizations, nationalizations, finances, and the like, which the loftier regions of communism allow us to avoid. One assumes, however, that under socialism the issue of the seizure of power is by definition already achieved, and that therefore, in that (utopian?) situation, "class struggle" now applies more to the construction of socialism as such rather than to the defeat of the class enemy.

The paper under discussion here is in fact a kind of shell game, in which, when you think you are talking about the armed forces, you are in reality talking about utopia, and when you think you are talking about revolution, you are deep into the future talking about the problems of socialism itself. It is as though Jonathan Swift were to complain that the horrors of the potato famine could have been avoided had people only taken his modest proposal to heart. Or perhaps we might prefer a somewhat modified Eisenhower cartoon, in which the military leader now observes, "Well, if they don't want to join the army, let them form a political party instead!" Only there is no one there to add, "As I did!"

Index